KU-496-365

LINUX
SECURITY
COOKBOOK™

Daniel J. Barrett,
Richard E. Silverman, and
Robert G. Byrnes

O'REILLY®

Beijing · Cambridge · Farnham · Köln · Paris · Sebastopol · Taipei · Tokyo

Linux Security Cookbook™
by Daniel J. Barrett, Richard E. Silverman, and Robert G. Byrnes

Copyright © 2003 O'Reilly & Associates, Inc. All rights reserved.
Printed in the United States of America.

Published by O'Reilly & Associates, Inc., 1005 Gravenstein Highway North, Sebastopol, CA 95472.

O'Reilly & Associates books may be purchased for educational, business, or sales promotional use. Online editions are also available for most titles (*safari.oreilly.com*). For more information, contact our corporate/institutional sales department: (800) 998-9938 or *corporate@oreilly.com*.

Editor:	Mike Loukides
Production Editor:	Jane Ellin
Cover Designer:	Hanna Dyer
Interior Designer:	David Futato

Printing History:

June 2003:	First Edition.

Nutshell Handbook, the Nutshell Handbook logo, and the O'Reilly logo are registered trademarks of O'Reilly & Associates, Inc. The *Cookbook* series designations, *Linux Security Cookbook*, the image of a campfire scene, and related trade dress are trademarks of O'Reilly & Associates, Inc. Many of the designations used by manufacturers and sellers to distinguish their products are claimed as trademarks. Where those designations appear in this book, and O'Reilly & Associates, Inc. was aware of a trademark claim, the designations have been printed in caps or initial caps.

While every precaution has been taken in the preparation of this book, the publisher and authors assume no responsibility for errors or omissions, or for damages resulting from the use of the information contained herein.

ISBN: 0-596-00391-9
[M]   [12/03]

LINUX
SECURITY
COOKBOOK™

Other Linux resources from O'Reilly

Related titles

Linux in a Nutshell	LPI Linux Certification in a Nutshell
Linux Network Administrator's Guide	Learning Red Hat Linux
Running Linux	Linux Server Hacks
Linux Device Drivers	Linux Security Cookbook
Understanding the Linux Kernel	Managing RAID on Linux
Building Secure Servers with Linux	Linux Web Server CD Bookshelf
	Building Embedded Linux Systems

Linux Books Resource Center

linux.oreilly.com is a complete catalog of O'Reilly's books on Linux and Unix and related technologies, including sample chapters and code examples.

ONLamp.com is the premier site for the open source web platform: Linux, Apache, MySQL and either Perl, Python, or PHP.

Conferences

O'Reilly & Associates bring diverse innovators together to nurture the ideas that spark revolutionary industries. We specialize in documenting the latest tools and systems, translating the innovator's knowledge into useful skills for those in the trenches. Visit *conferences.oreilly.com* for our upcoming events.

Safari Bookshelf (*safari.oreilly.com*) is the premier online reference library for programmers and IT professionals. Conduct searches across more than 1,000 books. Subscribers can zero in on answers to time-critical questions in a matter of seconds. Read the books on your Bookshelf from cover to cover or simply flip to the page you need. Try it today with a free trial.

Table of Contents

Preface . . . . **xi**

1. System Snapshots with Tripwire **1**

   1.1 Setting Up Tripwire   4

   1.2 Displaying the Policy and Configuration   5

   1.3 Modifying the Policy and Configuration   6

   1.4 Basic Integrity Checking   7

   1.5 Read-Only Integrity Checking   8

   1.6 Remote Integrity Checking   9

   1.7 Ultra-Paranoid Integrity Checking   11

   1.8 Expensive, Ultra-Paranoid Security Checking   13

   1.9 Automated Integrity Checking   13

  1.10 Printing the Latest Tripwire Report   14

  1.11 Updating the Database   15

  1.12 Adding Files to the Database   16

  1.13 Excluding Files from the Database   17

  1.14 Checking Windows VFAT Filesystems   17

  1.15 Verifying RPM-Installed Files   18

  1.16 Integrity Checking with rsync   19

  1.17 Integrity Checking Manually   20

2. Firewalls with iptables and ipchains **23**

   2.1 Enabling Source Address Verification   24

   2.2 Blocking Spoofed Addresses   26

   2.3 Blocking All Network Traffic   28

   2.4 Blocking Incoming Traffic   28

   2.5 Blocking Outgoing Traffic   30

2.6	Blocking Incoming Service Requests	30
2.7	Blocking Access from a Remote Host	31
2.8	Blocking Access to a Remote Host	32
2.9	Blocking Outgoing Access to All Web Servers on a Network	33
2.10	Blocking Remote Access, but Permitting Local	34
2.11	Controlling Access by MAC Address	35
2.12	Permitting SSH Access Only	36
2.13	Prohibiting Outgoing Telnet Connections	37
2.14	Protecting a Dedicated Server	38
2.15	Preventing pings	39
2.16	Listing Your Firewall Rules	39
2.17	Deleting Firewall Rules	41
2.18	Inserting Firewall Rules	42
2.19	Saving a Firewall Configuration	42
2.20	Loading a Firewall Configuration	43
2.21	Testing a Firewall Configuration	45
2.22	Building Complex Rule Trees	46
2.23	Logging Simplified	47

3.	**Network Access Control**	**49**
3.1	Listing Your Network Interfaces	51
3.2	Starting and Stopping the Network Interface	52
3.3	Enabling/Disabling a Service (xinetd)	53
3.4	Enabling/Disabling a Service (inetd)	54
3.5	Adding a New Service (xinetd)	55
3.6	Adding a New Service (inetd)	56
3.7	Restricting Access by Remote Users	57
3.8	Restricting Access by Remote Hosts (xinetd)	58
3.9	Restricting Access by Remote Hosts (xinetd with libwrap)	59
3.10	Restricting Access by Remote Hosts (xinetd with tcpd)	60
3.11	Restricting Access by Remote Hosts (inetd)	61
3.12	Restricting Access by Time of Day	62
3.13	Restricting Access to an SSH Server by Host	64
3.14	Restricting Access to an SSH Server by Account	64
3.15	Restricting Services to Specific Filesystem Directories	65
3.16	Preventing Denial of Service Attacks	67
3.17	Redirecting to Another Socket	69
3.18	Logging Access to Your Services	70
3.19	Prohibiting root Logins on Terminal Devices	71

4. Authentication Techniques and Infrastructures **72**

4.1   Creating a PAM-Aware Application   74

4.2   Enforcing Password Strength with PAM   75

4.3   Creating Access Control Lists with PAM   76

4.4   Validating an SSL Certificate   78

4.5   Decoding an SSL Certificate   79

4.6   Installing a New SSL Certificate   80

4.7   Generating an SSL Certificate Signing Request (CSR)   81

4.8   Creating a Self-Signed SSL Certificate   83

4.9   Setting Up a Certifying Authority   84

4.10 Converting SSL Certificates from DER to PEM   87

4.11 Getting Started with Kerberos   88

4.12 Adding Users to a Kerberos Realm   92

4.13 Adding Hosts to a Kerberos Realm   93

4.14 Using Kerberos with SSH   94

4.15 Using Kerberos with Telnet   96

4.16 Securing IMAP with Kerberos   98

4.17 Using Kerberos with PAM for System-Wide Authentication   100

5. Authorization Controls **102**

5.1   Running a root Login Shell   104

5.2   Running X Programs as root   105

5.3   Running Commands as Another User via sudo   106

5.4   Bypassing Password Authentication in sudo   106

5.5   Forcing Password Authentication in sudo   108

5.6   Authorizing per Host in sudo   108

5.7   Granting Privileges to a Group via sudo   110

5.8   Running Any Program in a Directory via sudo   110

5.9   Prohibiting Command Arguments with sudo   111

5.10 Sharing Files Using Groups   111

5.11 Permitting Read-Only Access to a Shared File via sudo   112

5.12 Authorizing Password Changes via sudo   113

5.13 Starting/Stopping Daemons via sudo   114

5.14 Restricting root's Abilities via sudo   115

5.15 Killing Processes via sudo   115

5.16 Listing sudo Invocations   117

5.17 Logging sudo Remotely   118

5.18 Sharing root Privileges via SSH   118

5.19	Running root Commands via SSH	120
5.20	Sharing root Privileges via Kerberos su	121

6. Protecting Outgoing Network Connections **124**

6.1	Logging into a Remote Host	125
6.2	Invoking Remote Programs	126
6.3	Copying Files Remotely	127
6.4	Authenticating by Public Key (OpenSSH)	129
6.5	Authenticating by Public Key (OpenSSH Client, SSH2 Server, OpenSSH Key)	131
6.6	Authenticating by Public Key (OpenSSH Client, SSH2 Server, SSH2 Key)	133
6.7	Authenticating by Public Key (SSH2 Client, OpenSSH Server)	134
6.8	Authenticating by Trusted Host	135
6.9	Authenticating Without a Password (Interactively)	138
6.10	Authenticating in cron Jobs	140
6.11	Terminating an SSH Agent on Logout	141
6.12	Tailoring SSH per Host	142
6.13	Changing SSH Client Defaults	143
6.14	Tunneling Another TCP Session Through SSH	144
6.15	Keeping Track of Passwords	146

7. Protecting Files **147**

7.1	Using File Permissions	148
7.2	Securing a Shared Directory	149
7.3	Prohibiting Directory Listings	150
7.4	Encrypting Files with a Password	151
7.5	Decrypting Files	152
7.6	Setting Up GnuPG for Public-Key Encryption	152
7.7	Listing Your Keyring	154
7.8	Setting a Default Key	155
7.9	Sharing Public Keys	156
7.10	Adding Keys to Your Keyring	157
7.11	Encrypting Files for Others	158
7.12	Signing a Text File	159
7.13	Signing and Encrypting Files	159
7.14	Creating a Detached Signature File	160
7.15	Checking a Signature	161
7.16	Printing Public Keys	162

7.17 Backing Up a Private Key 162
7.18 Encrypting Directories 164
7.19 Adding Your Key to a Keyserver 165
7.20 Uploading New Signatures to a Keyserver 165
7.21 Obtaining Keys from a Keyserver 166
7.22 Revoking a Key 168
7.23 Maintaining Encrypted Files with Emacs 169
7.24 Maintaining Encrypted Files with vim 170
7.25 Encrypting Backups 171
7.26 Using PGP Keys with GnuPG 173

8. Protecting Email **175**
8.1 Encrypted Mail with Emacs 175
8.2 Encrypted Mail with vim 177
8.3 Encrypted Mail with Pine 178
8.4 Encrypted Mail with Mozilla 179
8.5 Encrypted Mail with Evolution 180
8.6 Encrypted Mail with mutt 181
8.7 Encrypted Mail with elm 182
8.8 Encrypted Mail with MH 183
8.9 Running a POP/IMAP Mail Server with SSL 183
8.10 Testing an SSL Mail Connection 188
8.11 Securing POP/IMAP with SSL and Pine 188
8.12 Securing POP/IMAP with SSL and mutt 190
8.13 Securing POP/IMAP with SSL and Evolution 191
8.14 Securing POP/IMAP with stunnel and SSL 192
8.15 Securing POP/IMAP with SSH 193
8.16 Securing POP/IMAP with SSH and Pine 195
8.17 Receiving Mail Without a Visible Server 197
8.18 Using an SMTP Server from Arbitrary Clients 198

9. Testing and Monitoring **202**
9.1 Testing Login Passwords (John the Ripper) 203
9.2 Testing Login Passwords (CrackLib) 205
9.3 Finding Accounts with No Password 206
9.4 Finding Superuser Accounts 207
9.5 Checking for Suspicious Account Use 207
9.6 Checking for Suspicious Account Use, Multiple Systems 209
9.7 Testing Your Search Path 211

9.8 Searching Filesystems Effectively   212

9.9 Finding setuid (or setgid) Programs   215

9.10 Securing Device Special Files   217

9.11 Finding Writable Files   218

9.12 Looking for Rootkits   219

9.13 Testing for Open Ports   220

9.14 Examining Local Network Activities   226

9.15 Tracing Processes   231

9.16 Observing Network Traffic   233

9.17 Observing Network Traffic (GUI)   238

9.18 Searching for Strings in Network Traffic   240

9.19 Detecting Insecure Network Protocols   243

9.20 Getting Started with Snort   247

9.21 Packet Sniffing with Snort   248

9.22 Detecting Intrusions with Snort   250

9.23 Decoding Snort Alert Messages   252

9.24 Logging with Snort   253

9.25 Partitioning Snort Logs Into Separate Files   255

9.26 Upgrading and Tuning Snort's Ruleset   256

9.27 Directing System Messages to Log Files (syslog)   257

9.28 Testing a syslog Configuration   261

9.29 Logging Remotely   262

9.30 Rotating Log Files   263

9.31 Sending Messages to the System Logger   264

9.32 Writing Log Entries via Shell Scripts   265

9.33 Writing Log Entries via Perl   267

9.34 Writing Log Entries via C   268

9.35 Combining Log Files   269

9.36 Summarizing Your Logs with logwatch   271

9.37 Defining a logwatch Filter   272

9.38 Monitoring All Executed Commands   273

9.39 Displaying All Executed Commands   275

9.40 Parsing the Process Accounting Log   278

9.41 Recovering from a Hack   279

9.42 Filing an Incident Report   280

Index 283

Preface

If you run a Linux machine, you must think about security. Consider this story told by Scott, a system administrator we know:

> In early 2001, I was asked to build two Linux servers for a client. They just wanted the machines installed and put online. I asked my boss if I should secure them, and he said no, the client would take care of all that. So I did a base install, no updates. The next morning, we found our network switch completely saturated by a denial of service attack. We powered off the two servers, and everything returned to normal. Later I had the fun of figuring out what had happened. Both machines had been rooted, via ftpd holes, within *six hours* of going online. One had been scanning lots of other machines for ftp and portmap exploits. The other was blasting SYN packets at some poor cablemodem in Canada, saturating our 100Mb network segment. And you know, they had been rooted *independently*, and the exploits had required no skill whatsoever. Just typical script kiddies.

Scott's story is not unusual: today's Internet is full of port scanners—both the automated and human kinds—searching for vulnerable systems. We've heard of systems infiltrated *one hour* after installation. Linux vendors have gotten better at delivering default installs with most vital services turned off instead of left on, but you still need to think about security from the moment you connect your box to the Net...and even earlier.

A Cookbook About Security?!?

Computer security is an ongoing process, a constant contest between system administrators and intruders. It needs to be monitored carefully and revised frequently. So... how the heck can this complex subject be condensed into a bunch of cookbook recipes?

Let's get one thing straight: this book is absolutely not a total security solution for your Linux computers. Don't even think it. Instead, we've presented a handy guide filled with easy-to-follow recipes for *improving* your security and performing common *tasks* securely. Need a quick way to send encrypted email within Emacs? It's in here. How about restricting access to your network services at particular times of day? Look inside. Want to firewall your web server? Prevent IP spoofing? Set up key-based SSH authentication? We'll show you the specific commands and configuration file entries you need.

In short: this book won't teach you security, but it will demonstrate helpful solutions to targeted problems, guiding you to close common security holes, and saving you the trouble of looking up specific syntax.

Intended Audience

Here are some good reasons to read this book:

- You need a quick reference for practical, security-related tasks.
- You think your system is secure, but haven't done much to check or ensure this. Think again. If you haven't followed the recipes in this book, or done something roughly equivalent, your system probably has holes.
- You are interested in Linux security, but fear the learning curve. Our book introduces a quick sampling of security topics, with plenty of code for experimenting, which may lead you to explore further.

The book is primarily for intermediate-level Linux users. We assume you know the layout of a Linux system (*/etc*, */usr/bin*, */var/spool*, and so forth), have written shell and Perl scripts, and are comfortable with commands like chmod, chgrp, umask, diff, ln, and emacs or vi. Many recipes require root privileges, so you'll get the most out of this book if you administer a Linux system.

Roadmap of the Book

Like a regular cookbook, ours is designed to be opened anywhere and browsed. The recipes can be read independently, and when necessary we provide cross-references to related recipes by number: for example, the notation [3.7] means "see Chapter 3, Recipe 7."

The chapters are presented roughly in the order you would use them when setting up a new Linux system. Chapter 1, *System Snapshots with Tripwire*, covers the first vital, security-related activity after setup, taking a snapshot of your filesystem state. From there we discuss protecting your system from unwanted network connections in Chapter 2, *Firewalls with iptables and ipchains*, and Chapter 3, *Network Access Control*.

Once your system is snapshotted and firewalled, it's time to add users. Recipes for login security are found in Chapter 4, *Authentication Techniques and Infrastructures*. And in case you need to share superuser privileges with multiple users, we follow with Chapter 5, *Authorization Controls*.

Now that you have users, they'll want to secure their own network connections, files, and email. Recipes for these topics are presented in Chapter 6, *Protecting Outgoing Network Connections*, Chapter 7, *Protecting Files*, and Chapter 8, *Protecting Email*, respectively.

Finally, as your system happily chugs away, you'll want to watch out for attacks and security holes. Chapter 9, *Testing and Monitoring*, is a grab-bag of recipes for checking your filesystem, network traffic, processes, and log files on an ongoing basis.

Our Security Philosophy

Computer security is full of tradeoffs among risks, costs, and benefits. In theory, nothing less than 100% security will protect your system, but 100% is impossible to achieve, and even getting close may be difficult and expensive. Guarding against the many possibilities for intrusion, not to mention counter-possibilities and counter-counter-possibilities, can be (and is) a full-time job.

As an example, suppose you are a careful communicator and encrypt all the mail messages you send to friends using GnuPG, as we discuss in Chapter 8. Let's say you even verified all your friends' public encryption keys so you know they haven't been forged. On the surface, this technique prevents hostile third parties from reading your messages in transit over the Internet. But let's delve a little deeper. Did you perform the encryption on a secure system? What if the GnuPG binary (gpg) has been compromised by a cracker, replaced by an insecure lookalike? What if your text editor was compromised? Or the shared libraries used by the editor? Or your kernel? Even if your kernel file on disk (*vmlinuz*) is genuine, what if its runtime state (in memory) has been modified? What if there's a keyboard sniffer running on your system, capturing your keystrokes before encryption occurs? There could even be an eavesdropper parked in a van outside your building, watching the images from your computer monitor by capturing stray electromagnetic emissions.

But enough about your system: what about your friends' computers? Did your friends choose strong passphrases so their encryption keys can't be cracked? After decrypting your messages, do they store them on disk, unencrypted? If their disks get backed up onto tape, are the tapes safely locked away or can they be stolen? And speaking of theft, are all your computers secured under lock and key? And who holds the keys? Maybe your next-door neighbor, to whom you gave a copy of your house-key, is a spy.

If you're the security chief at a Fortune 500 company or in government, you probably need to think about this complex web of issues on a regular basis. If you're a home user with a single Linux system and a cable modem, the costs of maintaining a large, multitiered security infrastructure, striving toward 100% security, very likely outweigh the benefits.

Regardless, you can still improve your security in steps, as we demonstrate in this book. Encrypting your sensitive files is better than not encrypting them. Installing a firewall, using SSH for remote logins, and performing basic intrusion and integrity checking all contribute toward your system safety. Do you need higher security? That depends on the level of risk you're willing to tolerate, and the price you're willing (and able) to pay.

In this cookbook, we present security tools and their common uses. We do not, and cannot, address every possible infiltration of your computer systems. Every recipe has caveats, exceptions, and limitations: some stated, and others merely implied by the "facts of life" of computer security in the real world.

Supported Linux Distributions

We developed and tested these recipes on the following Linux distributions:

- Red Hat Linux 8.0, kernel 2.4.18
- SuSE Linux 8.0, kernel 2.4.18
- Red Hat Linux 7.0, kernel 2.2.22 (for the ipchains recipes in Chapter 2)

In addition, our technical review team tested recipes on Red Hat 6.2, SuSE 8.1, Debian 3.0, and Mandrake 9.0. Overall, most recipes should work fine on most distributions, as long as you have the necessary programs installed.

Trying the Recipes

Most recipes provide commands or scripts you can run, or a set of configuration options for a particular program. When trying a recipe, please keep in mind:

- Our default shell for recipes is bash. If you use another shell, you might need different syntax for setting environment variables and other shell-specific things.
- If you create a Linux shell script (say, "myscript") in your current directory, but the current directory (".") is not in your search path, you can't run it simply by typing the script name:

  ```
  $ myscript
  bash: myscript: command not found
  ```

  because the shell won't find it. To invoke the script, specify that it's in the current directory:

  ```
  $ ./myscript
  ```

  Alternatively, you could add the current directory to your search path, but we recommend against this. [9.7]

- Linux commands may behave differently when run in an interactive shell, a script, or a batch job (e.g., via cron). Each method may have a different environment (for example, search path), and some commands even are coded to behave differently depending how they are invoked. If a recipe does not behave as you expect in a script, try running it interactively, and vice versa. You can see your environment with the env command, and your shell variables with the set built-in command.

- Different Linux distributions may place important binaries and configuration files in locations different from those in our recipes. Programs are assumed to be in your search path. You might need to add directories to your path, such as */sbin*, */usr/sbin*, and */usr/kerberos/bin*. If you cannot find a file, try the locate command:*

  ```
  $ locate sshd.config
  /etc/ssh/sshd_config
  ```

  or in the worst case, the find command from the root of the filesystem, as root:

  ```
  # find / -name sshd_config -print
  ```

- Make sure you have the most recent versions of programs involved in the recipe, or at least stable versions, and that the programs are properly installed.

Finally, each Linux system is unique. While we have tested these recipes on various machines, yours might be different enough to produce unexpected results.

 Before you run any recipe, make sure you understand how it will affect security on your system.

Conventions Used in This Book

The following typographic conventions are used in this book:

Italic is used to indicate new terms and for comments in code sections. It is also used for URLs, FTP sites, filenames, and directory names. Some code sections begin with a line of italicized text, which usually specifies the file that the code belongs in.

Constant width is used for code sections and program names.

Constant width italic is used to indicate replaceable parts of code.

Constant width bold is used to indicate text typed by the user in code sections.

We capitalize the names of software packages or protocols, such as Tripwire or FTP, in contrast to their associated programs, denoted tripwire and ftp.

---

* Contained in the RPM package *slocate* (for Red Hat) or *findutils-locate* (for SuSE).

We use the following standards for shell prompts, so it's clear if a command must be run by a particular user or on a particular machine:

Shell Prompt	Meaning
$	Ordinary user prompt
#	Root shell prompt
myhost$	Shell prompt on host *myhost*
myhost#	Root prompt on host *myhost*
myname$	Shell prompt for user *myname*
myname@myhost$	Shell prompt for user *myname* on host *myhost*

 This icon indicates a tip, suggestion, or general note.

 This icon indicates a warning or caution.

We'd Like to Hear from You

Please address comments and questions concerning this book to the publisher:

O'Reilly & Associates, Inc.
1005 Gravenstein Highway North
Sebastopol, CA 95472
(800) 998-9938 (in the United States or Canada)
(707) 829-0515 (international or local)
(707) 829-0104 (fax)

We have a web page for this book, where we list errata, examples, or any additional information. You can access this page at:

http://www.oreilly.com/catalog/linuxsckbk/

To comment or ask technical questions about this book, send email to:

bookquestions@oreilly.com

For more information about our books, conferences, Resource Centers, and the O'Reilly Network, see our web site at:

http://www.oreilly.com

Acknowledgments

First and foremost, we thank our editor, Mike Loukides, for his guidance and patience as we completed the book. Working with you is always a pleasure. We thank our technical review team, Olaf Gellert, Michael A. Johnson, Nico Kadel, Klaus Möller, Sandra O'Brien, Colin Phipps, Marco Thorbrügge, and Kevin Timm, for their insightful comments that improved the text. We also thank Paul Shelman, Beth Reagan, John Kling, Jill Gaffney, Patrick Romain, Rick van Rein, Wouter Hanegraaff, Harvey Newstrom, and "Scott" the sysadmin.

Dan would like to thank his family, Lisa and Sophie, for their support and love during the writing of this book. Richard would like to thank H. David Todd and Douglas Bigelow for giving him the chance that led to his career, lo these many years ago. Bob would like to thank his wife, Alison, for her support and understanding during too many nights and weekends when he was glued to his keyboard.

System Snapshots with Tripwire

1.0   Introduction

Suppose your system is infiltrated by the infamous Jack the Cracker. Being a conscientious evildoer, he quickly modifies some system files to create back doors and cover his tracks. For instance, he might substitute a hacked version of */bin/login* to admit him without a password, and a bogus */bin/ls* could skip over and hide traces of his evil deeds. If these changes go unnoticed, your system could remain secretly compromised for a long time. How can this situation be avoided?

Break-ins of this kind can be detected by an *integrity checker*: a program that periodically inspects important system files for unexpected changes. The *very first* security measure you should take when creating a new Linux machine, before you make it available to networks and other users, is to "snapshot" (record) the initial state of your system files with an integrity checker. If you don't, you cannot reliably detect alterations to these files later. This is vitally important!

Tripwire is the best known open source integrity checker. It stores a snapshot of your files in a known state, so you can periodically compare the files against the snapshot to discover discrepancies. In our example, if */bin/login* and */bin/ls* were in Tripwire's snapshot, then any changes in their size, inode number, permissions, or other attributes would catch Tripwire's attention. Notably, Tripwire detects changes in a file's *content*, even a single character, by verifying its checksum.

 `tripwire` Version 1.2, supplied in SuSE 8.0, is positively ancient and supports an outdated syntax. Before attempting any recipes in this chapter, upgrade to the latest `tripwire` (2.3 or higher) at *http://sourceforge.org/projects/tripwire* or *http://www.tripwire.org*.

Tripwire is driven by two main components: a policy and a database. The *policy* lists all files and directories that Tripwire should snapshot, along with rules for identifying violations (unexpected changes). For example, a simple policy could treat any changes in */root*, */bin*, and */lib* as violations. The Tripwire *database* contains the snapshot itself, created by evaluating the policy against your filesystems. Once setup is complete, you can compare filesystems against the snapshot at any time, and Tripwire will report any discrepancies. This is a Tripwire *integrity check*, and it generates an *integrity check report*, as in Figure 1-1.

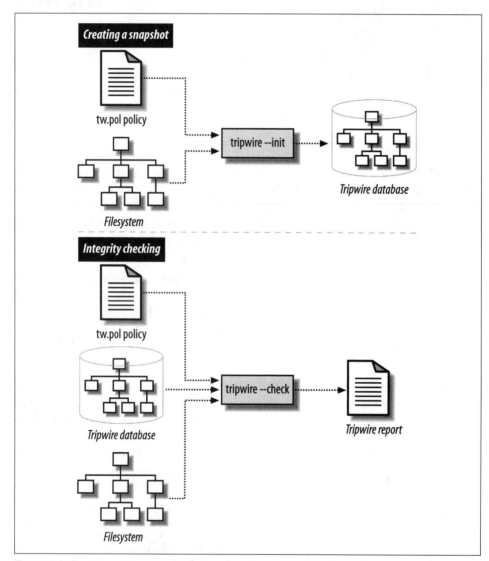

Figure 1-1. Creating a Tripwire snapshot, and performing an integrity check

Along with the policy and database, Tripwire also has a *configuration*, stored in a configuration file, that controls global aspects of its behavior. For example, the configuration specifies the locations of the database, policy file, and `tripwire` executable.

Important Tripwire-related files are encrypted and signed to prevent tampering. Two cryptographic keys are responsible for this protection. The *site key* protects the policy file and the configuration file, and the *local key* protects the database and generated reports. Multiple machines with the same policy and configuration may share a site key, whereas each machine must have its own local key for its database and reports.

Although Tripwire is a security tool, it can be compromised itself if you are not careful to protect its sensitive files. The most secret, quadruple-hyper-encrypted Tripwire database is useless if Jack the Cracker simply deletes it! Likewise, Jack could hack the `tripwire` executable (*/usr/sbin/tripwire*) or interfere with its notifications to the system administrator. Our recipes will describe several configurations—at increasing levels of paranoia and expense—to thwart such attacks.

Tripwire has several weaknesses:

- Its lengthy output can make your eyes glaze over, not the most helpful state for finding security violations.
- If you update your critical files frequently, then you must update the database frequently, which can be tiresome.
- Its batch-oriented approach (periodic checks, not real-time) leaves a window of opportunity. Suppose you modify a file, and then a cracker modifies it again before the next integrity check. Tripwire will rightfully flag the file, but you'll wrongly blame the discrepancy on your change instead of the cracker's. Your Tripwire database will be "poisoned" (contain invalid data) on the next update.
- It doesn't compile easily in some Linux and Unix environments.

Regardless, Tripwire can be a valuable security tool if used carefully and methodically.

 Before connecting any Linux computer to a network, or making the machine available to other users in any way, TAKE A SNAPSHOT. We cannot stress this enough. A machine's first snapshot MUST capture a legitimate, uncompromised state or it is worthless. (That's why this topic is the *first* chapter in the book.)

In addition to Tripwire, we also present a few non-Tripwire techniques for integrity checking, involving `rpm` [1.15], `rsync` [1.16], and `find`. [1.17]

There are other integrity checkers around, such as Aide (*http://www.cs.tut.fi/~rammer/aide.html*) and Samhain (*http://la-samhna.de/samhain*), though we do not cover them. Finally, you might also check out runtime kernel integrity checkers, like `kstat` (*http://www.s0ftpj.org*) and `prosum` (*http://prosum.sourceforge.net*).

1.1   Setting Up Tripwire

Problem

You want to prepare a computer to use Tripwire for the first time.

Solution

After you have installed Tripwire, do the following:

```
# cd /etc/tripwire
# ./twinstall.sh
# tripwire --init
# rm twcfg.txt twpol.txt
```

Discussion

The script `twinstall.sh` performs the following tasks within the directory *letc/ tripwire*:

* Creates the site key and the local key, prompting you to enter their passphrases. (If the keys exist, this step is skipped.) The site key is stored in *site.key*, and the local key in *hostname-local.key*, where *hostname* is the hostname of the machine.

* Signs the default configuration file, *twcfg.txt*, with the site key, creating *tw.cfg*.

* Signs the default policy file, *twpol.txt*, with the site key, creating *tw.pol*.

If for some reason your system doesn't have `twinstall.sh`, equivalent manual steps are:

```
Helpful variables:
DIR=/etc/tripwire
SITE_KEY=$DIR/site.key
LOCAL_KEY=$DIR/`hostname`-local.key

Generate the site key:
# twadmin --generate-keys --site-keyfile $SITE_KEY

Generate the local key:
# twadmin --generate-keys --local-keyfile $LOCAL_KEY

Sign the configuration file:
# twadmin --create-cfgfile --cfgfile $DIR/tw.cfg \
        --site-keyfile $SITE_KEY $DIR/twcfg.txt

Sign the policy file:
# twadmin --create-polfile --cfgfile $DIR/tw.cfg \
        --site-keyfile $SITE_KEY $DIR/twpol.txt

Set appropriate permissions:
# cd $DIR
```

```
# chown root:root $SITE_KEY $LOCAL_KEY tw.cfg tw.pol
# chmod 600 $SITE_KEY $LOCAL_KEY tw.cfg tw.pol
```

(Or chmod 640 to allow a root group to access the files.)

These steps assume that your default configuration and policy files exist: *twcfg.txt* and *twpol.txt*, respectively. They should have been supplied with the Tripwire distribution. Undoubtedly you'll need to edit them to match your system. [1.3] The names *twcfg.txt* and *twpol.txt* are mandatory if you run twinstall.sh, as they are hard-coded inside the script.*

Next, tripwire builds the Tripwire database and signs it with the local key:

```
# tripwire --init
```

Enter the local key passphrase to complete the operation. If tripwire produces an error message like "Warning: File System Error," then your default policy probably refers to nonexistent files. These are not fatal errors: tripwire still ran successfully. At some point you should modify the policy to remove these references. [1.3]

The last step, which is optional but recommended, is to delete the plaintext (unencrypted) policy and configuration files:

```
# rm twcfg.txt twpol.txt
```

You are now ready to run integrity checks.

See Also

twadmin(8), tripwire(8). If Tripwire isn't included in your Linux distribution, it can be downloaded from the Tripwire project page at *http://sourceforge.net/projects/ tripwire* or *http://www.tripwire.org*. (Check both to make sure you're getting the latest version.) Basic documentation is installed in */usr/share/doc/tripwire** but does not include the full manual, so be sure to download it (in PDF or source formats) from the SourceForge project page. The commercial Tripwire is found at *http://www. tripwire.com*.

1.2   Displaying the Policy and Configuration

Problem

You want to view Tripwire's policy or configuration, but they are stored in non-human–readable, binary files, or they are missing.

---

* If they are different on your system, read *twinstall.sh* to learn the appropriate names.

Solution

Generate the active configuration file:

```
# cd /etc/tripwire
# twadmin --print-cfgfile > twcfg.txt
```

Generate the active policy file:

```
# cd /etc/tripwire
# twadmin --print-polfile > twpol.txt
```

Discussion

Tripwire's active configuration file *tw.cfg* and policy file *tw.pol* are encrypted and signed and therefore non-human–readable. To view them, you must first convert them to plaintext.

Tripwire's documentation advises you to delete the plaintext versions of the configuration and policy after re-signing them. If your plaintext files were missing to start with, this is probably why.

Although you can redirect the output of twadmin to any files you like, remember that twinstall.sh requires the plaintext policy and configuration files to have the names we used, *twcfg.txt* and *twpol.txt*. [1.1]

See Also

twadmin(8).

1.3 Modifying the Policy and Configuration

Problem

You want to change the set of files and directories that tripwire examines, or change tripwire's default behavior.

Solution

Extract the policy and configuration to plaintext files: [1.2]

```
# cd /etc/tripwire
# twadmin --print-polfile > twpol.txt
# twadmin --print-cfgfile > twcfg.txt
```

Modify the policy file *twpol.txt* and/or the configuration file *twcfg.txt* with any text editor. Then re-sign the modified files: [1.1]

```
# twadmin --create-cfgfile --cfgfile /etc/tripwire/tw.cfg \
        --site-keyfile site_key etc/tripwire/twcfg.txt
```

```
# twadmin --create-polfile --cfgfile /etc/tripwire/tw.cfg \
        --site-keyfile site_key etc/tripwire/twpol.txt
```

and reinitialize the database: [1.1]

```
# tripwire --init
# rm twcfg.txt twpol.txt
```

Discussion

This is much like setting up Tripwire from scratch [1.1], except our existing, crypto-graphically-signed policy and configuration files are first converted to plaintext. [1.2]

You'll want to modify the policy if `tripwire` complains that a file does not exist:

```
### Error: File could not be opened.
```

Edit the policy file and remove or comment out the reference to this file if it does not exist on your system. Then re-sign the policy file.

You don't need to follow this procedure if you're simply updating the database after an integrity check [1.11], only if you've modified the policy or configuration.

See Also

twadmin(8), tripwire(8).

1.4   Basic Integrity Checking

Problem

You want to check whether any files have been altered since the last Tripwire snapshot.

Solution

```
# tripwire --check
```

Discussion

This command is the lifeblood of Tripwire: has your system changed? It compares the current state of your filesystem against the Tripwire database, according to the rules in your active policy. The results of the comparison are written to standard output and also stored as a timestamped, signed Tripwire report.

You can also perform a limited integrity check against one or more files in the database. If your tripwire policy contains this rule:

```
(
  rulename = "My funky files",
  severity = 50
```

```
        )
        {
          /sbin/e2fsck                          -> $(SEC_CRIT) ;
          /bin/cp                               -> $(SEC_CRIT) ;
          /usr/tmp                              -> $(SEC_INVARIANT) ;
          /etc/csh.cshrc                        -> $(SEC_CONFIG) ;
        }
```

you can check selected files and directories with:

```
# tripwire --check /bin/cp /usr/tmp
```

or all files in the given rule with:

```
# tripwire --check --rule-name "My funky files"
```

or all rules with severities greater than or equal to a given value:

```
# tripwire --check --severity 40
```

See Also

tripwire(8), and the Tripwire manual for policy syntax. You can produce a help message with:

```
$ tripwire --check --help
```

1.5   Read-Only Integrity Checking

Problem

You want to store Tripwire's most vital files on read-only media, such as a CD-ROM or write-protected disk, to guard against compromise, and then run integrity checks.

Solution

1. Copy the site key, local key, and tripwire binary onto the desired disk, write-protect it, and mount it. Suppose it is mounted at /mnt/cdrom.

```
# mount /mnt/cdrom
# ls -l /mnt/cdrom
total 2564
-r--r-----    1 root     root           931 Feb 21 12:20 site.key
-r--r-----    1 root     root           931 Feb 21 12:20 myhost-local.key
-r-xr-xr-x    1 root     root       2612200 Feb 21 12:19 tripwire
```

2. Generate the Tripwire configuration file in plaintext: [1.2]

```
# DIR=/etc/tripwire
# cd $DIR
# twadmin --print-cfgfile > twcfg.txt
```

3. Edit the configuration file to point to these copies: [1.3]

```
/etc/tripwire/twcfg.txt:
ROOT=/mnt/cdrom
SITEKEYFILE=/mnt/cdrom/site.key
LOCALKEYFILE=/mnt/cdrom/myhost-local.key
```

4. Sign your modified Tripwire configuration file: [1.3]

```
# SITE_KEY=/mnt/cdrom/site.key
# twadmin --create-cfgfile --cfgfile $DIR/tw.cfg \
          --site-keyfile $SITE_KEY $DIR/twcfg.txt
```

5. Regenerate the tripwire database [1.3] and unmount the CD-ROM:

```
# /mnt/cdrom/tripwire --init
# umount /mnt/cdrom
```

Now, whenever you want to perform an integrity check [1.4], insert the read-only disk and run:

```
# mount /mnt/cdrom
# /mnt/cdrom/tripwire --check
# umount /mnt/cdrom
```

Discussion

The site key, local key, and tripwire binary (*/usr/sbin/tripwire*) are the only files you need to protect from compromise. Other Tripwire-related files, such as the database, policy, and configuration, are signed by the keys, so alterations would be detected. (Back them up frequently, however, in case an attacker deletes them!)

Before copying */usr/sbin/tripwire* to CD-ROM, make sure it is statically linked (which is the default configuration) so it does not depend on any shared runtime libraries that could be compromised:

```
$ ldd /usr/sbin/tripwire
not a dynamic executable
```

See Also

twadmin(8), tripwire(8), ldd(1), mount(8).

1.6   Remote Integrity Checking

Problem

You want to perform an integrity check, but to increase security, you store vital Tripwire files off-host.

In this recipe and others, we use two machines: your original machine to be checked, which we'll call *trippy*, and a second, trusted machine we'll call *trusty*. *trippy* is the untrusted machine whose integrity you want to check with Tripwire. *trusty* is a secure machine, typically with no incoming network access.

Solution

Store copies of the site key, local key, and `tripwire` binary on a trusted remote machine that has no incoming network access. Use `rsync`, securely tunneled through `ssh`, to verify that the originals and copies are identical, and to trigger an integrity check.

The initial setup on remote machine *trusty* is:

```
#!/bin/sh
REMOTE_MACHINE=trippy
RSYNC='/usr/bin/rsync -a --progress --rsh=/usr/bin/ssh'
SAFE_DIR=/usr/local/tripwire/${REMOTE_MACHINE}
VITAL_FILES="/usr/sbin/tripwire
    /etc/tripwire/site.key
    /etc/tripwire/${REMOTE_MACHINE}-local.key"

mkdir $SAFE_DIR
for file in $VITAL_FILES
do
    $RSYNC ${REMOTE_MACHINE}:$file $SAFE_DIR/
done
```

Prior to running every integrity check on the local machine, verify these three files by comparing them to the remote copies. The following code should be run on *trusty*, assuming the same variables as in the preceding script (`REMOTE_MACHINE`, etc.):

```
#!/bin/sh
cd $SAFE_DIR
rm -f log
for file in $VITAL_FILES
do
    base=`basename $file`
    $RSYNC -n ${REMOTE_MACHINE}:$file . | fgrep -x "$base" >> log
done
if [ -s log ] ; then
    echo 'Security alert!'
else
    ssh ${REMOTE_MACHINE} -l root /usr/sbin/tripwire --check
fi
```

Discussion

`rsync` is a handy utility for synchronizing files on two machines. In this recipe we tunnel `rsync` through `ssh`, the Secure Shell, to provide secure authentication and to encrypt communication between *trusty* and *trippy*. (This assumes you have an appropriate SSH infrastructure set up between *trusty* and *trippy*, e.g., [6.4]. If not, rsync can be used insecurely without SSH, but we don't recommend it.)

The --progress option of rsync produces output only if the local and remote files differ, and the -n option causes rsync not to copy files, merely reporting what it would do. The fgrep command removes all output but the filenames in question. (We use fgrep because it matches fixed strings, not regular expressions, since filenames commonly contain special characters like "." found in regular expressions.) The fgrep -x option matches whole lines, or in this case, filenames. Thus, the file *log* is empty if and only if the local and remote files are identical, triggering the integrity check.

You might be tempted to store the Tripwire database remotely as well, but it's not necessary. Since the database is signed with the local key, which is kept off-host, tripwire would alert you if the database changed unexpectedly.

Instead of merely checking the important Tripwire files, *trusty* could copy them to *trippy* before each integrity check:

```
# scp -p tripwire trippy:/usr/sbin/tripwire
# scp -p site.key trippy-local.key trippy:/etc/tripwire/
# ssh trippy -l root /usr/sbin/tripwire --check
```

Another tempting alternative is to mount *trippy*'s disks remotely on *trusty*, preferably read-only, using a network filesystem such as NFS or AFS, and then run the Tripwire check on *trusty*. This method, however, is only as secure as your network filesystem software.

See Also

rsync(1), ssh(1).

1.7 Ultra-Paranoid Integrity Checking

Problem

You want highly secure integrity checks, at the expense of speed and convenience.

Solution

Securely create a bootable CD-ROM containing a minimal Linux system, the tripwire binary, and your local and site keys. Disconnect your computer from all networks, boot on the CD-ROM, and perform an integrity check of your computer's disks, using executable programs on the CD-ROM only.

Back up your Tripwire database, configuration, and policy frequently, in case an attacker deletes them from your system.

Discussion

This cumbersome but more secure method requires at least two computers, one of them carefully trusted. As before, we'll call the trusted system *trusty* and the Tripwire machine *trippy*. Our goal is to run secure Tripwire checks on *trippy*.

The first important step is to create a bootable CD-ROM securely. This means:

- Create the CD-ROM on *trusty*, a virgin Linux machine built directly from trusted source or binary packages, that has never been on a network or otherwise accessible to third parties. Apply all necessary security patches to bring *trusty* up to date.
- Configure the CD-ROM's startup scripts to disable all networking.
- Populate the CD-ROM directly from trusted source or binary packages.
- Create your Tripwire site key and local key on *trusty*.

Second, boot *trippy* on the CD-ROM, mount the local disks, and create *trippy*'s Tripwire database, using the tripwire binary and keys on the CD-ROM. Since the Tripwire database, policy, and configuration files are signed with keys on the CD-ROM, these files may safely reside on *trippy*, rather than the CD-ROM.

Third, you must boot *trippy* on the CD-ROM before running an integrity check. Otherwise, if you simply mount the CD-ROM on *trippy* and run the tripwire binary from the CD-ROM, you are not protected against:

- Compromised shared libraries on *trippy*, if your tripwire binary is dynamically linked.
- A compromised Linux kernel on *trippy*.
- A compromised mount point for the CD-ROM on *trippy*.

See, we told you this recipe was for the paranoid. But if you want higher security with Tripwire, you might need this level of caution.

For more convenience, you could schedule a cron job to reboot *trippy* nightly from the CD-ROM, which runs the Tripwire check and then reboots *trippy* normally. Do not, however, schedule this cron job on *trippy* itself, since cron could be compromised. Instead, schedule it on *trusty*, perhaps triggering the reboot via an SSH batch job. [6.10]

See Also

A good starting point for making a self-contained bootable CD-ROM or floppy is tomsrtbt at *http://www.toms.net/rb*.

Consider including post-mortem security tools on the CD-ROM, such as the Coroner's Toolkit. [9.41]

1.8 Expensive, Ultra-Paranoid Security Checking

Problem

You want highly secure integrity checks and are willing to shell out additional money for them.

Solution

Store your files on a dual-ported disk array. Mount the disk array read-only on a second, trusted machine that has no network connection. Run your Tripwire scans on the second machine.

Discussion

A dual-ported disk array permits two machines to access the same physical disk. If you've got money to spare for increased security, this might be a reasonable approach to securing Tripwire.

Once again, let *trippy* be your machine in need of Tripwire scans. *trusty* is a highly secure second machine, built directly from trusted source or binary packages with all necessary security patches applied, that has no network connection and has never been accessible to third parties.

trippy's primary storage is kept on a dual-ported disk array. Mount this array on *trusty* read-only. Perform all Tripwire-related operations on *trusty*: initializing the database, running integrity checks, and so forth. The Tripwire database, binaries, keys, policy, and configuration are likewise kept on *trusty*. Since *trusty* is inaccessible via any network, your Tripwire checks will be as reliable as the physical security of *trusty*.

1.9 Automated Integrity Checking

Problem

You want to schedule integrity checks at specific times or intervals.

Solution

Use cron. For example, to perform an integrity check every day at 3:00 a.m.:

```
root's crontab file:
0 3 * * * /usr/sbin/tripwire --check
```

Discussion

This is not a production-quality recipe. An intruder could compromise cron, substituting another job or simply preventing yours from running. For more reliability, run the cron job on a trusted remote machine:

Remote crontab entry on trusty:
```
0 3 * * * ssh -n -l root trippy /usr/sbin/tripwire --check
```

but if an intruder compromises sshd on *trippy*, you're again out of luck. Likewise, some rootkits [9.12] can subvert the exec call to tripwire even if invoked remotely. For maximum security, run not only the cron job but also the integrity check on a trusted remote machine. [1.8]

Red Hat Linux comes preconfigured to run tripwire every night via the cron job */etc/cron.daily/tripwire-check*. However, a Tripwire database is not supplied with the operating system: you must initialize one yourself. [1.1] If you don't, cron will send daily email to root about a failed tripwire invocation.

See Also

tripwire(8), crontab(1), crontab(5), cron(8).

1.10   Printing the Latest Tripwire Report

Problem

You want to display the results of the most recent integrity check.

Solution

```
#!/bin/sh
DIR=/var/lib/tripwire/report
HOST=`hostname -s`
LAST_REPORT=`ls -1t $DIR/$HOST-*.twr | head -1`
twprint --print-report --twrfile "$LAST_REPORT"
```

Discussion

Tripwire reports are stored in the location indicated by the REPORTFILE variable in the Tripwire configuration file. A common value is:

```
REPORTFILE = /var/lib/tripwire/report/$(HOSTNAME)-$(DATE).twr
```

The HOSTNAME variable contains the hostname of your machine (big surprise), and DATE is a numeric timestamp such as 20020409-040521 (April 9, 2002, at 4:05:21). So for host *trippy*, this report filename would be:

/var/lib/tripwire/report/trippy-20020409-040521.twr

When tripwire runs, it can optionally send reports by email. This notification should not be considered reliable since email can be suppressed, spoofed, or otherwise compromised. Instead, get into the habit of examining the reports yourself.

The twprint program can print reports not only for integrity checks but also for the Tripwire database. To do the latter:

```
# twprint --print-dbfile --dbfile /var/lib/tripwire/`hostname -s`.twd
Tripwire(R) 2.3.0 Database
Database generated by:        root
Database generated on:        Mon Apr  1 22:33:52 2002
Database last updated on:     Never
... contents follow ...
```

See Also

twprint(8).

1.11   Updating the Database

Problem

Your latest Tripwire report contains discrepancies that tripwire should ignore in the future.

Solution

Update the Tripwire database relative to the most recent integrity check report:

```
#!/bin/sh
DIR=/var/lib/tripwire/report
HOST=`hostname -s`
LAST_REPORT=`ls -1t $DIR/$HOST-*.twr | head -1`
tripwire --update --twrfile "$LAST_REPORT"
```

Discussion

Updates are performed with respect to an integrity check report, not with respect to the current filesystem state. Therefore, if you've modified some files since the last check, you cannot simply run an update: you must run an integrity check first. Otherwise the update won't take the changes into account, and the next integrity check will still flag them.

Updating is significantly faster than reinitializing the database. [1.3]

See Also

tripwire(8).

1.12 Adding Files to the Database

Problem

Tell `tripwire` to include a file or directory in its database.

Solution

Generate the active policy file in human-readable format. [1.2] Add the given file or directory to the active policy file.

To mark the file */bin/ls* for inclusion:

```
/bin/ls  -->  $(SEC_BIN) ;
```

To mark the entire directory tree */etc* for inclusion:

```
/etc     -->  $(SEC_BIN) ;
```

To mark */etc* and its files, but not recurse into subdirectories:

```
/etc     -->  $(SEC_BIN) (recurse=1) ;
```

To mark only the */etc* directory but none of its files or subdirectories:

```
/etc     -->  $(SEC_BIN) (recurse=0);
```

Then reinitialize the database. [1.3]

Discussion

The policy is a list of rules stored in a policy file. A rule looks like:

```
filename -> rule ;
```

which means that the given file (or directory) should be considered compromised if the given rule is broken. For instance,

```
/bin/login -> +pisug ;
```

means that */bin/login* is suspect if its file permissions (p), inode number (i), size (s), user (u), or group (g) have changed since the last snapshot. We won't document the full policy syntax because Tripwire's manual is quite thorough. Our recipe uses a predefined rule in a global variable, `SEC_BIN`, designating a binary file that should not change.

The recurse=n attribute for a directory tells tripwire to recurse n levels deep into the filesystem. Zero means to consider only the directory file itself.

It's actually quite likely that you'll need to modify the policy. The default policy supplied with Tripwire is tailored to a specific type of system or Linux distribution, and contains a number of files not necessarily present on yours.

See Also

The Tripwire manual has detailed documentation on the policy file format.

1.13   Excluding Files from the Database

Problem

You want to add some, but not all, files in a given directory to the Tripwire database.

Solution

Mark a directory hierarchy for inclusion:

```
/etc -> rule
```

Immediately after, mark some files to be excluded:

```
!/etc/not.me
!/etc/not.me.either
```

You can exclude a subdirectory too:

```
!/etc/dirname
```

Discussion

The exclamation mark (!) prevents the given file or subdirectory from being added to Tripwire's database.

See Also

The Tripwire manual has detailed documentation on the policy file format.

1.14   Checking Windows VFAT Filesystems

Problem

When checking the integrity of a VFAT filesystem, `tripwire` always complains that files have changed when they haven't.

Solution

Tell `tripwire` not to compare inode numbers.

```
filename -> rule -i ;
```

For example:

```
/mnt/windows/system  -> $(SEC_BIN) -i ;
```

Discussion

Modern Linux kernels do not assign constant inode numbers in VFAT filesystems.

See Also

The Tripwire manual has detailed documentation on the policy file format.

1.15   Verifying RPM-Installed Files

Problem

You have installed some RPM packages, perhaps long ago, and want to check whether any files have changed since the installation.

Solution

```
# rpm -Va [packages]
```

Debian Linux has a similar tool called debsums.

Discussion

If your system uses RPM packages for installing software, this command conveniently compares the installed files against the RPM database. It notices changes in file size, ownership, timestamp, MD5 checksum, and other attributes.

The output is a list of (possibly) problematic files, one per line, each preceded by a string of characters with special meaning. For example:

```
$ rpm -Va
SM5....T c /etc/syslog.conf
.M......   /var/lib/games/trojka.scores
missing    /usr/lib/perl5/5.6.0/Net/Ping.pm
..?.....   /usr/X11R6/bin/XFree86
.....U..   /dev/audio
S.5....T   /bin/ls
```

The first line indicates that *syslog.conf* has an unexpected size (S), permissions (M), checksum (5), and timestamp (T). This is perhaps not surprising, since *syslog.conf* is a configuration file you'd be likely to change after installation. In fact, that is exactly what the "c" means: a configuration file. Similarly, *troijka.scores* is a game score file likely to change. The file *Ping.pm* has apparently been removed, and *XFree86* could not be checked (?) because we didn't run rpm as root. The last two files definitely deserve investigation: */dev/audio* has a new owner (U), and */bin/ls* has been modified.

This technique is valid only if your RPM database and `rpm` command have not been compromised by an attacker. Also, it checks only those files installed from RPMs.

See Also

rpm(8) lists the full set of file attributes checked.

1.16   Integrity Checking with rsync

Problem

You want to snapshot and check your files but you can't use Tripwire. You have lots of disk space on a remote machine.

Solution

Use `rsync` to copy your important files to the remote machine. Use `rsync` again to compare the copies on the two machines.

Discussion

Let *trippy* and *trusty* be your two machines as before. You want to ensure the integrity of the files on *trippy*.

1. On *trippy*, store the `rsync` binary on a CD-ROM mounted at */mnt/cdrom*.

2. On *trusty*, copy the files from *trippy*:

   ```
   trusty# rsync -a -v --rsync-path=/mnt/cdrom/rsync --rsh=/usr/bin/ssh \
                  trippy:/ /data/trippy-backup
   ```

3. Check integrity from *trusty*:

   ```
   trusty# rsync -a -v -n --rsync-path=/mnt/cdrom/rsync --rsh=/usr/bin/ssh \
                  trippy:/ /data/trippy-backup
   ```

The first `rsync` actually performs copying, while the second merely reports differences, thanks to the -n option. If there are no differences, the output will look something like this:

```
receiving file list ... done
wrote 16 bytes   read 7478 bytes   4996.00 bytes/sec
total size is 3469510  speedup is 462.97
```

but if any files differ, their names will appear after the "receiving file list" message:

```
receiving file list ... done
/bin/ls
/usr/sbin/sshd
wrote 24 bytes   read 7486 bytes   5006.67 bytes/sec
total size is 3469510  speedup is 461.99
```

Any listed files—in this case /bin/ls and /usr/sbin/sshd—should be treated as suspicious.

This method has important limitations, most notably that it does not check inode numbers or device numbers. A real integrity checker is better.

See Also

rsync(1).

1.17 Integrity Checking Manually

Problem

You can't use Tripwire for administrative or political reasons, but you want to snapshot your files for later comparison. You don't have enough disk space to mirror your files.

Solution

Run a script like the following that stores pertinent information about each file of interest, such as checksum, inode number, and timestamp:

```
#!/bin/sh
for file
do
    date=`/usr/bin/stat "$file" | /bin/grep '^Modify:' | /usr/bin/cut -f2- -d' '`
    sum=`/usr/bin/md5sum "$file" | /usr/bin/awk '{print $1}'`
    inode=`/bin/ls -id "$file" | /usr/bin/awk '{print $1}'`
    /bin/echo -e "$file\t$inode\t$sum\t$date"
done
```

Store this script as /usr/local/bin/idfile (for example). Use find to run this script on your important files, creating a snapshot. Store it on read-only media. Periodically create a new snapshot and compare the two with diff.

This is not a production-quality integrity checker. It doesn't track file ownership or permissions. It checks only ordinary files, not directories, device special files, or symbolic links. Its tools (md5sum, stat, etc.) are not protected against tampering.

Discussion

1. Run the idfile script to create a snapshot file:

   ```
   # find /dir -xdev -type f -print0 | \
     xargs -0 -r /usr/local/bin/idfile > /tmp/my_snapshot
   ```

   This creates a snapshot file, basically a poor man's Tripwire database.

   ```
   /bin/arch2222    7ba4330c353be9dd527e7eb46d27f923Wed Aug 30 17:54:25 2000
   /bin/ash 2194    cef0493419ea32a7e26eceff8e5dfa90Wed Aug 30 17:40:11 2000
   ```

```
/bin/awk 2171      b5915e362f1a33b7ede6d7965a4611e4Sat Feb 23 23:37:18 2002
...
```

Note that `idfile` will process */tmp/my_snapshot* itself, which will almost certainly differ next time you snapshot. You can use `grep -v` to eliminate the */tmp/my_snapshot* line from the output.

Be aware of the important options and limitations of `find`. [9.8]

2. In preparation for running the `idfile` script later from CD-ROM, modify `idfile` so all commands are relative to */mnt/cdrom/bin*:

```
#!/mnt/cdrom/bin/sh
BIN=/mnt/cdrom/bin
for file
do
    date=`$BIN/stat "$file" | $BIN/grep '^Modify:' | $BIN/cut -f2- -d' '`
    md5sum=`$BIN/sum "$file" | $BIN/awk '{print $1}'`
    inode=`$BIN/ls -id "$file" | $BIN/awk '{print $1}'`
    $BIN/echo -e "$file\t$inode\t$sum\t$date"
done
```

3. Burn a CD-ROM with the following contents:

Directory	Files
/	my_snapshot
/bin	awk, cut, echo, diff, find, grep, ls, mdsum, sh, stat, xargs, idfile

4. Mount the CD-ROM at */mnt/cdrom*.

5. As needed, rerun the `find` and do a `diff`, using the binaries on the CD-ROM:

```
#!/bin/sh
BIN=/mnt/cdrom/bin
$BIN/find /dir -xdev -type f -print0 | \
  xargs -0 -r $BIN/idfile > /tmp/my_snapshot2
$BIN/diff /tmp/my_snapshot2 /mnt/cdrom/my_snapshot
```

This approach is not production-quality; it has some major weaknesses:

- Creating the snapshot can be very slow, and creating new snapshots frequently may be cumbersome.

- It doesn't check some important attributes of a file, such as ownership and permissions. Tailor the `idfile` script to your needs.

- It checks only ordinary files, not directories, device special files, or symbolic links.

- By running `ls`, `md5sum`, and the other programs in sequence, you leave room for race conditions during the generation of the snapshot. A file could change between the invocations of two of these tools.

- If any of the executables are dynamically linked against libraries on the system, and these libraries are compromised, the binaries on the CD-ROM can theoretically be made to operate incorrectly.

- If the mount point */mnt/cdrom* is compromised, your CD-ROM can be spoofed.

See Also

find(1), diff(1). Use a real integrity checker if possible. If you can't use Tripwire, consider Aide (*http://www.cs.tut.fi/~rammer/aide.html*) or Samhain (*http://la-samhna.de/samhain*).

## CHAPTER 2

Firewalls with iptables and ipchains

2.0   Introduction

Your network's first barrier against unwanted infiltrators is your firewall. You *do* have a firewall in place, right? If you think you don't need one, monitor your incoming network traffic some time: you might be amazed by the attention you're receiving. For instance, one of our home computers has never run a publicly accessible service, but it's hit 10–150 times per day by Web, FTP, and SSH connection requests from unfamiliar hosts. Some of these could be legitimate, perhaps web crawlers creating an index; but when the hits are coming from *dialup12345.nowhere.aq* in faraway Antarctica, it's more likely that some script kiddie is probing your ports. (Or the latest Windows worm is trying in vain to break in.)

Linux has a wonderful firewall built right into the kernel, so you have no excuse to be without one. As a superuser, you can configure this firewall with interfaces called ipchains and iptables. ipchains models a stateless packet filter. Each packet reaching the firewall is evaluated against a set of rules. *Stateless* means that the decision to accept, reject, or forward a packet is not influenced by previous packets.

iptables, in contrast, is *stateful*: the firewall can make decisions based on previous packets. Consider this firewall rule: "Drop a response packet if its associated request came from *server.example.com.*" iptables can manage this because it can associate requests with responses, but ipchains cannot. Overall, iptables is significantly more powerful, and can express complex rules more simply, than ipchains.

ipchains is found in kernel Versions 2.2 and up, while iptables requires kernel Version 2.4 or higher.* The two cannot be used together: one or the other is chosen when the kernel is compiled.

---

* Kernel 2.0 has another interface called ipfwadm, but it's so old we won't cover it.

A few caveats before you use the recipes in this chapter:

- We're definitely not providing a complete course in firewall security. ipchains and iptables can implement complex configurations, and we're just scratching the surface. Our goal, as usual, is to present useful recipes.

- The recipes work individually, but not necessarily when combined. You must think carefully when mixing and matching firewall rules, to make sure you aren't passing or blocking traffic unintentionally. Assume all rules are flushed at the beginning of each recipe, using iptables -F or ipchains -F as appropriate. [2.17]

- The recipes do not set default policies (-P option) for the chains. The default policy specifies what to do with an otherwise unhandled packet. You should choose intelligent defaults consistent with your site security policy. One example for iptables is:

```
# iptables -P INPUT DROP
# iptables -P OUTPUT ACCEPT
# iptables -P FORWARD DROP
```

and for ipchains:

```
# ipchains -P input DENY
# ipchains -P output ACCEPT
# ipchains -P forward DENY
```

These permit outgoing traffic but drop incoming or forwarded packets.

The official site for iptables is *http://www.netfilter.org*, where you can also find the *Linux 2.4 Packet Filtering Howto* at *http://www.netfilter.org/documentation/HOWTO/packet-filtering-HOWTO.html*. Another nice iptables article is at *http://www.samag.com/documents/s=1769/sam0112a/0112a.htm*.

2.1 Enabling Source Address Verification

Problem

You want to prevent remote hosts from spoofing incoming packets as if they had come from your local machine.

Solution

Turn on source address verification in the kernel. Place the following code into a system boot file (i.e., linked into the */etc/rc.d* hierarchy) that executes before any network devices are enabled:

```
#!/bin/sh
echo -n "Enabling source address verification..."
echo 1 > /proc/sys/net/ipv4/conf/default/rp_filter
echo "done"
```

Our Firewall Philosophy

In designing a set of firewall rules for a Linux host, there are several different models we could follow. They correspond to different positions or functions of the host in your network.

Single computer
> The host has a single network interface, and the firewall's purpose is to protect that host from the outside world. The principle distinction here is "this host" versus "everything else." One example is a home computer connected to a cable modem.

Multi-homed host
> The host has multiple network interfaces connected to different networks, but is *not* acting as a router. In other words, it has an address on each of its connected networks, but it does not forward traffic across itself, nor interconnect those networks for other hosts. Such a host is called *multi-homed* and may be directly connected to various networks. In this case, firewall rules must distinguish among the different interfaces, addresses, and networks to which the host/router is attached, perhaps implementing different security policies on different networks. For example, the host might be connected to the Internet on one side, and a trusted private network on the other.

Router
> The host has multiple network interfaces and is configured as a router. That is, the kernel's "IP forwarding" flag is on, and the host will forward packets between its connected networks as directed by its routing table. In this case, firewall rules not only must control what traffic may reach the host, but also might restrict what traffic can *cross* the host (as router), bound for other hosts.

For this chapter, we decided to take the first approach—single computer—as our model. The other models are also valid and common, but they require a more detailed understanding of topics beyond the scope of this book, such as IP routing, routing protocols (RIP, OSPF, etc.), address translation (NAT/NAPT), etc.

We also assume your single computer has source address verification turned on, to prevent remote hosts from pretending to be local. [2.1] Therefore we don't address such spoofing directly in the firewall rules.

Or, to perform the same task after network devices are enabled:

```
#!/bin/sh
CONF_DIR=/proc/sys/net/ipv4/conf
CONF_FILE=rp_filter
if [ -e ${CONF_DIR}/all/${CONF_FILE} ]; then
    echo -n "Setting up IP spoofing protection..."
    for f in ${CONF_DIR}/*/${CONF_FILE}; do
        echo 1 > $f
    done
    echo "done"
fi
```

A quicker method may be to add this line to /etc/sysctl.conf:

```
net.ipv4.conf.all.rp_filter = 1
```

and run sysctl to reread the configuration immediately:

```
# sysctl -p
```

Discussion

Source address verification is a kernel-level feature that drops packets that *appear* to come from your internal network, but do not. Enabling this feature should be your first network-related security task. If your kernel does not support it, you can set up the same effect using firewall rules, but it takes more work. [2.2]

See Also

sysctl(8). Source address verification is explained in the IPCHAINS-HOWTO at *http://www.linux.org/docs/ldp/howto/IPCHAINS-HOWTO-5.html#ss5.7.*

2.2   Blocking Spoofed Addresses

Problem

You want to prevent remote hosts from pretending to be local to your network.

Solution

For a single machine, to prevent remote hosts from pretending to be that machine, use the following:

For iptables:

```
# iptables -A INPUT -i external_interface -s your_IP_address -j REJECT
```

For ipchains:

```
# ipchains -A input -i external_interface -s your_IP_address -j REJECT
```

If you have a Linux machine acting as a firewall for your internal network (say, 192.168.0.*) with two network interfaces, one internal and one external, and you want to prevent remote machines from spoofing internal IP addresses to the external interface, use the following:

For iptables:

```
# iptables -A INPUT -i external_interface -s 192.168.0.0/24 -j REJECT
```

For ipchains:

```
# ipchains -A input -i external_interface -s 192.168.0.0/24 -j REJECT
```

Drop Versus Reject

The Linux firewall can refuse packets in two manners. iptables calls them DROP and REJECT, while ipchains uses the terminology DENY and REJECT. DROP (or DENY) simply swallows the packet, never to be seen again, and emits no response. REJECT, in contrast, responds to the packet with a friendly message back to the sender, something like "Hello, I have rejected your packet."

DROP and REJECT have pros and cons. In general, REJECT is more compliant with standards: hosts are supposed to send rejection notices. Used within your network, rejects make things easier to debug if problems occur. DROP gives a bit more security, but it's hard to say how much, and it increases the risk of other network-related problems for you. A DROP policy makes it appear to peers that your host is turned off or temporarily unreachable due to network problems. Attempts to connect to TCP services will take a long time to fail, as clients will receive no explicit rejection (TCP "reset" message), and will keep trying to connect. This may have unexpected consequences beyond the blocking the service. For example, some services automatically attempt to use the IDENT protocol (RFC 1413) to identify their clients. If you DROP incoming IDENT connections, some of your outgoing protocol sessions may be mysteriously slow to start up, as the remote server times out attempting to identify you.

On the other hand, REJECT can leave you open to denial of service attacks, with you as the unwitting patsy. Suppose a Hostile Third Party sends you packets with a forged source address from a victim site, *V*. In response, you reject the packets, returning them not to the Hostile Third Party, but to victim *V*, owner of the source address. *Voilà*—you are unintentionally flooding *V* with rejections. If you're a large site with hundreds or thousands of hosts, you might choose DROP to prevent them from being abused in such a manner. But if you're a home user, you're probably less likely to be targeted for this sort of attack, and perhaps REJECT is fine. To further complicate matters, the Linux kernel has features like ICMP rate-limiting that mitigate some of these concerns. We'll avoid religious arguments and simply say, "Choose the solution best for your situation."

In this chapter, we stick with REJECT for simplicity, but you may feel free to tailor the recipes more to your liking with DROP or DENY. Also note that iptables supports a variety of rejection messages: "Hello, my port is unreachable," "Bummer, that network is not accessible," "Sorry I'm not here right now, but leave a message at the beep," and so forth. (OK, we're kidding about one of those.) See the --reject-with option.

Discussion

For a single machine, simply enable source address verification in the kernel. [2.1]

See Also

iptables(8), ipchains(8).

2.3   Blocking All Network Traffic

Problem

You want to block all network traffic by firewall.

Solution

For iptables:

```
# iptables -F
# iptables -A INPUT -j REJECT
# iptables -A OUTPUT -j REJECT
# iptables -A FORWARD -j REJECT
```

For ipchains:

```
# ipchains -F
# ipchains -A input -j REJECT
# ipchains -A output -j REJECT
# ipchains -A forward -j REJECT
```

Discussion

You could also stop your network device altogether with ifconfig [3.2] or even unplug your network cable. It all depends on what level of control you need.

The target REJECT sends an error packet in response to the incoming packet. You can tailor iptables's error packet using the option --reject-with. Alternatively, you can specify the targets DROP (iptables) and DENY (ipchains) that simply absorb the packet and produce no response. See the sidebar "Drop Versus Reject."

See Also

iptables(8), ipchains(8).

    Rules in a chain are evaluated in sequential order.

2.4   Blocking Incoming Traffic

Problem

You want to block all incoming network traffic, except from your system itself. Do not affect outgoing traffic.

Solution

For iptables:

```
# iptables -F INPUT
# iptables -A INPUT -m state --state ESTABLISHED -j ACCEPT
# iptables -A INPUT -j REJECT
```

For ipchains:

```
# ipchains -F input
# ipchains -A input -i lo -j ACCEPT
# ipchains -A input -p tcp --syn -j REJECT
# ipchains -A input -p udp --dport 0:1023 -j REJECT
```

Discussion

The iptables recipe takes advantage of statefulness, permitting incoming packets only if they are part of established outgoing connections. All other incoming packets are rejected.

The ipchains recipe accepts all packets from yourself. The source can be either your actual IP address or the loopback address, 127.0.0.1; in either case, the traffic is delivered via the loopback interface, lo. We then reject TCP packets that initiate connections (--syn) and all UDP packets on privileged ports. This recipe has a disadvantage, however, which is that you have to list the UDP port numbers. If you run other UDP services on nonprivileged ports (1024 and up), you'll have to modify the port list. But even so there's a catch: some outgoing services allocate a randomly numbered, nonprivileged port for return packets, and you don't want to block it.

Don't simply drop all input packets, e.g.:

```
# ipchains -F input
# ipchains -A input -j REJECT
```

as this will block responses returning from your legitimate outgoing connections.

iptables also supports the --syn flag to process TCP packets:

```
# iptables -A INPUT -p tcp --syn -j REJECT
```

As with ipchains, this rule blocks TCP/IP packets used to initiate connections. They have their SYN bit set but the ACK and FIN bits unset.

If you block all incoming traffic, you will block ICMP messages required by Internet standards (RFCs); see *http//rfc.net/rfc792.html* and *http://www.cymru.com/ Documents/icmp-messages.html*.

See Also

iptables(8), ipchains(8).

2.5   Blocking Outgoing Traffic

Problem

Drop all outgoing network traffic. If possible, do not affect incoming traffic.

Solution

For iptables:

```
# iptables -F OUTPUT
# iptables -A OUTPUT -m state --state ESTABLISHED -j ACCEPT
# iptables -A OUTPUT -j REJECT
```

For ipchains:

```
# ipchains -F output
# ipchains -A output -p tcp ! --syn -j ACCEPT
# ipchains -A output -j REJECT
```

Depending on your shell, you might need to escape the exclamation point.

Discussion

This recipe takes advantage of iptables's statefulness. iptables can tell the difference between outgoing traffic initiated from the local machine and outgoing traffic in response to established incoming connections. The latter is permitted, but the former is not.

ipchains is stateless but can recognize (and reject) packets with the SYN bit set and the ACK and FIN bits cleared, thereby permitting established and incoming TCP connections to function. However, this technique is insufficient for UDP exchanges: you really need a stateful firewall for that.

See Also

iptables(8), ipchains(8).

2.6   Blocking Incoming Service Requests

Problem

You want to block connections to a particular network service, for example, HTTP.

Solution

To block all incoming HTTP traffic:

For iptables:

```
# iptables -A INPUT -p tcp --dport www -j REJECT
```

For ipchains:

```
# ipchains -A input -p tcp --dport www -j REJECT
```

To block incoming HTTP traffic but permit local HTTP traffic:

For iptables:

```
# iptables -A INPUT -p tcp -i lo --dport www -j ACCEPT
# iptables -A INPUT -p tcp --dport www -j REJECT
```

For ipchains:

```
# ipchains -A input -p tcp -i lo --dport www -j ACCEPT
# ipchains -A input -p tcp --dport www -j REJECT
```

Discussion

You can also block access at other levels such as TCP-wrappers. [3.9][3.11]

See Also

iptables(8), ipchains(8).

2.7   Blocking Access from a Remote Host

Problem

You want to block incoming traffic from a particular host.

Solution

To block all access by that host:

For iptables:

```
# iptables -A INPUT -s remote_IP_address -j REJECT
```

For ipchains:

```
# ipchains -A input -s remote_IP_address -j REJECT
```

To block requests for one particular service, say, the SMTP mail service:

For iptables:

```
# iptables -A INPUT -p tcp -s remote_IP_address --dport smtp -j REJECT
```

For ipchains:

```
# ipchains -A input -p tcp -s remote_IP_address --dport smtp -j REJECT
```

To admit some hosts but block all others:

For iptables:

```
# iptables -A INPUT -s IP_address_1 [-p protocol --dport service] -j ACCEPT
# iptables -A INPUT -s IP_address_2 [-p protocol --dport service] -j ACCEPT
# iptables -A INPUT -s IP_address_3 [-p protocol --dport service] -j ACCEPT
# iptables -A INPUT [-p protocol --dport service] -j REJECT
```

For ipchains:

```
# ipchains -A input -s IP_address_1 [-p protocol --dport service] -j ACCEPT
# ipchains -A input -s IP_address_2 [-p protocol --dport service] -j ACCEPT
# ipchains -A input -s IP_address_3 [-p protocol --dport service] -j ACCEPT
# ipchains -A input [-p protocol --dport service] -j REJECT
```

Discussion

You can also block access at other levels such as TCP-wrappers. [3.9][3.11]

See Also

iptables(8), ipchains(8).

2.8   Blocking Access to a Remote Host

Problem

You want to block outgoing traffic to a particular host.

Solution

To block all access:

For iptables:

```
# iptables -A OUTPUT -d remote_IP_address -j REJECT
```

For ipchains:

```
# ipchains -A output -d remote_IP_address -j REJECT
```

To block a particular service, such as a remote web site:

For iptables:

```
# iptables -A OUTPUT -p tcp -d remote_IP_address --dport www -j REJECT
```

For ipchains:

```
# ipchains -A output -p tcp -d remote_IP_address --dport www -j REJECT
```

Discussion

Perhaps you've discovered that a particular web site has malicious content on it, such as a trojan horse. This recipe will prevent all of your users from accessing that site. (We don't consider "redirector" web sites, such as *http://www.anonymizer.com*, which would get around this restriction.)

See Also

iptables(8), ipchains(8).

2.9   Blocking Outgoing Access to All Web Servers on a Network

Problem

You want to prevent outgoing access to a network, e.g., all web servers at *yahoo.com*.

Solution

Figure out how to specify the *yahoo.com* network, e.g., 64.58.76.0/24, and reject web access:

For iptables:

```
# iptables -A OUTPUT -p tcp -d 64.58.76.0/24 --dport www -j REJECT
```

For ipchains:

```
# ipchains -A output -p tcp -d 64.58.76.0/24 --dport www -j REJECT
```

Discussion

Here the network is specified using Classless InterDomain Routing (CIDR) mask format, *a.b.c.d/N*, where *N* is the number of bits in the netmask. In this case, N=24, so the first 24 bits are the network portion of the address.

See Also

iptables(8), ipchains(8).

You can supply hostnames instead of IP addresses in your firewall rules. If DNS reports multiple IP addresses for that hostname, a separate rule will be created for each IP address. For example, *www.yahoo.com* has (at this writing) 11 IP addresses:

```
$ host www.yahoo.com
www.yahoo.com is an alias for www.yahoo.akadns.net.
www.yahoo.akadns.net has address 216.109.125.68
www.yahoo.akadns.net has address 64.58.76.227
...
```

So you could block access to Yahoo, for example, and view the results by:

iptables:

```
# iptables -A OUTPUT -d www.yahoo.com -j REJECT
# iptables -L OUTPUT
```

ipchains:

```
# ipchains -A output -d www.yahoo.com -j REJECT
# ipchains -L output
```

Security experts recommend that you use only IP addresses in your rules, not hostnames, since an attacker could poison your DNS and circumvent rules defined for hostnames. However, the hostnames are relevant only at the moment you run iptables or ipchains to define a rule, as the program looks up the underlying IP addresses immediately and stores them in the rule. So you could conceivably use hostnames for convenience when defining your rules, then check the results (via the output of iptables-save or ipchains-save [2.19]) to confirm the IP addresses.

2.10   Blocking Remote Access, but Permitting Local

Problem

You want only local users to access a TCP service; remote requests should be denied.

Solution

Permit connections via the loopback interface and reject all others.

For iptables:

```
# iptables -A INPUT -p tcp -i lo --dport service -j ACCEPT
# iptables -A INPUT -p tcp --dport service -j REJECT
```

For ipchains:

```
# ipchains -A input -p tcp -i lo --dport service -j ACCEPT
# ipchains -A input -p tcp --dport service -j REJECT
```

Alternatively, you can single out your local IP address specifically:

For iptables:

```
# iptables -A INPUT -p tcp ! -s your_IP_address --dport service -j REJECT
```

For ipchains:

```
# ipchains -A input -p tcp ! -s your_IP_address --dport service -j REJECT
```

Depending on your shell, you might need to escape the exclamation point.

Discussion

The local IP address can be a network specification, of course, such as *a.b.c.d/N*.

You can permit an unrelated set of machines to access the service but reject everyone else, like so:

For iptables:

```
# iptables -A INPUT -p tcp -s IP_address_1 --dport service -j ACCEPT
# iptables -A INPUT -p tcp -s IP_address_2 --dport service -j ACCEPT
# iptables -A INPUT -p tcp -s IP_address_3 --dport service -j ACCEPT
# iptables -P INPUT -j REJECT
```

For ipchains:

```
# ipchains -A input -p tcp -s IP_address_1 --dport service -j ACCEPT
# ipchains -A input -p tcp -s IP_address_2 --dport service -j ACCEPT
# ipchains -A input -p tcp -s IP_address_3 --dport service -j ACCEPT
# ipchains -P input -j REJECT
```

See Also

iptables(8), ipchains(8). Chapter 3 covers diverse, non-firewall approaches to block incoming service requests.

2.11   Controlling Access by MAC Address

Problem

You want only a particular machine, identified by its MAC address, to access your system.

Solution

```
# iptables -F INPUT
# iptables -A INPUT -i lo -j ACCEPT
# iptables -A INPUT -m mac --mac-source 12:34:56:89:90:ab -j ACCEPT
# iptables -A INPUT -j REJECT
```

ipchains does not support this feature.

Discussion

This technique works only within your local subnet. If you receive a packets from a machine outside your subnet, it will contain your gateway's MAC address, not that of the original source machine.

MAC addresses can be spoofed. Suppose you have a machine called *mackie* whose MAC address is trusted by your firewall. If an intruder discovers this fact, and *mackie* is down, the intruder could spoof *mackie*'s MAC address and your firewall would be none the wiser. On the other hand, if *mackie* is up during the spoofing, its kernel will start screaming (via syslog) about duplicate MAC addresses.

Note that our recipe permits local connections from your own host; these arrive via the loopback interface.

See Also

iptables(8), ipchains(8).

2.12 Permitting SSH Access Only

Problem

You want to permit incoming SSH access but no other incoming access. Allow local connections to all services, however.

Solution

For iptables:

```
# iptables -F INPUT
# iptables -A INPUT -p tcp --dport ssh -j ACCEPT
# iptables -A INPUT -i lo -j ACCEPT
# iptables -A INPUT -j REJECT
```

For ipchains:

```
# ipchains -F input
# ipchains -A input -p tcp --dport ssh -j ACCEPT
# ipchains -A input -i lo -j ACCEPT
# ipchains -A input -j REJECT
```

Discussion

A common setup is to permit access to a remote machine only by SSH. If you want this access limited to certain hosts or networks, list them by IP address as follows:

For iptables:

```
# iptables -A INPUT -p tcp -s 128.220.13.4 --dport ssh -j ACCEPT
# iptables -A INPUT -p tcp -s 71.54.121.19 --dport ssh -j ACCEPT
# iptables -A INPUT -p tcp -s 152.16.91.0/24 --dport ssh -j ACCEPT
# iptables -A INPUT -j REJECT
```

For ipchains:

```
# ipchains -A input -p tcp -s 128.220.13.4 --dport ssh -j ACCEPT
# ipchains -A input -p tcp -s 71.54.121.19 --dport ssh -j ACCEPT
# ipchains -A input -p tcp -s 152.16.91.0/24 --dport ssh -j ACCEPT
# ipchains -A input -j REJECT
```

The REJECT rule in the preceding iptables and ipchains examples prevents *all* other incoming connections. If you want to prevent only SSH connections (from nonapproved hosts), use this REJECT rule instead:

For iptables:

```
# iptables -A INPUT -p tcp --dport ssh -j REJECT
```

For ipchains:

```
# ipchains -A input -p tcp --dport ssh -j REJECT
```

Alternatively you can use TCP-wrappers. [3.9] [3.11] [3.13]

See Also

iptables(8), ipchains(8), ssh(1).

2.13   Prohibiting Outgoing Telnet Connections

Problem

You want to block outgoing Telnet connections.

Solution

To block all outgoing Telnet connections:

For iptables:

```
# iptables -A OUTPUT -p tcp --dport telnet -j REJECT
```

For ipchains:

```
# ipchains -A output -p tcp --dport telnet -j REJECT
```

To block all outgoing Telnet connections except to yourself from yourself:

For iptables:

```
# iptables -A OUTPUT -p tcp -o lo --dport telnet -j ACCEPT
# iptables -A OUTPUT -p tcp --dport telnet -j REJECT
```

For ipchains:

```
# ipchains -A output -p tcp -i lo --dport telnet -j ACCEPT
# ipchains -A output -p tcp --dport telnet -j REJECT
```

Discussion

Telnet is notoriously insecure in its most common form, which transmits your login name and password in plaintext over the network. This recipe is a sneaky way to encourage your users to find a more secure alternative, such as ssh. (Unless your users are running Telnet in a secure fashion with Kerberos authentication. [4.15])

See Also

iptables(8), ipchains(8), telnet(1).

2.14 Protecting a Dedicated Server

Problem

You want to run a specific set of services on your machine, accessible to the outside world. All other services should be rejected and logged. Internally, however, local users can access all services.

Solution

Suppose your services are www, ssh, and smtp.

For iptables:

```
# iptables -F INPUT
# iptables -A INPUT -i lo -j ACCEPT
# iptables -A INPUT -m multiport -p tcp --dport www,ssh,smtp -j ACCEPT
# iptables -A INPUT -j LOG -m limit
# iptables -A INPUT -j REJECT
```

For ipchains:

```
# ipchains -F input
# ipchains -A input -i lo -j ACCEPT
# ipchains -A input -p tcp --dport www -j ACCEPT
# ipchains -A input -p tcp --dport ssh -j ACCEPT
# ipchains -A input -p tcp --dport smtp -j ACCEPT
# ipchains -A input -l -j REJECT
```

Discussion

Local connections from your own host arrive via the loopback interface.

See Also

iptables(8), ipchains(8).

2.15 Preventing pings

Problem

You don't want remote sites to receive responses if they ping you.

Solution

For iptables:

```
# iptables -A INPUT -p icmp --icmp-type echo-request -j DROP
```

For ipchains:

```
# ipchains -A input -p icmp --icmp-type echo-request -j DENY
```

Discussion

In this case, we use DROP and DENY instead of REJECT. If you're trying to hide from pings, then replying with a rejection kind of defeats the purpose, eh?

Don't make the mistake of dropping all ICMP messages, e.g.:

```
WRONG!! DON'T DO THIS!
# iptables -A INPUT -p icmp -j DROP
```

because pings are only one type of ICMP message, and you might not want to block all types. That being said, you might want to block some others, like redirects and source quench. List the available ICMP messages with:

```
$ iptables -p icmp -h
$ ipchains -h icmp
```

See Also

iptables(8), ipchains(8). The history of ping, by its author, is at *http://ftp.arl.mil/~mike/ping.html*.

2.16 Listing Your Firewall Rules

Problem

You want to see your firewall rules.

Solution

For iptables:

```
# iptables -L [chain]
```

For ipchains:

```
# ipchains -L [chain]
```

For more detailed output, append the -v option.

If iptables takes a long time to print the rule list, try appending the -n option to disable reverse DNS lookups. Such lookups of local addresses, such as 192.168.0.2, may cause delays due to timeouts.

Discussion

An iptables rule like:

```
# iptables -A mychain -p tcp -s 1.2.3.4 -d 5.6.7.8 --dport smtp -j chain2
```

has a listing like:

```
Chain mychain (3 references)
target     prot opt source              destination
chain2     tcp  --  1.2.3.4             5.6.7.8              tcp dpt:smtp
```

which is basically a repeat of what you specified: any SMTP packets from IP address 1.2.3.4 to 5.6.7.8 should be forwarded to target chain2. Here's a similar ipchains rule that adds logging:

```
# ipchains -A mychain -p tcp -s 1.2.3.4 -d 5.6.7.8 --dport smtp -l -j chain2
```

Its listing looks like:

```
Chain mychain (3 references):
target    prot opt     source       destination     ports
chain2    tcp  ----l-  1.2.3.4      5.6.7.8         any -> smtp
```

A detailed listing (-L -v) adds packet and byte counts and more:

```
Chain mychain (3 references):
pkts bytes  target prot opt    tosa tosx ifname source    destination ports
15   2640   chain2 tcp  ----l- 0xFF 0x00 any    1.2.3.4   5.6.7.8     any -> smtp
```

Another way to view your rules is in the output of iptables-save or ipchains-save [2.19], but this more concise format is not as readable. It's meant only to be processed by iptables-restore or ipchains-restore, respectively:

```
# ipchains-save
... Saving 'mychain'.
-A foo -s 1.2.3.4/255.255.255.255 -d 5.6.7.8/255.255.255.255 25:25 -p 6 -j chain2 -l
```

See Also

iptables(8), ipchains(8).

2.17   Deleting Firewall Rules

Problem

You want to delete firewall rules, individually or all at once.

Solution

To delete rules *en masse*, also called *flushing* a chain, do the following:

For iptables:

```
# iptables -F [chain]
```

For ipchains:

```
# ipchains -F [chain]
```

To delete rules individually:

For iptables:

```
# iptables -D chain rule_number
```

For ipchains:

```
# ipchains -D chain rule_number
```

Discussion

Rules are numbered beginning with 1. To list the rules:

```
# iptables -L
```

```
# ipchains -L
```

select one to delete (say, rule 4 on the input chain), and type:

```
# iptables -D INPUT 4
```

```
# ipchains -D input 4
```

If you've previously saved your rules and want your deletions to remain in effect after the next reboot, re-save the new configuration. [2.19]

See Also

iptables(8), ipchains(8).

2.18 Inserting Firewall Rules

Problem

Rather than appending a rule to a chain, you want to insert or replace one elsewhere in the chain.

Solution

Instead of the -A option, use -I to insert or -R to replace. You'll need to know the numeric position, within the existing rules, of the new rule. For instance, to insert a new rule in the fourth position in the chain:

```
# iptables -I chain 4 ...specification...

# ipchains -I chain 4 ...specification...
```

To replace the second rule in a chain:

```
# iptables -R chain 2 ...specification...

# ipchains -R chain 2 ...specification...
```

Discussion

When you insert a rule at position N in a chain, the old rule N becomes rule N+1, rule N+1 becomes rule N+2, and so on. To see the rules in a chain in order, so you can determine the right numeric offset, list the chain with -L. [2.16]

See Also

iptables(8), ipchains(8).

2.19 Saving a Firewall Configuration

Problem

You want to save your firewall configuration.

Solution

Save your settings:

For iptables:

```
# iptables-save > /etc/sysconfig/iptables
```

For ipchains:

```
# ipchains-save > /etc/sysconfig/ipchains
```

The destination filename is up to you, but some Linux distributions (notably Red Hat) refer to the files we used, inside their associated */etc/init.d* scripts.

Discussion

ipchains-save and iptables-save print your firewall rules in a text format, readable by ipchains-restore and iptables-restore, respectively. [2.20]

 Our recipes using iptables-save, iptables-restore, ipchains-save, and ipchains-restore will work for both Red Hat and SuSE. However, SuSE by default takes a different approach. Instead of saving and restoring rules, SuSE builds rules from variables set in */etc/sysconfig/ SuSEfirewall2*.

See Also

iptables-save(8), ipchains-save(8), iptables(8), ipchains(8).

2.20   Loading a Firewall Configuration

Problem

You want to load your firewall rules, e.g., at boot time.

Solution

Use ipchains-restore or iptables-restore. Assuming you've saved your firewall configuration in */etc/sysconfig*: [2.19]

For iptables:

```
#!/bin/sh
echo 1 > /proc/sys/net/ipv4/ip_forward        (optional)
iptables-restore < /etc/sysconfig/iptables
```

For ipchains:

```
#!/bin/sh
echo 1 > /proc/sys/net/ipv4/ip_forward        (optional)
ipchains-restore < /etc/sysconfig/ipchains
```

To tell Red Hat Linux that firewall rules should be loaded at boot time:

```
# chkconfig iptables on
```

```
# chkconfig ipchains on
```

Discussion

Place the load commands in one of your system *rc* files. Red Hat Linux already has *rc* files "iptables" and "ipchains" in */etc/init.d* that you can simply enable using chkconfig. SuSE Linux, in contrast, has a script */sbin/SuSEpersonal-firewall* that invokes iptables or ipchains rules, and it's optionally started by */etc/init.d/personal-firewall.initial* and */etc/init.d/personal-firewall.final* at boot time.

To roll your own solution, you can write a script like the following and invoke it from an *rc* file of your choice:

```
#!/bin/sh
# Uncomment either iptables or ipchains
PROGRAM=/usr/sbin/iptables
#PROGRAM=/sbin/ipchains

FIREWALL=`/bin/basename $PROGRAM`
RULES_FILE=/etc/sysconfig/${FIREWALL}
LOADER=${PROGRAM}-restore
FORWARD_BIT=/proc/sys/net/ipv4/ip_forward

if [ ! -f ${RULES_FILE} ]
then
    echo "$0: Cannot find ${RULES_FILE}" 1>&2
    exit 1
fi

case "$1" in
    start)
        echo 1 > ${FORWARD_BIT}
        ${LOADER} < ${RULES_FILE} || exit 1
        ;;
    stop)
        ${PROGRAM} -F              # Flush all rules
        ${PROGRAM} -X              # Delete user-defined chains
        echo 0 > ${FORWARD_BIT}
        ;;
    *)
        echo "Usage: $0 start|stop" 1>&2
        exit 1
        ;;
esac
```

Make sure you load your firewall rules for all appropriate runlevels where networking is enabled. On most systems this includes runlevels 2 (multiuser without NFS), 3 (full multiuser), and 5 (X11). Check */etc/inittab* to confirm this, and use chkconfig to list the status of the networking service at each runlevel:

```
$ chkconfig --list network
network         0:off   1:off   2:on    3:on    4:on    5:on    6:off
```

See Also

iptables-load(8), ipchains-load(8), iptables(8), ipchains(8).

2.21 Testing a Firewall Configuration

Problem

You want to create and test an ipchains configuration nondestructively, i.e., without affecting your active firewall.

Solution

Using ipchains, create a chain for testing:

```
# ipchains -N mytest
```

Insert your rules into this test chain:

```
# ipchains -A mytest ...
# ipchains -A mytest ....
```

Specify a test packet:

```
SA=source_address
SP=source_port
DA=destination_address
DP=destination_port
P=protocol
I=interface
```

Simulate sending the packet through the test chain:

```
# ipchains -v -C mytest -s $SA --sport $SP -d $DA --dport $DP -p $P -i $I
```

At press time, iptables does not have a similar feature for testing packets against rules. iptables 1.2.6a has a -C option and provides this teaser:

```
# iptables -v -C mytest -p $P -s $SA --sport $SP -d $DA --dport $DP -i $I
iptables: Will be implemented real soon. I promise ;)
```

but the iptables FAQ (*http://www.netfilter.org/documentation/FAQ/netfilter-faq.html*) indicates that the feature might never be implemented, since checking a single packet against a *stateful* firewall is meaningless: decisions can depend on previous packets.

Discussion

This process constructs a packet with its interface, protocol, source, and destination. The response is either "accepted," "denied," or "passed through chain" for user-defined chains. With -v, you can watch each rule match or not.

The mandatory parameters are:

```
-C chain_name
-s source_addr --sport source_port
-d dest_addr --dport dest_port
-p protocol
-i interface_name
```

For a more realistic test of your firewall, use nmap to probe it from a remote machine. [9.13]

See Also

ipchains(8).

2.22   Building Complex Rule Trees

Problem

You want to construct complex firewall behaviors, but you are getting lost in the complexity.

Solution

Be modular: isolate behaviors into their own chains. Then connect the chains in the desired manner.

For iptables:

```
# iptables -N CHAIN1
# iptables -N CHAIN2
# iptables -N CHAIN3
# iptables -N CHAIN4
# iptables -N CHAIN5
```

Add your rules to each chain. Then connect the chains; for example:

```
# iptables -A INPUT ...specification... -j CHAIN1
# iptables -A CHAIN1 ...specification... -j CHAIN2
# iptables -A CHAIN2 ...specification... -j CHAIN3
# iptables -A INPUT ...specification... -j CHAIN4
# iptables -A INPUT ...specification... -j CHAIN5
```

to create a rule structure as in Figure 2-1.

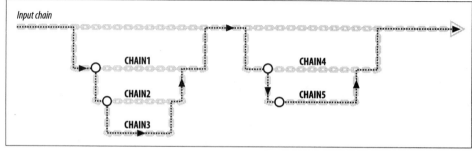

Figure 2-1. Building rule chain structures in iptables or ipchains

For ipchains:

```
# ipchains -N chain1
# ipchains -N chain2
# ipchains -N chain3
# ipchains -N chain4
# ipchains -N chain5
```

Add your rules to each chain. Then connect the chains, for example:

```
# ipchains -A input ...specification... -j chain1
# ipchains -A chain1 ...specification... -j chain2
# ipchains -A chain2 ...specification... -j chain3
# ipchains -A input ...specification... -j chain4
# ipchains -A input ...specification... -j chain5
```

to create the same rule structure as in Figure 2-1.

Discussion

Connecting chains is like modular programming with subroutines. The rule:

```
# iptables -A CHAIN1 ...specification... -j CHAIN2
```

creates a jump point to CHAIN2 from this rule in CHAIN1, if the rule is satisfied. Once CHAIN2 has been traversed, control returns to the next rule in CHAIN1, similar to returning from a subroutine.

See Also

iptables(8), ipchains(8).

2.23 Logging Simplified

Problem

You want your firewall to log and drop certain packets.

Solution

For iptables, create a new rule chain that logs and drops in sequence:

```
# iptables -N LOG_DROP
# iptables -A LOG_DROP -j LOG --log-level warning --log-prefix "dropped" -m limit
# iptables -A LOG_DROP -j DROP
```

Then use it as a target in any relevant rules:

```
# iptables ...specification... -j LOG_DROP
```

For ipchains:

```
# ipchains ...specification... -l -j DROP
```

Discussion

iptables's LOG target causes the kernel to log packets that match your given specification. The --log-level option sets the syslog level [9.27] for these log messages and --log-prefix adds an identifiable string to the log entries. The further options --log-prefix, --log-tcp-sequence, --log-tcp-options, and --log-ip-options affect the information written to the log; see iptables(8).

LOG is usually combined with the limit module (-m *limit*) to limit the number of redundant log entries made per time period, to prevent flooding your logs. You can accept the defaults (3 per hour, in bursts of at most 5 entries) or tailor them with --limit and --limit-burst, respectively.

ipchains has much simpler logging: just add the -l option to the relevant rules.

See Also

iptables(8), ipchains(8).

## CHAPTER 3

Network Access Control

3.0   Introduction

One of your most vital security tasks is to maintain control over incoming network connections. As system administrator, you have many layers of control over these connections. At the lowest level—hardware—you can unplug network cables, but this is rarely necessary unless your computer has been badly cracked beyond all trust. More practically, you have the following levels of control in software, from general to service-specific:

Network interface
>   The interface can be brought entirely down and up.

Firewall
>   By setting firewall rules in the Linux kernel, you control the handling of incoming (and outgoing and forwarded) packets. This topic is covered in Chapter 2.

A superdaemon or Internet services daemon
>   A superdaemon controls the invocation (or not) of specific network services, based on various criteria. Suppose your system receives an incoming request for a Telnet connection. Your superdaemon could accept or reject it based on the source address, the time of day, the count of other Telnet connections open... or it could simply forbid all Telnet access. Superdaemons typically have a set of configuration files for controlling your many services conveniently in one place.

Individual network services
>   Any network service, such as sshd or ftpd, may have built-in access control facilities of its own. For example, sshd has its AllowUsers configuration keyword, ftpd has */etc/ftpaccess*, and various services require user authentication.

These levels all play a part when a network service request arrives. Suppose remote user joeblow tries to FTP into the smith account on *server.example.com*, as in Figure 3-1:

>   If *server.example.com* is physically connected to the network...
>   *And* its network interface is up...

And its kernel firewall permits FTP packets from Joe's host…
And a superdaemon is running…
And the superdaemon is configured to invoke ftpd…
And the superdaemon accepts FTP connections from Joe's machine…
And ftpd is installed and executable…
And the ftpd configuration in */etc/ftpaccess* accepts the connection…
And joeblow authenticates as smith…

then the connection succeeds. (Assuming nothing else blocks it, such as a network outage.)

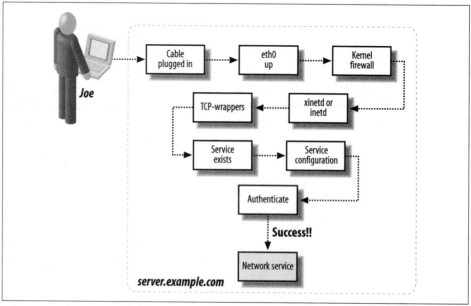

Figure 3-1. Layers of security for incoming network connections

System administrators must be aware of all these levels of control. In this chapter we'll discuss:

ifconfig

A low-level program for controlling network interfaces, bringing them up and down and setting parameters.

xinetd

A superdaemon that controls the invocation of other daemons. It is operated by configuration files, usually in the directory */etc/xinetd.d*, one file per service. For example, */etc/xinetd.d/finger* specifies how the finger daemon should be invoked on demand:

```
/etc/xinetd.d/finger:
service finger
{
```

```
    server = /usr/sbin/in.fingerd        path to the executable
    user = nobody                        run as user "nobody"
    wait = no                            run multithreaded
    socket_type = stream                 a stream-based service
}
```

Red Hat includes xinetd.

inetd

Another older superdaemon like xinetd. Its configuration is found in */etc/inetd. conf*, one service per line. An analogous entry to the previous xinetd example looks like this:

/etc/inetd.conf:
```
finger  stream  tcp  nowait  nobody  /usr/sbin/in.fingerd  in.fingerd
```

SuSE includes inetd.

TCP-wrappers

A layer that controls incoming access by particular hosts or domains, as well as other criteria. It is specified in */etc/hosts.allow* (allowed connections) and */etc/ hosts.deny* (disallowed connections). For example, to forbid all finger connections:

/etc/hosts.deny:
```
finger : ALL : DENY
```

or to permit finger connections only from hosts in the *friendly.org* domain:

/etc/hosts.allow:
```
finger : *.friendly.org
finger : ALL : DENY
```

We won't reproduce the full syntax supported by these files, since it's in the manpage, hosts.allow(5). But be aware that TCP-wrappers can also do IDENT checking, invoke arbitrary external programs, and other important tasks. Both Red Hat and SuSE include TCP-wrappers.

 All recipes in this chapter come with a large caveat: they do not actually restrict access by host, but by IP source address. For example, we can specify that only host 121.108.19.42 can access a given service on our system. Source addresses, however, can be spoofed without much difficulty. A machine that falsely claims to be 121.108.19.42 could potentially bypass such restrictions. If you truly need to control access by host rather than source address, then a preferable technique is cryptographic host authentication such as SSH server authentication, host-based client authentication, or IPSec.

3.1   Listing Your Network Interfaces

Problem

You want a list of your network interfaces.

Solution

To list all interfaces, whether up or down, whose drivers are loaded:

```
$ ifconfig -a
```

To list all interfaces that are up:

```
$ ifconfig
```

To list a single interface, commonly *eth0*:

```
$ ifconfig eth0
```

Discussion

If you are not root, ifconfig might not be in your path: try */sbin/ifconfig*.

When invoked with the -a option, ifconfig lists all network interfaces that are up or down, but it will miss physical interfaces whose drivers are not loaded. For example, suppose you have a box with two Ethernet cards installed (*eth0* and *eth1*) from different manufacturers, with different drivers, but only one (*eth0*) is configured in Linux (i.e., there is an */etc/sysconfig/network-scripts/ifcfg-** file for it). The other interface you don't normally use. ifconfig -a will not show the second interface until you run ifconfig eth1 to load the driver.

See Also

ifconfig(8).

3.2 Starting and Stopping the Network Interface

Problem

You want to prevent all remote network connections, incoming and outgoing, on your network interfaces.

Solution

To shut down one network interface, say, *eth0*:

```
# ifconfig eth0 down
```

To bring up one network interface, say, *eth0*:

```
# ifconfig eth0 up
```

To shut down all networking:

```
# /etc/init.d/network stop
```

or:

```
# service network stop          Red Hat
```

To bring up all networking:

```
# /etc/init.d/network start
```

or:

```
# service network start         Red Hat
```

Discussion

Linux provides three levels of abstraction for enabling and disabling your network interfaces (short of unplugging the network cable):

/sbin/ifconfig
> The lowest level, to enable/disable a single network interface. It has other functions as well for configuring an interface in various ways.

/sbin/ifup, /sbin/ifdown
> This mid-level pair of scripts operates on a single network interface, bringing it up or down respectively, by invoking ifconfig with appropriate arguments. They also initialize DHCP and handle a few other details. These are rarely invoked directly by users.

/etc/init.d/network
> A high-level script that operates on all network interfaces, not just one. It runs ifup or ifdown for each interface as needed, and also handles other details: adding routes, creating a lock file to indicate that networking is enabled, and much more. It even toggles the loopback interface, which might be more than you intended, if you just want to block outside traffic.

The scripts ifup, ifdown, and network are pretty short and well worth reading.

See Also

ifconfig(8). usernetctl(8) describes how non-root users may modify parameters of network interfaces using ifup and ifdown, if permitted by the system administrator.

3.3   Enabling/Disabling a Service (xinetd)

Problem

You want to prevent a specific TCP service from being invoked on your system by xinetd.

Solution

If the service's name is "myservice," locate its configuration in */etc/xinetd.d/myservice* or */etc/xinetd.conf* and add:

```
disable = yes
```

to its parameters. For example, to disable telnet, edit */etc/xinetd.d/telnet*:

```
service telnet
{
    ...
    disable = yes
}
```

Then inform xinetd by signal to pick up your changes:

```
# kill -USR2 `pidof xinetd`
```

To permit access, remove the disable line and resend the SIGUSR2 signal.

Discussion

Instead of disabling the service, you could delete its xinetd configuration file (e.g., */etc/xinetd.d/telnet*), or even delete the service's executable from the machine, but such deletions are harder to undo. (Don't remove the executable *and* leave the service enabled, or xinetd will still try to run it and will complain.)

Alternatively use ipchains or iptables [2.7] if you want to keep the service runnable but restrict the network source addresses allowed to invoke it. Specific services might also have their own, program-level controls for restricting allowed client addresses.

See Also

xinetd(8). The xinetd home page is *http://www.synack.net/xinetd*.

3.4   Enabling/Disabling a Service (inetd)

Problem

You want to prevent a specific TCP service from being invoked on your system by inetd.

Solution

To disable, comment out the service's line in */etc/inetd.conf* by preceding it with a hash mark (#). For example, for the Telnet daemon:

```
/etc/inetd.conf:
# telnet  stream  tcp  nowait  root  /usr/sbin/in.telnetd  in.telnetd
```

Then inform inetd by signal to pick up your changes. (Here the hash mark is the root shell prompt, not a comment symbol.)

```
# kill -HUP `pidof inetd`
```

To enable, uncomment the same line and send SIGHUP again.

Discussion

Instead of disabling the service, you could delete the line in the inetd configuration file, or even delete its executable from the machine, but such deletions are harder to undo. (Don't remove the executable *and* leave the service enabled, or inetd will still try to run it, and will complain.) Alternatively, use ipchains or iptables [2.6] to keep the service runnable, just not by remote request.

See Also

inetd(8), inetd.conf(5).

3.5   Adding a New Service (xinetd)

Problem

You want to add a new network service, controlled by xinetd.

Solution

Create a new configuration file in */etc/xinetd.d* with at least the following information:

```
service SERVICE_NAME             Name from /etc/services; see services(5)
{
    server = /PATH/TO/SERVER     The service executable
    server_args = ANY_ARGS_HERE  Any arguments; omit if none
    user = USER                  Run the service as this user
    socket_type = TYPE           stream, dgram, raw, or seqpacket
    wait = YES/NO                yes = single-threaded, no = multithreaded
}
```

Name the file *SERVICE_NAME*. Then signal xinetd to read your new service file. [3.3]

Discussion

To create an xinetd configuration file for your service, you must of course know your service's desired properties and behavior. Is it stream based? Datagram based? Single-threaded or multithreaded? What arguments does the server executable take, if any?

xinetd configuration files have a tremendous number of additional keywords and values. See xinetd.conf(5) for full details.

xinetd reads all files in */etc/xinetd.d* only if */etc/xinetd.conf* tells it to, via this line:

```
includedir /etc/xinetd.d
```

Check your */etc/xinetd.conf* to confirm the location of its `includedir`.

See Also

xinetd(8), xinetd.conf(5), services(5). The xinetd home page is *http://www.synack. net/xinetd.*

3.6   Adding a New Service (inetd)

Problem

You want to add a new network service, controlled by `inetd`.

Solution

Add a new line to */etc/inetd.conf* of the form:

```
SERVICE_NAME  SOCKET_TYPE  PROTOCOL  THREADING  USER  /PATH/TO/SERVER  ARGS
```

Then signal inetd to reread */etc/inetd.conf*. [3.4]

Discussion

The values on the line are:

1. *Service name*. A service listed in */etc/services*. If it's not, add an entry by selecting a service name, port number, and protocol. See services(5).
2. *Socket type*. Either `stream`, `dgram`, `raw`, `rdm`, or `seqpacket`.
3. *Protocol*. Typically `tcp` or `udp`.
4. *Threading*. Use `wait` for single-threaded, or `nowait` for multithreaded.
5. *User*. The service will run as this user.
6. *Path* to server executable.
7. *Server arguments*, separated by whitespace. You must begin with the zero[th] argument, the server's basename itself. For example, for */usr/sbin/in.telnetd*, the zero[th] argument would be *in.telnetd*.

A full example is:

```
telnet  stream  tcp  nowait  root  /usr/sbin/in.telnetd  in.telnetd
```

A line in *inetd.conf* may contain a few other details as well, specifying buffer sizes, a local host address for listening, and so forth. See the manpage.

See Also

inetd(8), inetd.conf(5), services(5).

3.7 Restricting Access by Remote Users

Problem

You want only particular remote users to have access to a TCP service. You cannot predict the originating hosts.

Solution

Block the service's incoming TCP port with a firewall rule [2.6], run an SSH server, and permit users to tunnel in via SSH port forwarding. Thus, SSH authentication will permit or deny access to the service. Give your remote users SSH access by public key.

For example, to reach the news server (TCP port 119) on your site *server.example. com*, a remote user on host *myclient* could consruct the following tunnel from (arbitrary) local port 23456 to the news server via SSH:

```
myclient$ ssh -f -N -L 23456:server.example.com:119 server.example.com
```

and then connect to the tunnel, for example with the tin newsreader:

```
myclient$ export NNTPSERVER=localhost
myclient$ tin -r -p 23456
```

Discussion

SSH tunneling, or port forwarding, redirects a TCP connection to flow through an SSH client and server in a mostly-transparent manner.[*] [6.14] This tunnel connects from a local port to a remote port, encrypting traffic on departure and decrypting on arrival. For example, to tunnel NNTP (Usenet news service, port 119), the newsreader talks to an SSH client, which forwards its data across the tunnel to the SSH server, which talks to the NNTP server, as in Figure 3-2.

By blocking a service's port (119) to the outside world, you have prevented all remote access to that port. But SSH travels over a different port (22) not blocked by the firewall.

---

[*] It's not transparent to services sensitive to the details of their sockets, such as FTP, but in most cases the communication is fairly seamless.

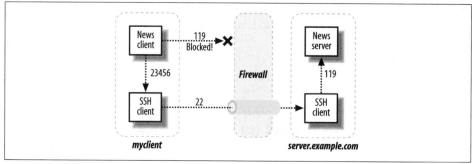

Figure 3-2. Tunneling NNTP with SSH

Alternatively, investigate whether your given service has its own user authentication. For example, wu-ftpd has the file /etc/ftpaccess, sshd has its AllowUsers keyword, and so forth.

See Also

ssh(1), sshd(8), tin(1).

3.8 Restricting Access by Remote Hosts (xinetd)

Problem

You want only particular remote hosts to access a TCP service via xinetd.

Solution

Use *xinetd.conf*'s only_from and no_access keywords:

```
service ftp
{
    only_from = 192.168.1.107
    ...
}

service smtp
{
    no_access = haxor.evil.org
    ...
}
```

Then reset xinetd so your changes take effect. [3.3]

Discussion

This is perhaps the simplest way to specify access control per service. But of course it works only for services launched by xinetd.

only_from and no_access can appear multiple times in a service entry:

```
{
    no_access = haxor.evil.org    deny a particular host
    no_access += 128.220.         deny all hosts in a network
    ...
}
```

If a connecting host is found in both the only_from and no_access lists, xinetd takes one of the following actions:

- If the host matches entries in both lists, but one match is *more specific* than the other, the more specific match prevails. For example, 128.220.13.6 is more specific than 128.220.13.

- If the host matches *equally* specific entries in both lists, xinetd considers this a configuration error and will not start the requested service.

So in this example:

```
service whatever
{
    no_access = 128.220.      haxor.evil.org    client.example.com
    only_from = 128.220.10.   .evil.org         client.example.com
}
```

connections from 128.220.10.3 are allowed, but those from 128.220.11.2 are denied. Likewise, *haxor.evil.org* cannot connect, but any other hosts in *evil.org* can. *client. example.com* is incorrectly configured, so its connection requests will be refused. Finally, any host matching none of the entries will be denied access.

See Also

xinetd.conf(5).

3.9   Restricting Access by Remote Hosts (xinetd with libwrap)

Problem

You want only particular remote hosts to access a TCP service via xinetd, when xinetd was compiled with libwrap support.

Solution

Control access via */etc/hosts.allow* and */etc/hosts.deny*. For example, to permit Telnet connections only from 192.168.1.100 and hosts in the *example.com* domain, add this to */etc/hosts.allow*:

```
in.telnetd : 192.168.1.100
in.telnetd : *.example.com
in.telnetd : ALL : DENY
```

Then reset xinetd so your changes take effect. [3.3]

Discussion

If you want to consolidate your access control in */etc/hosts.allow* and */etc/hosts.deny*, rather than use xinetd-specific methods [3.8], or if you prefer the *hosts.allow* syntax and capabilities, this technique might be for you. These files support a rich syntax for specifying hosts and networks that may, or may not, connect to your system via specific services.

This works only if xinetd was compiled with libwrap support enabled. To detect this, look at the output of:

```
$ strings /usr/sbin/xinetd | grep libwrap
libwrap refused connection to %s from %s
%s started with libwrap options compiled in.
```

If you see printf-style format strings like the above, your xinetd has libwrap support.

See Also

xinetd(8), hosts.allow(5).

3.10 Restricting Access by Remote Hosts (xinetd with tcpd)

Problem

You want only particular remote hosts to access a TCP service via xinetd, when xinetd was *not* compiled with libwrap support.

Solution

Set up access control rules in */etc/hosts.allow* and/or */etc/hosts.deny*. For example, to permit telnet connections only from 192.168.1.100 and hosts in the *example.com* domain, add to */etc/hosts.allow*:

```
in.telnetd : 192.168.1.100
in.telnetd : *.example.com
in.telnetd : ALL : DENY
```

Then modify */etc/xinetd.conf* or */etc/xinetd.d/servicename* to invoke tcpd in place of your service:

Old /etc/xinetd.conf or /etc/xinetd.d/telnet:
```
service telnet
{
    ...
    flags = ...
    server = /usr/sbin/in.telnetd
    ...
}
```

New /etc/xinetd.conf or /etc/xinetd.d/telnet:
```
service telnet
{
    ...
    flags = ... NAMEINARGS
    server = /usr/sbin/tcpd
    server_args = /usr/sbin/in.telnetd
    ...
}
```

Then reset xinetd so your changes take effect. [3.3]

Discussion

This technique is only for the rare case when, for some reason, you don't want to use xinetd's built-in access control [3.8] and your xinetd does not have libwrap support compiled in. It mirrors the original inetd method of access control using TCP-wrappers. [3.11]

You must include the flag NAMEINARGS, which tells xinetd to look in the server_args line to find the service executable name (in this case, */usr/sbin/in.telnetd*).

See Also

xinetd(8), hosts.allow(5), tcpd(8).

3.11   Restricting Access by Remote Hosts (inetd)

Problem

You want only particular remote hosts to access a TCP service via inetd.

Solution

Use `tcpd`, specifying rules in */etc/hosts.allow* and/or */etc/hosts.deny*. Here's an example of wrapping the Telnet daemon, `in.telnetd`, to permit connections only from IP address 192.168.1.100 or the *example.com* domain. Add to */etc/hosts.allow*:

```
in.telnetd : 192.168.1.100
in.telnetd : *.example.com
in.telnetd : ALL : DENY
```

Then modify the appropriate configuration files to substitute `tcpd` for your service, and restart `inetd`.

Discussion

The control files */etc/hosts.allow* and */etc/hosts.deny* define rules by which remote hosts may access local TCP services. The access control daemon `tcpd` processes the rules and determines whether or not to launch a given service.

First set up your access control rules in */etc/hosts.allow* and/or */etc/hosts.deny*. Then modify */etc/inetd.conf* to invoke the service through `tcpd`:

Old /etc/inetd.conf:
```
telnet  stream  tcp  nowait  root  /usr/sbin/in.telnetd  in.telnetd
```

New /etc/inetd.conf:
```
telnet  stream  tcp  nowait  root  /usr/sbin/tcpd  /usr/sbin/in.telnetd
```

Finally restart `inetd` so your changes take effect. [3.4]

See Also

hosts.allow(5), tcpd(8), inetd.conf(5).

3.12   Restricting Access by Time of Day

Problem

You want a service to be available only at certain times of day.

Solution

For `xinetd`, use its `access_times` attribute. For example, to make `telnetd` accessible from 8:00 a.m. until 5:00 p.m. (17:00) each day:

/etc/xinetd.conf or /etc/xinetd.d/telnet:
```
service telnet
{
    ...
```

```
    access_times = 8:00-17:00
}
```

For inetd, we'll implement this manually using the m4 macro processor and cron. First, invent some strings to represent times of day, such as "working" to mean 8:00 a.m. and "playing" to mean 5:00 p.m. Then create a script (say, inetd-services) that uses m4 to select lines in a template file, creates the inetd configuration file, and signals inetd to reread it:

/usr/local/sbin/inetd-services:
```
#!/bin/sh
m4 "$@" /etc/inetd.conf.m4 > /etc/inetd.conf.$$
mv /etc/inetd.conf.$$ /etc/inetd.conf
kill -HUP `pidof inetd`
```

Copy the original */etc/inetd.conf* file to the template file, */etc/inetd.conf.m4*. Edit the template to enable services conditionally according to the value of a parameter, say, TIMEOFDAY. For example, the Telnet service line that originally looks like this:

```
telnet stream tcp nowait root /usr/sbin/tcpd in.telnetd
```

might now look like:

```
ifelse(TIMEOFDAY,working,telnet stream tcp nowait root /usr/sbin/tcpd in.telnetd)
```

which means "if TIMEOFDAY is working, include the Telnet line, otherwise don't." Finally, set up *crontab* entries to enable or disable services at specific times of day, by setting the TIMEOFDAY parameter:

```
0  8 * * * /usr/local/sbin/inetd-services -DTIMEOFDAY=working
0 17 * * * /usr/local/sbin/inetd-services -DTIMEOFDAY=playing
```

Discussion

For xinetd, we can easily control each service using the access_times parameter. Times are specified on a 24-hour clock.

For inetd, we need to work a bit harder, rebuilding the configuration file at different times of day to enable and disable services. The recipe can be readily extended with additional parameters and values, like we do with TIMEOFDAY. Notice that the xinetd solution uses time ranges, while the inetd solution uses time instants (i.e., the minute that cron triggers inetd-services).

See Also

xinetd.conf(5), inetd.conf(5), m4(1), crontab(5).

3.13 Restricting Access to an SSH Server by Host

Problem

You want to limit access to sshd from specific remote hosts.

Solution

Use sshd's built-in TCP-wrappers support. Simply add rules to the files */etc/hosts. allow* and */etc/hosts.deny*, specifying sshd as the service. For example, to permit only 192.168.0.37 to access your SSH server, insert these lines into */etc/hosts.allow*:

```
sshd: 192.168.0.37
sshd: ALL: DENY
```

Discussion

There is no need to invoke tcpd or any other program, as sshd processes the rules directly.

 TCP-wrappers support in sshd is optional, selected at compile time. Red Hat 8.0 includes it but SuSE does not. If you're not sure, or your sshd seems to ignore settings in */etc/hosts.allow* and */etc/hosts.deny*, check if it was compiled with this support:

```
$ strings /usr/sbin/sshd | egrep 'hosts\.(allow|deny)'
/etc/hosts.allow
/etc/hosts.deny
```

If the egrep output is empty, TCP-wrappers support is not present. Download OpenSSH from *http://www.openssh.com* (or use your vendor's source RPM) and rebuild it:

```
$ ./configure --with-libwrap ...other desired options...
$ make
# make install
```

See Also

sshd(8), hosts_access(5).

3.14 Restricting Access to an SSH Server by Account

Problem

You want only certain accounts on your machine to accept incoming SSH connections.

Solution

Use sshd's `AllowUsers` keyword in */etc/ssh/sshd_config*. For example, to permit SSH connections from anywhere to access the smith and jones accounts, but no other accounts:

```
/etc/ssh/sshd_config:
AllowUsers smith jones
```

To allow SSH connections from *remote.example.com* to the smith account, but no other incoming SSH connections:

```
AllowUsers smith@remote.example.com
```

Note this does *not* say anything about the remote user "smith@remote.example. com." It is a rule about connections *from* the site *remote.example.com to* your local smith account.

After modifying *sshd_config*, restart sshd to incorporate your changes.

Discussion

`AllowUsers` specifies a list of local accounts that may accept SSH connections. The list is definitive: any account not listed cannot receive SSH connections.

The second form of the syntax (user@host) looks unfortunately like an email address, or a reference to a remote user, but it is no such thing. The line:

```
AllowUsers user@remotehost
```

means "allow the remote system called *remotehost* to connect via SSH to my local account *user*."

A listing in the `AllowUsers` line does not guarantee acceptance by sshd: the remote user must still authenticate through normal means (password, public key, etc.), not to mention passing any other roadblocks on the way (firewall rules, etc.).

See Also

sshd_config(5).

3.15 Restricting Services to Specific Filesystem Directories

Problem

You want to create a chroot cage to restrict a service to a particular directory (and its subdirectories) in your filesystem.

Solution

Create a *chroot cage* by running the GNU chroot program instead of the service. Pass the service executable as an argument. In other words, change this:

```
/etc/xinetd.conf or /etc/xinetd.d/myservice:
service myservice
{
    ...
    server        = /usr/sbin/myservice -a -b
    ...
}
```

into this:

```
service myservice
{
    ...
    user = root
    server = /usr/sbin/chroot
    server_args = /var/cage /usr/sbin/myservice -a -b
    ...
}
```

Discussion

chroot takes two arguments: a directory and a program. It forces the program to behave as if the given directory were the root of the filesystem, "/". This effectively prevents the program from accessing any files not under the chroot cage directory, since those files have no names in the chroot'ed view of the filesystem. Even if the program runs with root privileges, it cannot get around this restriction. The system call invoked by chroot (which also is named chroot) is one-way: once it is invoked, there is no system call to undo it in the context of the calling process or its children.

A chroot cage is most effective if the program relinquishes its root privileges after it starts—many daemons can be configured to do this. A root program confined to a chroot cage can still wreak havoc by creating and using new device special files, or maliciously using system calls that are not related to the filesystem (like reboot!).

In normal operation, a program may access many files not directly related to its purpose, and this can restrict the practicality of chroot. You might have to duplicate so much of your filesystem inside the cage as to negate the cage's usefulness—especially if the files are sensitive (e.g., your password file, for authentication), or if they change. In the former case, it's better if the service itself contains special support for chroot, where it can choose to perform the chroot operation after it has accessed all the general system resources it needs. In the latter case, you can use hard links to make files already named outside the cage accessible from inside it—but that works only for files residing on the same filesystem as the cage. Symbolic links will not be effective, as they will be followed in the context of the cage.

In order for chroot to work, it must be run as root, and the given "cage" directory must contain a Linux directory structure sufficient to run myservice. In the preceding example, /var/cage will have to contain /var/cage/usr/sbin/myservice, /var/cage/lib (which must include any libraries that myservice may use), and so forth. Otherwise you'll see errors like:

```
chroot: cannot execute program_name: No such file or directory
```

This can be a bit of a detective game. For example, to get this simple command working:

```
# chroot /var/cage /usr/bin/who
```

the directory /var/cage will need to mirror:

/usr/bin/who
/lib/ld-linux.so.2
/lib/libc.so.6
/var/log/wtmp
/var/run/utmp

The commands ldd and strings can help identify which shared libraries and which files are used by the service, e.g.:

```
$ ldd /usr/sbin/myservice
... output...
$ strings /usr/sbin/myservice | grep /
... output...
```

See Also

chroot(1), xinetd.conf(5), strings(1), ldd(1). If there's no ldd manpage on your system, type ldd --help for usage.

3.16 Preventing Denial of Service Attacks

Problem

You want to prevent denial of service (DOS) attacks against a network service.

Solution

For xinetd, use the cps, instances, max_load, and per_source keywords.

```
/etc/xinetd.conf or /etc/xinetd.d/myservice:
service myservice
{
    ...
    cps = 10 30        Limit to 10 connections per second.
                       If the limit is exceeded, sleep for 30 seconds.
```

```
        instances = 4          Limit to 4 concurrent instances of myservice.
        per_source = 2         Limit to 2 simultaneous sessions per source IP address.
                               Specify UNLIMITED for no limit, the default.
        max_load = 3.0         Reject new requests if the one-minute system load average exceeds 3.0.
    }
```

For inetd, use the inetd -R option to specify the maximum number of times a service may be invoked per minute. The default is 256.

Discussion

These keywords can be used individually or in combination. The cps keyword limits the number of connections per second that your service will accept. If the limit is exceeded, then xinetd will disable the service temporarily. You determine how long to disable the service via the second argument, in seconds.

The instances keyword limits the number of concurrent instances of the given service. By default there is no limit, though you can state this explicitly with:

```
    instances = UNLIMITED
```

The per_source keyword is similar: instead of limiting server instances, it limits sessions for each source IP address. For example, to prevent any remote host from having multiple FTP connections to your site:

```
    /etc/xinetd.conf or /etc/xinetd.d/ftp:
    service ftp
    {
        ...
        per_source = 1
    }
```

Finally, the max_load keyword disables a service if the local system load average gets too high, to prevent throttling the CPU.

inetd is less flexible: it has a -R command option that limits the number of invocations for each service per minute. The limit applies to all services, individually. If the limit is exceeded, inetd logs a message of the form:

```
    telnet/tcp server failing (looping), service terminated
```

Actually, the service isn't terminated, it's just disabled for ten minutes. This time period cannot be adjusted.

Some firewalls have similar features: for example, iptables can limit the total number of incoming connections. On the other hand, iptables does not support the per_source functionality: it cannot limit the total per source address.

See Also

xinetd.conf(5).

3.17 Redirecting to Another Socket

Problem

You want to redirect a connection to another host and/or port, on the same or a different machine.

Solution

Use xinetd's redirect keyword:

```
/etc/xinetd.conf or /etc/xinetd.d/myservice:
service myservice
{
    ...
    server = path to original service
    redirect = IP_address  port_number
}
```

The server keyword is required, but its value is ignored. xinetd will not activate a service unless it has a server setting, even if the service being is redirected.

Discussion

For example, to redirect incoming finger connections (port 79) to another machine at 192.168.14.21:

```
/etc/xinetd.conf or /etc/xinetd.d/finger:
service finger
{
    ...
    server = /usr/sbin/in.fingerd
    redirect = 192.168.14.21 79
}
```

Of course you can redirect connections to an entirely different service, such as qotd on port 17:

```
service finger
{
    ...
    server = /usr/sbin/in.fingerd
    redirect = 192.168.14.21 17
}
```

Now incoming finger requests will instead receive an amusing "quote of the day," as long as the qotd service is enabled on the other machine. You can also redirect requests to another port on the same machine.

See Also

xinetd.conf(5). A tutorial can be found at *http://www.macsecurity.org/resources/ xinetd/tutorial.shtml*.

3.18   Logging Access to Your Services

Problem

You want to know who is accessing your services via xinetd.

Solution

Enable logging in the service's configuration file:

```
/etc/xinetd.conf or /etc/xinetd.d/myservice:
service myservice
{
    ...
    log_type = SYSLOG facility level
    log_on_success = DURATION EXIT HOST PID USERID
    log_on_failure = ATTEMPT HOST USERID
}
```

xinetd logs to syslog by default. To log to a file instead, modify the preceding log_type line to read:

```
log_type = FILE filename
```

Discussion

xinetd can record diagnostic messages via syslog or directly to a file. To use syslog, choose a facility (daemon, local0, etc.) and optionally a log level (crit, warning, etc.), where the default is info.

```
log_type = SYSLOG daemon            facility = daemon, level = info
log_type = SYSLOG daemon warning    facility = daemon, level = warning
```

To log to a file, simply specify a filename:

```
log_type = FILE /var/log/myservice.log
```

Optionally you may set hard and soft limits on the size of the log file: see xinetd. conf(5).

Log messages can be generated when services successfully start and terminate (via log_on_success) or when they fail or reject connections (via log_on_failure).

If logging doesn't work for you, the most likely culprit is an incorrect setup in */etc/syslog.conf*. It's easy to make a subtle configuration error and misroute your log messages. Run our syslog testing script to see where your messages are going. [9.28]

See Also

xinetd.conf(5), syslog.conf(5), inetd.conf(5).

3.19 Prohibiting root Logins on Terminal Devices

Problem

You want to prevent the superuser, root, from logging in directly over a terminal or pseudo-terminal.

Solution

Edit */etc/securetty*. This file contains device names, one per line, that permit root logins. Make sure there are no pseudo-ttys (pty) devices listed, so root cannot log in via the network, and remove any others of concern to you. Lines do not contain the leading "/dev/" path, and lines beginning with a hash mark (#) are comments. For example:

```
/etc/securetty:
# serial lines
tty1
tty2
# devfs devices
vc/1
vc/2
```

Discussion

If possible, don't permit root to log in directly. If you do, you're providing a route for breaking into your system: an outsider can launch (say) a dictionary attack against the terminal in question. Instead, users should log in as themselves and gain root privileges in an appropriate manner, as we discuss in Chapter 5.

See Also

securetty(5). Documentation on devfs is at *http://www.atnf.csiro.au/people/rgooch/linux/docs/devfs.html*.

CHAPTER 4
Authentication Techniques and Infrastructures

4.0 Introduction

Before you can perform any operation on a Linux system, you must have an *identity*, such as a username, SSH key, or Kerberos credential. The act of proving your identity is called *authentication*, and it usually involves some kind of password or digital key. To secure your Linux system, you need to create and control identities carefully. Our recipes span the following authentication systems:

Pluggable Authentication Modules (PAM)
> An application-level, dynamically configurable system for *consistent* authentication. Instead of having applications handle authentication on their own, they can use the PAM API and libraries to take care of the details. Consistency is achieved when many applications perform the same authentication by referencing the same PAM module. Additionally, applications needn't be recompiled to change their authentication behavior: just edit a PAM configuration file (transparent to the application) and you're done.

Secure Sockets Layer (SSL) *
> A network protocol for reliable, bidirectional, byte-stream connections. It provides cryptographically assured privacy (encryption), integrity, optional client authentication, and mandatory server authentication. Its authentication relies on X.509 *certificates*: data structures that bind an entity's public key to a name. The binding is attested to by a second, certifying entity, by means of a digital signature; the entity owning the public key is the certificate's *subject*, and the certifying entity is the *issuer*. The issuer in turn has its own certificate, with itself as the subject, and so on, forming a chain of subjects and issuers. To verify a certificate's authenticity, software follows this chain, possibly through several levels of certificate hierarchy, until it reaches one of a set of built-in, terminal (*self-signed*)

---

* Or TLS, for *Transport Layer Security*.

certificates marked as *trusted* by the user or system. Linux includes a popular implementation of SSL, called OpenSSL.

Kerberos

A sophisticated, comprehensive authentication system, initially developed at the Massachusetts Institute of Technology as part of Project Athena in the 1980s. It involves a centralized authentication database maintained on one or more highly-secure hosts acting as Kerberos Key Distribution Centers (KDCs). Principals acting in a Kerberos system (users, hosts, or programs acting on a user's behalf) obtain credentials called "tickets" from a KDC, for individual services such as remote login, printing, etc. Each host participating in a Kerberos "realm" must be explicitly added to the realm, as must each human user.

Kerberos has two major versions, called Kerberos-4 and Kerberos-5, and two major Unix-based implementations, MIT Kerberos (*http://web.mit.edu/kerberos/www*) and Heimdal (*http://www.pdc.kth.se/heimdal*). We cover the MIT variant of Kerberos-5, which is included in Red Hat 8.0. SuSE 8.0 includes Heimdal; our recipes should guide you toward getting started there, although some details will be different. You could also install MIT Kerberos on SuSE.

Secure Shell (SSH)

Provides strong, cryptographic authentication for users to access remote machines. We present SSH recipes in Chapter 6.

Authentication is a complex topic, and we won't teach it in depth. Our recipes focus on basic setup and scenarios. In the real world, you'll need a stronger understanding of (say) Kerberos design and operation to take advantage of its many features, and to run it securely. For more information see the following web sites:

Linux-PAM
> *http://www.kernel.org/pub/linux/libs/pam*

OpenSSL
> *http://www.openssl.org*

Kerberos
> *http://web.mit.edu/kerberos/www*

SSH
> *http://www.openssh.com*

In addition, there are other important authentication infrastructures for Linux which we do not cover. One notable protocol is *Internet Protocol Security* (IPSec), which provides strong authentication and encryption at the IP level. A popular implementation, FreeS/WAN, is found at *http://www.freeswan.org*.

PAM Modules

A PAM module consists of a *shared library*: compiled code dynamically loaded into the memory space of a running process. A program that uses PAM loads modules based on per-program configuration assigned by the system administrator, and calls them via a standard API. Thus, a new PAM module effectively extends the capabilities of existing programs, allowing them to use new authentication, authorization, and accounting mechanisms transparently.

To add a new PAM module to your system, copy the compiled PAM module code library into the directory */lib/security*. For example, if your library is *pam_foo.so*:

```
# cp pam_foo.so /lib/security
# cd /lib/security
# chown root.root pam_foo.so
# chmod 755 pam_foo.so
```

Now you can set applications to use the new module by adding appropriate configuration lines to */etc/pam.conf*, or to files among */etc/pam.d/**. There are many ways to configure use of a module, and not all modules can be used in all possible ways. A module generally comes with suggested configurations. Modules may also depend on other software: LDAP, Kerberos, and so forth; see the module's documentation.

pam(8) explains the details of PAM operation and the module configuration language.

4.1   Creating a PAM-Aware Application

Problem

You want to write a program that uses PAM for authentication.

Solution

Select (or create) a PAM configuration in */etc/pam.d*. Then use the PAM API to perform authentication with respect to that configuration. For example, the following application uses the su configuration, which means every user but root must supply his login password:

```
#include <security/pam_appl.h>
#include <security/pam_misc.h>
#include <pwd.h>
#include <sys/types.h>
#include <stdio.h>
#define MY_CONFIG "su"
static struct pam_conv conv = { misc_conv, NULL };

main( )
{
```

```
    pam_handle_t *pamh;
    int result;
    struct passwd *pw;
    if ((pw = getpwuid(getuid( ))) == NULL)
      perror("getpwuid");
    else if ((result = pam_start(MY_CONFIG, pw->pw_name, &conv, &pamh)) != PAM_SUCCESS)
      fprintf(stderr, "start failed: %d\n", result);
    else if ((result = pam_authenticate(pamh, 0)) != PAM_SUCCESS)
      fprintf(stderr, "authenticate failed: %d\n", result);
    else if ((result = pam_acct_mgmt(pamh, 0)) != PAM_SUCCESS)
      fprintf(stderr, "acct_mgmt failed: %d\n", result);
    else if ((result = pam_end(pamh, result)) != PAM_SUCCESS)
      fprintf(stderr, "end failed: %d\n", result);
    else
      Run_My_Big_Application( );              /* Run your application code */
}
```

Compile the program, linking with libraries *libpam* and *libpam_misc*:

```
$ gcc myprogram.c -lpam -lpam_misc
```

Discussion

The PAM libraries include functions to start PAM and check authentication credentials. Notice how the details of authentication are completely hidden from the application: simply reference your desired PAM module (in this case, su) and examine the function return values. Even after your application is compiled, you can change the authentication behavior by editing configurations in */etc/pam.d*. Such is the beauty of PAM.

See Also

pam_start(3), pam_end(3), pam_authenticate(3), pam_acct_mgmt(3). The Linux PAM Developer's Guide is at *http://www.kernel.org/pub/linux/libs/pam/Linux-PAM-html/pam_appl.html*.

4.2 Enforcing Password Strength with PAM

Problem

You want your users to employ strong passwords.

Solution

Use the CrackLib [9.2] module of PAM, pam_cracklib, to test and enforce password strength requirements automatically. In some Linux distributions such as Red Hat 8.0, this feature is enabled by default. passwd and other PAM-mediated programs will complain if a new password is too short, too simple, too closely related to the previous password, etc.

You can adjust password strength and other variables by editing the parameters to the pam_cracklib module in */etc/pam.d/system-auth*. For example, to increase the number of consecutive times a user can enter an incorrect password, change the retry parameter from its default of 3:

```
password    required     /lib/security/pam_cracklib.so   retry=3
```

Discussion

PAM allows recursion via the pam_stack module—that is, one PAM module can invoke another. If you examine the contents of */etc/pam.d*, you will find quite a number of modules that recursively depend on system-auth, for example. This lets you define a single, systemwide authentication policy that propagates to other services.

Red Hat 8.0 has a sysadmin utility, authconfig, with a simple GUI for setting system authentication methods and policies: how authentication is performed (local passwords, Kerberos, LDAP), whether caching is done, etc. authconfig does its work by writing */etc/pam.d/system-auth*. Unfortunately, it does not preserve any customizations you might make to this file. So, if you make custom edits as described above, beware using authconfig—it will erase them!

See Also

pam(8), authconfig(8), pam_stack(8). See */usr/share/doc/pam-*/txts/README.pam_cracklib* for a list of parameters to tweak.

4.3   Creating Access Control Lists with PAM

Problem

You would like to apply an access control list (ACL) to an existing service that does not explicitly support ACLs (e.g., telnetd, imapd, etc.).

Solution

Use the listfile PAM module.

First, make sure the server in question uses PAM for authentication, and find out which PAM service name it uses. This may be in the server documentation, or it may be clear from examining the server itself and perusing the contents of */etc/pam.d*. For example, suppose you're dealing with the IMAP mail server. First notice that there is a file called *etc/pam.d/imap*. Further, the result of:

```
# locate imapd
...
/usr/sbin/imapd
```

shows that the IMAP server is in */usr/sbin/imapd*, and:

```
# ldd /usr/sbin/imapd
libpam.so.0 => /lib/libpam.so.0 (0x40027000)
...
```

shows that the server is dynamically linked against the PAM library (*libpam.so*), also suggesting that it uses PAM. In fact, the Red Hat 8.0 IMAP server uses PAM via that service name and control file ("imap").

Continuing with this example, create an ACL file for the IMAP service, let's say */etc/imapd.acl*, and make sure it is not world-writable:

```
# chmod o-w /etc/imapd.acl
```

Edit this file, and place in it the usernames of those accounts authorized to use the IMAP server, one name per line. Then, add the following to */etc/pam.d/imap*:

```
account required /lib/security/pam_listfile.so file=/etc/imapd.acl \
item=user sense=allow onerr=fail
```

With this configuration, only those users listed in the ACL file will be allowed access to the IMAP service. If the ACL file is missing, PAM will deny access for all accounts.

Discussion

The PAM "listfile" module is actually even more flexible than we've indicated. Entries in your ACL file can be not only usernames (item=user), but also:

- Terminal lines (item=tty)
- Remote host (item=rhost)
- Remote user (item=ruser)
- Group membership (item=group)
- Login shell (item=shell)

The sense keyword determines how the ACL file is interpreted. sense=allow means that access will be allowed only if the configured item is in the file, and denied otherwise. sense=deny means the opposite: access will be denied only if the item is in the file, and allowed otherwise.

The onerr keyword indicates what to do if some unexpected error occurs during PAM processing of the *listfile* module—for instance, if the ACL file does not exist. The values are succeed and fail. fail is a more conservative option from a security standpoint, but can also lock you out of your system because of a configuration mistake!

Another keyword, apply=[*user*|*@group*], limits the restriction in question to apply only to particular users or groups. This is intended for use with the tty, rhost, and shell items. For example, using item=rhost and apply=@foo would restrict access to connections from hosts listed in the ACL file, and furthermore only to local accounts in the foo group.

To debug problems with PAM modules, look for PAM-specific error messages in */var/log/messages* and */var/log/secure*. (If you don't see the expected messages, check your system logger configuration. [9.28])

Note that not all module parameters have defaults. Specifically, the file, item, and sense parameters must be supplied; if not, the module will fail with an error message like:

```
Dec  2 15:49:21 localhost login: PAM-listfile: Unknown sense or sense not specified
```

You generally do not need to restart servers using PAM: they usually re-initialize the PAM library for every authentication and reread your changed files. However, there might be exceptions.

There is no standard correspondence between a server's name and its associated PAM service. For instance, logins via Telnet are actually mediated by */bin/login*, and thus use the login service. The SSH server sshd uses the same-named PAM service (sshd), whereas the IMAP server imapd uses the imap (with no "d") PAM service. And many services in turn depend on other services, notably system-auth.

See Also

See */usr/share/doc/pam-*/txts/README.pam_listfile* for a list of parameters to tweak.

4.4   Validating an SSL Certificate

Problem

You want to check that an SSL certificate is valid.

Solution

If your system's certificates are kept in a file (as in Red Hat):

```
$ openssl ... -CAfile file_of_CA_certificates ...
```

If they are kept in a directory (as in SuSE):

```
$ openssl ... -CAdir directory_of_CA_certificates ...
```

For example, to check the certificate for the secure IMAP server on *mail.server.net* against the system trusted certificate list on a Red Hat host:

```
$ openssl s_client -quiet -CAfile /usr/share/ssl/cert.pem \
                          -connect mail.server.net:993
```

To check the certificate of a secure web site *https://www.yoyodyne.com/* from a SuSE host (recall HTTPS runs on port 443):

```
$ openssl s_client -quiet -CAdir /usr/share/ssl/certs -connect www.yoyodyne.com:443
```

If you happen to have a certificate in a file *cert.pem*, and you want to validate it, there is a separate validate command:

```
$ openssl validate -CA... -in cert.pem
```

Add -inform der if the certificate is in the binary DER format rather than PEM.

Discussion

Red Hat 8.0 comes with a set of certificates for some well-known Internet Certifying Authorities in the file */usr/share/ssl/cert.pem*. SuSE 8.0 has a similar collection, but it is instead stored in a directory with a particular structure, a sort of hash table implemented using symbolic links. Under SuSE, the directory */usr/share/ssl/certs* contains each certificate in a separate file, together with the links.

If the necessary root certificate is present in the given file, along with any necessary intermediate certificates not provided by the server, then openssl can validate the server certificate.

 If a server certificate is invalid or cannot be checked, an SSL connection will not fail. openssl will simply print a warning and continue connecting.

See Also

openssl(1).

4.5   Decoding an SSL Certificate

Problem

You want to view information about a given SSL certificate, stored in a PEM file.

Solution

```
$ openssl x509 -text -in filename
Certificate:
```

```
    Data:
        Version: 3 (0x2)
        Serial Number:
            d0:1e:40:90:00:00:27:4b:00:00:00:01:00:00:00:04
        Signature Algorithm: sha1WithRSAEncryption
        Issuer: C=US, ST=Utah, L=Salt Lake City, O=Xcert EZ by DST, CN=Xcert EZ by
DST/Email=ca@digsigtrust.com
        Validity
            Not Before: Jul 14 16:14:18 1999 GMT
            Not After : Jul 11 16:14:18 2009 GMT
        Subject: C=US, ST=Utah, L=Salt Lake City, O=Xcert EZ by DST, CN=Xcert EZ by
DST/Email=ca@digsigtrust.com
    ...
```

Discussion

This is a quick way to learn who issued a certificate, its begin and end dates, and other pertinent details.

See Also

openssl(1).

4.6   Installing a New SSL Certificate

Problem

You have a certificate that your SSL clients (mutt, openssl, etc.) cannot verify. It was issued by a Certifying Authority (CA) not included in your installed list of trusted issuers.

Solution

Add the CA's root certificate to the list, together with any other, intermediate certificates you may need. First, ensure the certificates are in PEM format. [4.10] A PEM format file looks like this:

```
-----BEGIN CERTIFICATE-----
MIID+DCCAuCgAwIBAgIRANAeQJAAACdLAAAAAQAAAQwDQYJKoZIhvcNAQEFBQAw
gYwxCzAJBgNVBAYTAlVTMQowCwYDVQQIEwRVdGFoMRcwFQYDVQQHEw5TYWx0IExh
...
wo3CbezcE9NGxX18
-----END CERTIFICATE-----
```

Then for Red Hat, simply add it to the file */usr/share/ssl/cert.pem*.

Note that only the base64-encoded data between the BEGIN CERTIFICATE and END CERTIFICATE lines is needed. Everything else is ignored. The existing file includes a textual description of each certificate as well, which you can generate [4.5] and include if you like.

For SuSE, supposing your CA certificate is in *newca.pem*, run:

```
# cp newca.pem /usr/share/ssl/certs
# /usr/bin/c_rehash
```

Discussion

Red Hat keeps certificates in a single file, whereas SuSE keeps them in a directory with a particular structure, a sort of hash table implemented using symbolic links. You can also use the hashed-directory approach with Red Hat if you like, since it includes the c_rehash program.

Many programs have their own certificate storage and do not use this system-wide list. Netscape and Mozilla use *~/.netscape/cert7.db*, KDE applications use *$KDEDIR/share/config/ksslcalist*, Evolution has its own list, and so on. Consult their documentation on how to add a new trusted CA.

Before installing a new CA certificate, you should be convinced that it's authentic, and that its issuer has adequate security policies. After all, you are going to trust the CA to verify web site identities for you! Take the same level of care as you would when adding a new GnuPG key as a trusted introducer. [7.9]

See Also

openssl(1).

4.7   Generating an SSL Certificate Signing Request (CSR)

Problem

You want to obtain an SSL certificate from a trusted certifying authority (CA).

Solution

Generate a Certificate Signing Request (CSR):

Red Hat:
```
$ make -f /usr/share/ssl/certs/Makefile filename.csr
```

SuSE or other:
```
$ umask 077
$ openssl req -new -out filename.csr -keyout privkey.pem
```

and send *filename.csr* to the CA.

Discussion

You can obtain a certificate for a given service from a well-known Certifying Authority, such as Verisign, Thawte, or Equifax. This is the simplest way to obtain a certificate, operationally speaking, as it will be automatically verifiable by many SSL clients. However, this approach costs money and takes time.

To obtain a certificate from a commercial CA, you create a Certificate Signing Request:

```
$ make -f /usr/share/ssl/certs/Makefile foo.csr
```

This generates a new RSA key pair in the file *foo.key*, and a certificate request in *foo.csr*. You will be prompted for a passphrase with which to encrypt the private key, which you will need to enter several times. You *must* remember this passphrase, or your private key is forever lost and the certificate, when you get it, will be useless.

openssl will ask you for the components of the certificate subject name:

```
Country Name (2 letter code) [GB]:
State or Province Name (full name) [Berkshire]:
Locality Name (eg, city) [Newbury]:
Organization Name (eg, company) [My Company Ltd]:
Organizational Unit Name (eg, section) []:
Common Name (eg, your name or your server's hostname) []:
Email Address []:
```

The most important part is the Common Name. It *must* be the DNS name with which your clients will be configured, not the canonical hostname or other aliases the host may have. Suppose you decide to run a secure mail server on your multipurpose machine *server.bigcorp.com*. Following good abstraction principles, you create an alias (a DNS CNAME record) *mail.bigcorp.com* for this host, so you can easily move mail service to another machine in the future without reconfiguring all its clients. When you generate a CSR for this mail server, what name should the Common Name field contain? The answer is *mail.bigcorp.com*, since your SSL clients will use this name to reach the server. If instead you used *server.bigcorp.com* for the Common Name, the SSL clients would compare the intended destination (*mail.bigcorp.com*) and the name in the server certificate (*server.bigcorp.com*) and complain that they do not match.

You will also be prompted for a *challenge password*. Enter one and make a note of it; you may be asked for it as part of your CA's certificate-issuing procedure.

When done, send the contents of *foo.csr* to your CA, following whatever procedure they have for getting it signed. They will return to you a real, signed certificate, which you can then install for use. [4.6] For instance, if this certificate were for IMAP/SSL on a Red Hat server, you would place the certificate and private key, unencrypted, in the file */usr/share/ssl/certs/imapd.pem* (replacing the Red Hat-supplied dummy certificate). First, make sure the certificate you've received is in PEM

---

format. [4.10] Suppose it's in the file *cert.pem*; then, decrypt your private key and append it to this file:

```
$ openssl rsa -in foo.key >> cert.pem
```

and then as root:

```
# chown root.root cert.pem
# chmod 400 cert.pem
```

The private key must be unencrypted so that the IMAP server can read it on startup; thus the key file must be protected accordingly.

See Also

openssl(1), req(1).

4.8   Creating a Self-Signed SSL Certificate

Problem

You want to create an SSL certificate but don't want to use a well-known certifying authority (CA), perhaps for reasons of cost.

Solution

Create a self-signed SSL certificate:

For Red Hat:

```
$ make -f /usr/share/ssl/certs/Makefile filename.crt
```

For SuSE or other:

```
$ umask 077
$ openssl req -new -x509 -days 365 -out filename.crt -keyout privkey.pem
```

Discussion

A certificate is *self-signed* if its subject and issuer are the same. A self-signed certificate does not depend on any higher, well-known issuing authority for validation, so it will have to be explicitly marked as trusted by your users. For instance, the first time you connect to such a server, client software (such as your web browser) will ask if you would like to trust this certificate in the future.

Self-signing is convenient but runs the risk of man-in-the-middle attacks on the first connection, before the client trusts the certificate. A more secure method is to pre-install this certificate on the client machine in a separate step, and mark it as trusted.

When you create the certificate, you will be prompted for various things, particularly a Common Name. Pay special attention to this, as when creating a certificate signing request (CSR). [4.7]

If you need many certificates, this method may be cumbersome, as your users will have to trust each certificate individually. Instead, use `openssl` to set up your own CA, and issue certificates under it. [4.9] This way, you need only add your one CA certificate to your client's trusted caches; any individual service certificates you create afterward will be automatically trusted.

 Self-signed certificates are fine for tests and for services not available to the public (i.e., inside a company intranet). For public access, however, use a certificate from a well-known CA. To use a standalone certificate properly, you are somewhat at the mercy of your users, who must be diligent about reading security warnings, verifying the certificate with you, and so forth. They will be tempted to bypass these steps, which is bad for your security and theirs.

See Also

openssl(1).

4.9   Setting Up a Certifying Authority

Problem

You want to create a simple Certifying Authority (CA) and issue SSL certificates yourself.

Solution

Use `CA.pl`, a Perl script supplied with OpenSSL. It ties together various `openssl` commands so you can easily construct a new CA and issue certificates under it. To create the CA:

```
$ /usr/share/ssl/misc/CA.pl -newca
```

To create a certificate, *newcert.pem*, signed by your CA:

```
$ /usr/share/ssl/misc/CA.pl -newreq
$ /usr/share/ssl/misc/CA.pl -sign
```

Discussion

First, realize that your newly created "CA" is more like a mockup than a real Certifying Authority:

- OpenSSL provides the basic algorithmic building blocks, but the CA.pl script is just a quick demonstration hack, not a full-blown program.

- A real CA for a production environment requires a much higher degree of security. It's typically implemented in specialized, tamper-resistant, cryptographic hardware—in a secure building with lots of guards—rather than a simple file on disk! You can emulate what a CA does using OpenSSL for testing purposes, but if you're going to use it for any sort of real application, first educate yourself on the topic of Public-Key Infrastructure, and know what kind of tradeoffs you're making.

That being said, CA.pl is still useful for some realistic applications. Suppose you are a business owner, and you need to enable secure web transactions for your partners on a set of HTTP servers you operate. There are several servers, and the set will change over time, so you want an easy way to allow these to be trusted. You use openssl to generate a CA key, and securely communicate its certificate to your partners, who add it to their trusted CA lists. You can then issue certificates for your various servers as they come online, and SSL server authentication will proceed automatically for your partners—and you have full control over certificate expiration and revocation, if you wish. Take appropriate care with the CA private key, commensurate with your (and your partners') security needs and the business threat level. This might mean anything from using a good passphrase to keeping the whole CA infrastructure on a box in a locked office not connected to the Net to using cryptographic hardware like CyberTrust SafeKeyper (which OpenSSL can do)—whatever is appropriate.

Let's create your Certifying Authority, consisting of a new root key, self-signed certificate, and some bookkeeping files under *demoCA*. CA.pl asks for a passphrase to protect the CA's private key, which is needed to sign requests.

```
$ /usr/share/ssl/misc/CA.pl -newca
CA certificate filename (or enter to create)
[press return]
Making CA certificate ...
Using configuration from /usr/share/ssl/openssl.cnf
Generating a 1024 bit RSA private key
.......++++++
.............++++++
writing new private key to './demoCA/private/cakey.pem'
Enter PEM pass phrase: ********
Verifying password - Enter PEM pass phrase: ********
-----
You are about to be asked to enter information that will be incorporated
into your certificate request.
What you are about to enter is what is called a Distinguished Name or a DN.
There are quite a few fields but you can leave some blank
For some fields there will be a default value,
If you enter '.', the field will be left blank.
-----
Country Name (2 letter code) [GB]:US
State or Province Name (full name) [Berkshire]: Washington
```

```
Locality Name (eg, city) [Newbury]: Redmond
Organization Name (eg, company) [My Company Ltd]: BigCorp
Organizational Unit Name (eg, section) []: Dept of Corporate Aggression
Common Name (eg, your name or your server's hostname) []: www.bigcorp.com
Email Address []: abuse@bigcorp.com
```

Now, you can create a certificate request:

```
$ /usr/share/ssl/misc/CA.pl -newreq
```

You will be presented with a similar dialog, but the output will be a file called *newreq.pem* containing both a new private key (encrypted by a passphrase you supply and must remember), and a certificate request for its public component.

Finally, have the CA sign your request:

```
$ /usr/share/ssl/misc/CA.pl -sign
Using configuration from /usr/share/ssl/openssl.cnf
Enter PEM pass phrase: ...enter CA password here...
Check that the request matches the signature
Signature ok
The Subjects Distinguished Name is as follows
countryName           :PRINTABLE:'US'
stateOrProvinceName   :PRINTABLE:'Washington'
localityName          :PRINTABLE:'Redmond'
organizationName      :PRINTABLE:'BigCorp'
commonName            :PRINTABLE:'Dept of Corporate Aggression'
Certificate is to be certified until Mar  5 15:25:09 2004 GMT (365 days)
Sign the certificate? [y/n]: y

1 out of 1 certificate requests certified, commit? [y/n] y
Write out database with 1 new entries
Data Base Updated
Signed certificate is in newcert.pem
```

Keep the private key from *newreq.pem* with the certificate in *newcert.pem*, and discard the certificate request.

If this key and certificate are for a server (e.g., Apache), you can use them in this format—although you will probably have to decrypt the private key and keep it in a protected file, so the server software can read it on startup:

```
$ openssl rsa -in newreq.pem
```

If the key and certificate are for client authentication, say for use in a web browser, you may need to bind them together in the PKCS-12 format to install it on the client:

```
$ openssl pkcs12 -export -inkey newreq.pem -in newcert.pem -out newcert.p12
```

You will be prompted first for the key passphrase (so openssl can read the private key), then for an "export" password with which to protect the private key in the new file. You will need to supply the export password when opening the *.p12* file elsewhere.

In any event, you will need to distribute your CA's root certificate to clients, so they can validate the certificates you issue with this CA. Often the format wanted for this purpose is DER (a *.crt* file):

```
$ openssl x509 -in demoCA/cacert.pem -outform der -out cacert.crt
```

See Also

openssl(1) and the Perl script */usr/share/ssl/misc/CA.pl.*

4.10 Converting SSL Certificates from DER to PEM

Problem

You have an SSL certificate in binary format, and you want to convert it to text-based PEM format.

Solution

```
$ openssl x509 -inform der -in filename -out filename.pem
```

Discussion

It may happen that you obtain a CA certificate in a different format. If it appears to be a binary file (often with the filename extension *.der* or *.crt*), it is probably the raw DER-encoded form; test this with:

```
$ openssl x509 -inform der -text -in filename
```

DER stands for Distinguished Encoding Rules, an encoding for ASN.1 data structures; X.509 certificates are represented using the ASN.1 standard. The openssl command uses PEM encoding by default. You can convert a DER-encoded certificate to PEM format thus:

```
$ openssl x509 -inform der -in filename -out filename.pem
```

See Also

openssl(1).

4.11   Getting Started with Kerberos

Problem

You want to set up an MIT Kerberos-5 Key Distribution Center (KDC).

Solution

1. Confirm that Kerberos is installed; if not, install the necessary Red Hat packages:

   ```
   $ rpm -q krb5-server krb5-workstation
   ```

2. Add */usr/kerberos/bin* and */usr/kerberos/sbin* to your search path.

3. Choose a realm name (normally your DNS domain), and in the following files:

   /etc/krb5.conf
   /var/kerberos/krb5kdc/kdc.conf
   /var/kerberos/krb5kdc/kadm5.acl

   replace all occurrences of EXAMPLE.COM with your realm and domain.

4. Create the KDC principal database, and choose a master password:

   ```
   # kdb5_util create
   ```

5. Start the KDC:

   ```
   # krb5kdc [-m]
   ```

6. Set up a Kerberos principal for yourself with administrative privileges, and a host principal for the KDC host. (Note the prompt is "kadmin.local:".) Suppose your KDC host is *kirby.dogood.org*:

   ```
   # kadmin.local [-m]
   kadmin.local: addpol users
   kadmin.local: addpol admin
   kadmin.local: addpol hosts
   kadmin.local: ank -policy users username
   kadmin.local: ank -policy admin username/admin
   kadmin.local: ank -randkey -policy hosts host/kirby.dogood.org
   kadmin.local: ktadd -k /var/kerberos/krb5kdc/kadm5.keytab \
                 kadmin/admin kadmin/changepw
   kadmin.local: quit
   ```

7. Start up the kadmin service:

   ```
   # kadmind [-m]
   ```

8. Test by obtaining your own Kerberos user credentials, and listing them:

   ```
   $ kinit
   $ klist
   ```

9. Test the Kerberos administrative system (note the prompt is "kadmin:"):

   ```
   $ kadmin
   kadmin: listprincs
   kadmin: quit
   ```

Discussion

When choosing a realm name, normally you should use the DNS domain of your organization. Suppose ours is *dogood.org*. Here's an example of replacing EXAMPLE. COM with your realm and domain names in */etc/krb5.conf*:

```
[libdefaults]
 default_realm = DOGOOD.ORG
[realms]
 DOGOOD.ORG = {
  kdc = kirby.dogood.org:88
  admin_server = kirby.dogood.org:749
  default_domain = dogood.org
 }
[domain_realm]
 .dogood.org = DOGOOD.ORG
 dogood.org = DOGOOD.ORG
```

The KDC principal database is the central repository of authentication information for the realm; it contains records for all principals (users and hosts) in the realm, including their authentication keys. These are strong random keys for hosts, or derived from passwords in the case of user principals.

```
# kdb5_util create
Initializing database '/var/kerberos/krb5kdc/principal' for realm 'DOGOOD.ORG',
master key name 'K/M@DOGOOD.ORG'
You will be prompted for the database Master Password.
It is important that you NOT FORGET this password.
Enter KDC database master key: ********
Re-enter KDC database master key to verify: ********
```

 Store the database master password in a safe place. The KDC needs it to start, and if you lose it, your realm database is useless and you will need to recreate it from scratch, including all user accounts.

kdb5_util stores the database in the files */var/kerberos/krb5kdc/principal** and stores the database master key in */var/kerberos/krb5kdc/.k5.DOGOOD.ORG*. The key allows the KDC to start up unattended (e.g., on a reboot), but at the cost of some security, since it can now be stolen if the KDC host is compromised. You may remove this key file, but if so, you must enter the master password by hand on system startup and at various other points. For this recipe, we assume that you leave the key file in place, but we'll indicate where password entry would be necessary if you removed it.

When you start the KDC (adding the *-m* option to enter the master password if necessary):

```
# krb5kdc [-m]
```

Protect Your Key Distribution Server

The KDC is the most sensitive part of the Kerberos system. The data in its database is equivalent to all your user's passwords; an attacker who steals it can impersonate any user or service in the system. For production use, KDCs should be locked down, particularly if your KDC master key is on disk to permit unattended restarts.

Typically, a KDC should run only Kerberos services (TGT server, kadmin, Kerberos-5-to-4 credentials conversion) and have no other inbound network access. Administration, typically infrequent, should be done only at the console. At MIT, for example, KDCs are literally locked in a safe, with only a network and power cable emerging to the outside world. If you truly require remote administration, a possible compromise is login access via SSH, using only public-key authentication (and perhaps also Kerberos, but the likely time you'll need to get in is when Kerberos isn't working!).

monitor its operation by watching its log file in another window:

```
$ tail -f /var/log/krb5kdc.log
Mar 05 03:05:01 kirbyg krb5kdc[4231](info): setting up network...
Mar 05 03:05:01 kirby krb5kdc[4231](info): listening on fd 7: 192.168.10.5 port 88
Mar 05 03:05:01 kirby krb5kdc[4231](info): listening on fd 8: 192.168.10.5 port 750
Mar 05 03:05:01 kirby krb5kdc[4231](info): set up 2 sockets
Mar 05 03:05:01 kirby krb5kdc[4232](info): commencing operation
```

Next, in the realm database set up a Kerberos principal for yourself with administrative privileges, and a host principal for the KDC host. Kerberos includes a secure administration protocol for modifying the KDC database from any host over the network, using the kadmin utility. Of course, we can't use that yet as setup is not complete. To bootstrap, we modify the database directly using root privilege to write the database file, with a special version of kadmin called kadmin.local. Add the -m option to supply the master password if needed. Supposing that your username is pat and the KDC host is *kirby.dogood.org*:

```
# kadmin.local [-m]
Authenticating as principal root/admin@DOGOOD.ORG with password.
kadmin.local:  addpol users
kadmin.local:  addpol admin
kadmin.local:  addpol hosts
kadmin.local:  ank -policy users pat
Enter password for principal "pat@DOGOOD.ORG": ********
Re-enter password for principal "pat@DOGOOD.ORG": ********
Principal "pat@DOGOOD.ORG" created.

kadmin.local:  ank -policy admin pat/admin
Enter password for principal "pat/admin@DOGOOD.ORG": ********
Re-enter password for principal "pat/admin@DOGOOD.ORG": ********
Principal "pat/admin@DOGOOD.ORG" created.

kadmin.local:  ank -randkey -policy hosts host/kirby.dogood.org
Principal "host/kirby.dogood.org@DOGOOD.ORG" created.
```

```
kadmin.local:  ktadd -k /etc/krb5.keytab host/kirby.dogood.org
Entry for principal host/kirby.dogood.org with kvno 3, encryption type
   Triple DES cbc mode with HMAC/sha1 added to keytab WRFILE:/etc/krb5.keytab.

kadmin.local:  ktadd -k /var/kerberos/krb5kdc/kadm5.keytab \
               kadmin/admin kadmin/changepw
Entry for principal kadmin/admin with kvno 3, encryption type
   Triple DES cbc mode with HMAC/sha1 added to keytab WRFILE:/var/kerberos/krb5kdc/
kadm5.keytab.
Entry for principal kadmin/changepw with kvno 3, encryption type
   Triple DES cbc mode with HMAC/sha1 added to keytab WRFILE:/var/kerberos/krb5kdc/
kadm5.keytab.

kadmin.local:  quit
```

The addpol command creates a *policy*—a collection of parameters and restrictions on accounts—which may be changed later. We create three policies for user, administrative, and host credentials, and begin applying them; this is a good idea even if not strictly needed, in case you want to start using policies later.

The ank command adds a new principal. The user and user administrative principals require passwords; for the host principal, we use the -randkey option, which generates a random key instead of using a password. When a user authenticates via Kerberos, she uses her password. A host also has credentials, but cannot supply a password, so a hosts's secret key is stored in a protected file, */etc/krb5.keytab*.

Now, we can start up and test the kadmin service, which you can monitor via its log file, */var/log/kadmind.log*:

```
# kadmind [-m]
```

First, try obtaining your Kerberos user credentials using kinit:

```
$ kinit
Password for pat@DOGOOD.ORG:
```

Having succeeded, use klist to examine your credentials:

```
$ klist
Ticket cache: FILE:/tmp/krb5cc_500
Default principal: pat@DOGOOD.ORG
Valid starting     Expires            Service principal
03/05/03 03:48:35  03/05/03 13:48:35  krbtgt/DOGOOD.ORG@DOGOOD.ORG

Kerberos 4 ticket cache: /tmp/tkt500
klist: You have no tickets cached
```

Now test the Kerberos administrative system, using the separate administrative password you assigned earlier:

```
$ kadmin
Authenticating as principal pat/admin@DOGOOD.ORG with password.
Enter password: ********
kadmin: listprincs
[list of all Kerberos principals in the database]
kadmin: quit
```

Finally, test the local host principal by using Kerberos authentication with OpenSSH [4.14] or Telnet [4.15].

If you left the KDC master disk on disk at the beginning of this recipe, you may set the KDC and kadmin servers to start automatically on boot:

```
# chkconfig krb5kdc on
# chkconfig kadmin on
```

Otherwise, you will need to start them manually after every system reset, using the -m switch and typing in the KDC master database password.

See Also

kadmin(8), kadmind(8), kdb5_util(8), krb5kdc(8), kinit(1), klist(1), chkconfig(8).

4.12   Adding Users to a Kerberos Realm

Problem

You want to add a new user to an existing MIT Kerberos-5 realm.

Solution

Use kadmin on any realm host:

```
$ kadmin
Authenticating as principal pat/admin@DOGOOD.ORG with password.
```

To add the user named joe:

```
kadmin: ank -policy users joe
Enter password for principal "joe@DOGOOD.ORG": ********
Re-enter password for principal "joe@DOGOOD.ORG": ********
Principal "joe@DOGOOD.ORG" created.
```

To give joe administrative privileges:

```
kadmin: ank -policy admin joe/admin
Enter password for principal "joe/admin@DOGOOD.ORG": ********
Re-enter password for principal "joe/admin@DOGOOD.ORG": ********
Principal "joe/admin@DOGOOD.ORG" created.
```

and tell Joe his temporary user and admin passwords, which he should immediately change with kpasswd. When finished:

```
kadmin: quit
```

Discussion

This is the same procedure we used while setting up your KDC. [4.11] You need not be on the KDC to do administration; you can do it remotely with kadmin. The program kadmin.local, which we used before, is only for bootstrapping or other exceptional situations.

See Also

kadmin(8).

4.13   Adding Hosts to a Kerberos Realm

Problem

You want to add a new host to an existing MIT Kerberos-5 realm.

Solution

Copy */etc/krb5.conf* from your KDC (or any other realm host) to the new host. Then run kadmin on the new host, say, *samaritan*:

```
samaritan# kadmin -p pat/admin
Authenticating as principal pat/admin@DOGOOD.ORG with password.
Enter password: ********
kadmin: ank -randkey -policy hosts host/samaritan.dogood.org
kadmin: ktadd -k /etc/krb5.keytab host/samaritan.dogood.org
kadmin: quit
```

Discussion

Assume the Kerberos realm we set up previously, *DOGOOD.ORG* [4.11], and suppose your new host is *samaritan.dogood.org*. Once the *DOGOOD.ORG* realm configuration file (*/etc/krb5.conf*) has been copied from the KDC to *samaritan*, we can take advantage of the kadmin protocol we set up on the KDC to administer the Kerberos database remotely, directly from *samaritan*. We add a host principal for our new machine and store the host's secret key in the local *keytab* file. (kadmin can find the Kerberos admin server from the *krb5.conf* file we just installed.)

```
samaritan# kadmin -p pat/admin
Authenticating as principal pat/admin@DOGOOD.ORG with password.
Enter password: ********

kadmin:  ank -randkey -policy hosts host/samaritan.dogood.org
Principal "host/samaritan.dogood.org@DOGOOD.ORG" created.

kadmin:  ktadd -k /etc/krb5.keytab host/samaritan.dogood.org
```

```
Entry for principal host/samaritan.dogood.org with kvno 3, encryption type
    Triple DES cbc mode with HMAC/sha1 added to keytab WRFILE:/etc/krb5.keytab.

kadmin: quit
```

That's it! Test by doing a kinit in your user account (pat):

```
# su - pat
pat@samaritan$ kinit
Password for pat@DOGOOD.ORG: ********
```

Having succeeded, use klist to examine your credentials:

```
pat@samaritan$ klist
Ticket cache: FILE:/tmp/krb5cc_500
Default principal: pat@DOGOOD.ORG

Valid starting     Expires            Service principal
03/05/03 03:48:35  03/05/03 13:48:35  krbtgt/DOGOOD.ORG@DOGOOD.ORG
```

and try connecting to yourself via ssh with Kerberos authentication, to test the operation of the host principal: [4.14]

```
pat@samaritan$ ssh -v1 samaritan
OpenSSH_3.4p1, SSH protocols 1.5/2.0, OpenSSL 0x0090602f
debug1: Reading configuration data /home/res/.ssh/config
...
debug1: Trying Kerberos v5 authentication.
debug1: Kerberos v5 authentication accepted.
...
pat@samaritan$
```

See Also

kadmin(8), kinit(1), klist(1), ssh(1).

4.14   Using Kerberos with SSH

Problem

You want to authenticate to your SSH server via Kerberos-5. We assume you already have an MIT Kerberos-5 infrastructure. [4.11]

Solution

Suppose your SSH server and client machines are *myserver* and *myclient*, respectively:

1. Make sure your OpenSSH distribution is compiled with Kerberos-5 support on both *myserver* and *myclient*. The Red Hat OpenSSH distribution comes this way, but if you're building your own, use:

   ```
   $ ./configure --with-kerberos5 ...
   ```

   before building and installing OpenSSH.

2. Configure the SSH server on *myserver*:

```
/etc/ssh/sshd_config:
KerberosAuthentication yes
KerberosTicketCleanup yes
```

Decide whether you want `sshd` to fall back to ordinary password authentication if Kerberos authentication fails:

```
KerberosOrLocalPasswd [yes|no]
```

3. Restart the SSH server:

```
myserver# /etc/init.d/sshd restart
```

4. On *myclient*, obtain a ticket-granting ticket if you have not already done so, and connect to *myserver* via SSH. Kerberos-based authentication should occur.

```
myclient$ kinit
Password for username@REALM: ********

myclient$ ssh -1 myserver              That's the number one, not a lower-case L
```

Discussion

We use the older SSH-1 protocol:

```
$ ssh -1 kdc
```

because OpenSSH supports Kerberos-5 only for SSH-1. This is not ideal, as SSH-1 is deprecated for its known security weaknesses, but SSH-2 has no standard support for Kerberos yet. However, there is a proposal to add it via GSSAPI (Generic Security Services Application Programming Interface, RFC 1964). A set of patches for OpenSSH implements this authentication mechanism, and is available from *http://www.sxw.org.uk/computing/patches/openssh.html*.

Continuing with our example using the built-in SSH-1 Kerberos support: if all works properly, ssh should log you in automatically without a password. Add the -v option to see more diagnostics:

```
$ ssh -1v myserver
OpenSSH_3.4p1, SSH protocols 1.5/2.0, OpenSSL 0x0090602f
debug1: Reading configuration data /home/res/.ssh/config
...
debug1: Trying Kerberos v5 authentication.
debug1: Kerberos v5 authentication accepted.
...
```

confirming the use of Kerberos authentication. You can also see the new "host/*hostname*" ticket acquired for the connection:

```
$ klist
Ticket cache: FILE:/tmp/krb5cc_500
Default principal: pat@DOGOOD.ORG
```

```
Valid starting      Expires             Service principal
03/05/03 03:48:35   03/05/03 13:48:35   krbtgt/DOGOOD.ORG@DOGOOD.ORG
03/05/03 06:19:10   03/05/03 15:55:06   host/myserver.dogood.org@DOGOOD.ORG
...
```

If Kerberos for SSH doesn't work, test it using the SSH server debug mode. In one window, run a test server on an alternate port (here 1234) in debug mode:

```
myserver# sshd -d -p 1234
```

and in another, connect with the client to the test server:

```
myclient$ ssh -v1p 1234 myserver
```

See if any enlightening diagnostic messages pop up on either side—you can increase the verbosity of the logging by repeating the -d and -v switches up to three times. If sshd reports "incorrect net address," try adding ListenAddress statements to */etc/ssh/ sshd_config*, explicitly listing the addresses on which you want the SSH server to listen; this can work around a bug in the handling of IPv4-in-IPv6 addresses, if your system has IPv6 enabled.

Note that if you use the same host as both client and server, you *cannot* use *localhost* instead of the hostname on the ssh command line. For Kerberos authentication, the SSH client requests a ticket for the host login service on the server; it does that by name, and there is no "localhost" principal (*host/localhost.dogood.org@DOGOOD. ORG*) in the KDC database. There couldn't be, because the database is global, whereas "localhost" means something different on every host.

If your Kerberos server is also an Andrew Filesystem kaserver, enable KerberosTgtPassing in */etc/ssh/sshd_config*:

```
KerberosTgtPassing yes
```

If you want to allow someone else to log into your account via Kerberos, you can add their Kerberos principal to your *~/.k5login* file. Be sure to also add your own as well if you create this file, since otherwise you will be unable to access your own account!

```
~/.k5login:
me@REALM
myfriend@REALM
```

See Also

sshd(8), sshd_config(5), kinit(1). OpenSSH also has support for Kerberos-4.

4.15   Using Kerberos with Telnet

Problem

You want to use Telnet securely, and you have an MIT Kerberos-5 environment.

Solution

Use the Kerberos-aware ("Kerberized") version of telnet. Assuming you have set up a Kerberos realm [4.11] and hosts [4.13], enable the Kerberized Telnet daemon on your desired destination machine:

```
/etc/xinetd.d/krb5-telnet:
service telnet
{
    ...
    disable = no
}
```

and disable the standard Telnet daemon:

```
/etc/xinetd.d/telnet:
service telnet
{
    ...
    disable = yes
}
```

Then restart xinetd on that machine [3.3] (suppose its hostname is *moof*):

```
moof# kill -HUP `pidof xinetd`
```

and check */var/log/messages* for any error messages. Then, on a client machine (say, *dogcow*) in the same realm, *DOGOOD.ORG*:

```
dogcow$ kinit -f
Password for pat@DOGOOD.ORG:

dogcow$ /usr/kerberos/bin/telnet -fax moof
Trying 10.1.1.6...
Connected to moof.dogood.org (10.1.1.6).
Escape character is '^]'.
Waiting for encryption to be negotiated...
[ Kerberos V5 accepts you as ``pat@DOGOOD.ORG'' ]
[ Kerberos V5 accepted forwarded credentials ]
Last login: Fri Mar  7 03:28:14 from localhost.localdomain
You have mail.
moof$
```

You now have an encrypted Telnet connection, strongly and automatically authenticated via Kerberos.

Discussion

Often, people think of Telnet as synonymous with "insecure," but this is not so. The Telnet protocol allows for strong authentication and encryption, though it is seldom implemented. With the proper infrastructure, Telnet can be quite secure, as shown here.

The -f flag to kinit requests forwardable credentials, and the same flag to telnet then requests that they be forwarded. Thus, your Kerberos credentials follow you from one host to the next, removing the need to run kinit again on the second host in order to use Kerberos there. This provides a more complete single-sign-on effect.

As shown, the Kerberized Telnet server still allows plaintext passwords if Kerberos authentication fails, or if the client doesn't offer it. To make telnetd require strong authentication, modify its xinetd configuration file:

```
/etc/xinetd.d/krb5-telnet:
service telnet
{
    ...
    service_args = -a valid
}
```

and restart xinetd again. Now when you try to telnet insecurely, it fails:

```
dogcow$ telnet moof
telnetd: No authentication provided.
Connection closed by foreign host.
```

If Kerberized authentication doesn't work, try the following to get more information:

```
dogcow$ telnet -fax
telnet> set authd
auth debugging enabled
telnet> set encd
Encryption debugging enabled
telnet> open moof
Trying 10.1.1.6...
```

which prints details about the Telnet authentication and encryption negotiation.

See Also

telnet(1), telnetd(8).

4.16   Securing IMAP with Kerberos

Problem

You want to take advantage of your MIT Kerberos-5 infrastructure for authentication to your mail server.

Solution

Use a mail client that supports GSSAPI Kerberos authentication via the IMAP AUTHENTICATE command, such as mutt or pine.

If you have set up an IMAP server using imapd, and a Kerberos realm [4.11], then most of the work is done: the Red Hat imapd comes with Kerberos support already built in and enabled. All that remains is to add Kerberos principals for the mail service on the server host.

If your username is homer and the mail server is marge, then:

```
marge# kadmin -p homer/admin
Authenticating as principal homer/admin@DOGOOD.ORG with password.
Enter password: ********

kadmin: ank -randkey -policy hosts imap/marge.dogood.org
Principal "imap/marge.dogood.org@DOGOOD.ORG" created.

kadmin: ktadd -k /etc/krb5.keytab imap/marge.dogood.org
Entry for principal imap/marge.dogood.org@DOGOOD.ORG with kvno 3,
  encryption type  Triple DES cbc mode with HMAC/sha1 added to keytab WRFILE:/etc/
krb5.keytab.

kadmin: quit
```

Now on any host in the Kerberos realm, your compatible mail client should automatically use your Kerberos credentials, if available:

```
$ kinit
Password for pat@DOGOOD.ORG: ********

$ klist
Ticket cache: FILE:/tmp/krb5cc_503
Default principal: pat@DOGOOD.ORG

Valid starting     Expires            Service principal
03/05/03 03:48:35  03/05/03 13:48:35  krbtgt/DOGOOD.ORG@DOGOOD.ORG
```

Then connect with your mail client, such as mutt: [8.12]

```
$ MAIL=imap://pat@marge.dogood.org/   mutt
```

or pine: [8.11]

```
$ pine -inbox-path='{pat@marge.dogood.org/imap}'
```

If it works correctly, you will be connected to your mailbox without being asked for a password, and you'll have acquired a Kerberos ticket for IMAP on the mail server:

```
$ klist
Ticket cache: FILE:/tmp/krb5cc_500
Default principal: pat@DOGOOD.ORG

Valid starting     Expires            Service principal
03/07/03 14:44:40  03/08/03 00:44:40  krbtgt/DOGOOD.ORG@DOGOOD.ORG
03/07/03 14:44:48  03/08/03 00:44:40  imap/marge.dogood.org@DOGOOD.ORG
```

Discussion

This technique works for POP as well. With pine, use Kerberos service principal *pop/marge.dogood.org@DOGOOD.ORG* and a mailbox path ending in */pop*. With mutt, however, we were unable to make this work in our Red Hat 8.0 system. There is some confusion about whether the Kerberos principal is *pop/...* or *pop-3/...*; also, the actual AUTH GSSAPI data transmitted by the client appears to be truncated, causing authentication failure. We assume this is a bug that will be fixed eventually.

For debugging, remember to examine the KDC syslog messages for clues.

See Also

mutt(1), pine(1). See the sidebar "SSL for Securing Mail" in Chapter 8, regarding the relationship between SSL and different forms of user authentication.

The Kerberos FAQ has more about GSSAPI: *http://www.faqs.org/faqs/kerberos-faq/general/section-84.html.*

4.17   Using Kerberos with PAM for System-Wide Authentication

Problem

You want your existing MIT Kerberos-5 realm to be used pervasively in system authentication.

Solution

Run authconfig (as root) and turn on the option "Use Kerberos 5." The needed parameters for realm, KDC, and Admin server should be prefilled automatically from */etc/krb5.conf*.

Discussion

Turning on the Kerberos option in authconfig alters various PAM configuration files in */etc/pam.d* to include Kerberos. In particular, it allows Kerberos in */etc/pam.d/system-auth*, which controls the authentication behavior of most servers and programs that validate passwords under Red Hat.

```
# grep -l system-auth /etc/pam.d/*
/etc/pam.d/authconfig
/etc/pam.d/authconfig-gtk
/etc/pam.d/chfn
...dozens more lines...
```

As a side effect, the general login process (e.g., via telnet, gdm/xdm, console, etc.) will automatically obtain Kerberos credentials on login, removing the need to run a separate kinit, as long as your Linux and Kerberos passwords are the same.

 Avoid authconfig if you have a custom PAM configuration. authconfig overwrites PAM files unconditionally; you will lose your changes.

The configuration produced by authconfig still allows authentication via local Linux passwords as well (from */etc/passwd* and */etc/shadow)*. By tailoring */etc/pam.d/system-auth*, however, you can produce other behavior. Consider these two lines:

```
/etc/pam.d/system-auth:
auth        sufficient      /lib/security/pam_unix.so likeauth nullok
auth        sufficient      /lib/security/pam_krb5.so use_first_pass
```

If you remove the second one, then local password validation will be forbidden, and Kerberos will be strictly required for authentication. Not all applications use PAM, however: in particular, Kerberized Telnet. So even if PAM ignores the local password database as shown, Kerberized Telnet will still do so if it falls back to password authentication. In this case, you could disable plain Telnet password authentication altogether. [4.15]

As a matter of overall design, however, consider having a fallback to local authentication, at least for a subset of accounts and for root authorization. Otherwise, if the network fails, you'll be locked out of all your machines! SSH public-key authentication, for example, would be a good complement to Kerberos: sysadmin accounts could have public keys in place to allow access in exceptional cases. [6.4]

See Also

authconfig(8), pam(8), and the documentation in the files */usr/share/doc/pam_krb5*/**.

## CHAPTER 5

Authorization Controls

5.0 Introduction

Authorization means deciding what a user may or may not do on a computer: for example, reading particular files, running particular programs, or connecting to particular network ports. Typically, permission is granted based on a credential such as a password or cryptographic key.

The superuser root, with uid 0, has full control over every file, directory, port, and dust particle on the computer. Therefore, your big, security-related authorization questions are:

- Who has root privileges on my computer?
- How are these privileges bestowed?

Most commonly, anyone knowing your root password has superuser powers, which are granted with the su command:

```
$ su
Password: *******
#
```

This technique is probably fine for a single person with one computer. But if you're a superuser on multiple machines, or if you have several superusers, things get more complicated. What if you want to give temporary or limited root privileges to a user? What if one of your superusers goes berserk: can you revoke his root privileges without impacting other superusers? If these tasks seem inconvenient or difficult, your system might benefit from additional infrastructure for authorization.

Here are some common infrastructures and our opinions of them:

Sharing the root password
> This is conceptually the simplest, but giving every superuser full access to everything is risky. Also, to revoke a rogue superuser's access you must change the root password, which affects all other superusers. Consider a finer grained

approach. When cooking a hamburger, after all, a flamethrower *will* work but a simple toaster oven might be more appropriate.

Multiple root accounts

Make several accounts with uid 0 and gid 0, but different usernames and passwords.

```
/etc/passwd:
root:x:0:0:root:/root:/bin/bash
root-bob:x:0:0:root:/root:/bin/bash
root-sally:x:0:0:root:/root:/bin/bash
root-vince:x:0:0:root:/root:/bin/bash
```

We do not recommend this method. It provides finer control than sharing the root password, but it's less powerful than the later methods we'll describe. Plus you'll break some common scripts that check for the literal username "root" before proceeding. See our recipe for locating superuser accounts so you can replace them and use another method. [9.4]

sudo

Most of this chapter is devoted to sudo recipes. This package has a system-wide configuration file, */etc/sudoers*, that specifies precisely which Linux commands may be invoked by given users on particular hosts with specific privileges. For example, the *sudoers* entry:

```
/etc/sudoers:
smith myhost = (root) /usr/local/bin/mycommand
```

means that user smith may invoke the command /usr/local/bin/mycommand on host *myhost* as user root. User smith can now successfully invoke this program by:

```
smith$ sudo -u root /usr/local/bin/mycommand
```

sudo lets you easily give out and quickly revoke root privileges without revealing the root password. (Users authenticate with their own passwords.) It also supports logging so you can discover who ran which programs via sudo. On the down side, sudo turns an ordinary user password into a (possibly limited) root password. And you must configure it carefully, disallowing arbitrary root commands and arbitrary argument lists, or else you can open holes in your system.

SSH

The Secure Shell can authenticate superusers by public key and let them execute root commands locally or remotely. Additionally, restricted privileges can be granted using SSH forced commands. The previous *sudoers* example could be achieved by SSH as:

```
~root/.ssh/authorized_keys:
command="/usr/local/bin/mycommand" ssh-dss fky7Dj7bGYxdHRYuHN ...
```

and the command would be invoked something like this:

```
$ ssh -l root -i private_key_name localhost
```

Kerberos ksu

> If your environment has a Kerberos infrastructure, you can use ksu, Kerberized su, for authorization. Like sudo, ksu checks a configuration file to make authorization decisions, but the file is per user rather than per system. That is, if user emma wants to invoke a command as user ben, then ben must grant this permission via configuration files in his account:
>
> *~ben/.k5login:*
> emma@EXAMPLE.COM
>
> *~ben/.k5users:*
> emma@EXAMPLE.COM /usr/local/bin/mycommand
>
> and emma would invoke it as:
>
> emma$ ksu ben -e mycommand
>
> Like SSH, ksu also performs strong authentication prior to authorization. Kerberos is installed by default in Red Hat 8.0 but not included with SuSE 8.0.

5.1   Running a root Login Shell

Problem

While logged in as a normal user, you need to run programs with root privileges as if root had logged in.

Solution

```
$ su -
```

Discussion

This recipe might seem trivial, but some Linux users don't realize that su alone does not create a full root environment. Rather, it runs a root shell but leaves the original user's environment largely intact. Important environment variables such as USER, MAIL, and PWD can remain unchanged.

su - (or equivalently, su -l or su --login) runs a login shell, clearing the original user's environment and running all the startup scripts in *~root* that would be run on login (e.g., *.bash_profile*).

Look what changes in your environment when you run su:

```
$ env > /tmp/env.user
$ su
# env > /tmp/env.rootshell
# diff  /tmp/env.user /tmp/env.rootshell
# exit
```

Now compare the environment of a root shell and a root login shell:

```
$ su -
# env > /tmp/env.rootlogin
# diff /tmp/env.rootshell /tmp/env.rootlogin
# exit
```

Or do a quick three-way diff:

```
$ diff3 /tmp/env.user /tmp/env.rootshell /tmp/env.rootlogin
```

See Also

su(1), env(1), environ(5). Your shell's manpage explains environment variables.

5.2 Running X Programs as root

Problem

While logged in as a normal user, you need to run an X window application as root. You get this error message:

```
** WARNING ** cannot open display
```

Solution

Create a shell script called, say, xsu:

```
#!/bin/sh
su - -c "exec env DISPLAY='$DISPLAY' \
    XAUTHORITY='${XAUTHORITY-$HOME/.Xauthority}' \
    "'"$SHELL"'" -c '$*'"
```

and run it with the desired command as its argument list:

```
# xsu  ...command line...
```

Discussion

The problem is that root's *.Xauthority* file does not have the proper authorization credentials to access your X display.

This script invokes a login shell [5.1] and the env program sets the environment variables DISPLAY and XAUTHORITY. The values are set to be the same as the invoking user's. Otherwise they would be set to root's values, but root doesn't own the display.

So in this solution, XAUTHORITY remains *~user/.Xauthority* instead of changing to *~root/.Xauthority*. Since root can read any user's *.Xauthority* file, including this one, it works.

This trick will not work if the user's home directory is NFS-mounted without remote root access.

See Also

env(1), su(1), xauth(1).

5.3 Running Commands as Another User via sudo

Problem

You want one user to run commands as another, without sharing passwords.

Solution

Suppose you want user smith to be able to run a given command as user jones.

```
/etc/sudoers:
smith  ALL = (jones) /usr/local/bin/mycommand
```

User smith runs:

```
smith$ sudo -u jones /usr/local/bin/mycommand
smith$ sudo -u jones mycommand                    If /usr/local/bin is in $PATH
```

User smith will be prompted for his own password, not jones's. The ALL keyword, which matches anything, in this case specifies that the line is valid on any host.

Discussion

sudo exists for this very reason!

To authorize root privileges for smith, replace "jones" with "root" in the above example.

See Also

sudo(8), sudoers(5).

5.4 Bypassing Password Authentication in sudo

Problem

You want one user to run a command as another user without supplying a password.

Careful sudo Practices

- Always edit */etc/sudoers* with the visudo program, not by invoking a text editor directly. visudo uses a lock to ensure that only one person edits */etc/sudoers* at a time, and verifies that there are no syntax errors before the file is saved.
- Never permit the following programs to be invoked with root privileges by sudo: su, sudo, visudo, any shell, and any program having a shell escape.
- Be meticulous about specifying argument lists for each command in */etc/sudoers*. If you aren't careful, even common commands like cat and chmod can be springboards to gain root privileges:

  ```
  $ sudo cat /etc/shadow > my.evil.file
  $ sudo cat ~root/.ssh/id_dsa > my.copy.of.roots.ssh.key
  $ sudo chmod 777 /etc/passwd; emacs /etc/passwd
  $ sudo chmod 4755 /usr/bin/less          (root-owned with a shell escape)
  ```
- Obviously, never let users invoke a program or script via sudo if the users have write permissions to the script. For example:

  /etc/sudoers:
  ```
  smith ALL = (root) /home/smith/myprogram
  ```
  would be a very bad idea, since smith can modify *myprogram* arbitrarily.

Solution

Use sudo's NOPASSWD tag, which indicates to sudo that no password is needed for authentication:

/etc/sudoers:
```
smith  ALL = (jones) NOPASSWD: /usr/local/bin/mycommand args
smith  ALL = (root) NOPASSWD: /usr/local/bin/my_batch_script ""
```

Discussion

By not requiring a password, you are trading security for convenience. If a sudo-enabled user leaves herself logged in at an unattended terminal, someone else can sit down and run privileged commands.

That being said, passwordless authorization is particularly useful for batch jobs, where no human operator is available to type a password.

See Also

sudo(8), sudoers(5).

5.5   Forcing Password Authentication in sudo

Problem

You want sudo always to prompt for a password.

Solution

When controlled by superuser:

```
/etc/sudoers:
Defaults timestamp_timeout = 0              systemwide
Defaults:smith  timestamp_timeout=0        per sudo user
```

When controlled by end-user, write a script that runs sudo -k after each sudo invocation. Call it "sudo" and put it in your search path ahead of /usr/bin/sudo:

```
~/bin/sudo:
#!/bin/sh
/usr/bin/sudo $@
/usr/bin/sudo -k
```

Discussion

After invoking sudo, your authorization privileges last for some number of minutes, determined by the variable timestamp_timeout in /etc/sudoers. During this period, you will not be prompted for a password. If your timestamp_timeout is zero, sudo always prompts for a password.

This feature can be enabled only by the superuser, however. Ordinary users can achieve the same behavior with sudo -k, which forces sudo to prompt for a password on your next sudo command. Our recipe assumes that the directory ~/bin is in your search path ahead of /usr/bin.

See Also

sudo(8), sudoers(5).

5.6   Authorizing per Host in sudo

Problem

You want to allow a user authorization privileges only on certain machines.

Solution

First, define a list of machines:

```
/etc/sudoers:
Host_Alias  SAFE_HOSTS = avocado, banana, cherry
```

Let smith run a program as jones on these machines:

```
smith  SAFE_HOSTS = (jones) /usr/local/bin/mycommand
```

Let smith run all programs as jones on these machines:

```
smith  SAFE_HOSTS = (jones) ALL
```

As an alternative, you can define a netgroup, in the */etc/netgroup* file:

```
safe-hosts (avocado,-,-) (banana,-,-) (cherry,-,-)
```

Then use the netgroup in the */etc/sudoers* file, with the "+" prefix:

```
Host_Alias  SAFE_HOSTS = +safe-hosts
```

You can also use the netgroup in place of the host alias:

```
smith  +safe_hosts = (jones) ALL
```

Discussion

This recipe assumes you have centralized your sudo configuration: the same *sudoers* file on all your computers. If not, you could grant per-machine privileges by installing a different *sudoers* file on each machine.

Netgroups can be useful for centralization if they are implemented as a shared NIS database. In that case, you can update the machines in netgroups without changing your */etc/sudoers* files.

The host alias is optional but helpful for organizing your *sudoers* file, so you needn't retype the set of hostnames repeatedly.

As another example, you could let users administer their own machines but not others:

```
/etc/sudoers:
bob bobs_machine = ALL
gert gerts_machine = ALL
ernie ernies_machine = ALL
```

(Though this is perhaps pointless infrastructure, since ALL would permit these people to modify their */etc/sudoers* file and their root password.)

See Also

sudo(8), sudoers(5).

5.7 Granting Privileges to a Group via sudo

Problem

Let a set of users run commands as another user.

Solution

Define a Linux group containing those users:

/etc/group:
```
mygroup:x:1200:joe,jane,hiram,krishna
```

Then create a sudo rule with the %groupname syntax:

/etc/sudoers:
```
# Let the group run a particular program:
%mygroup  ALL = (root) /usr/local/bin/mycommand arg1 arg2
# Give full superuser privileges to the group
%mygroup  ALL = (ALL) ALL
```

See Also

sudo(8), sudoers(5), group(5).

5.8 Running Any Program in a Directory via sudo

Problem

Authorize a user to run all programs in a given directory, but only those programs, as another user.

Solution

Specify a fully-qualified directory name instead of a command, ending it with a slash:

/etc/sudoers:
```
smith ALL = (root) /usr/local/bin/
```

```
smith$ sudo -u root /usr/local/bin/mycommand        Authorized
smith$ sudo -u root /usr/bin/emacs                  Rejected
```

This authorization does not descend into subdirectories.

```
smith$ sudo -u root /usr/local/bin/gnu/emacs        Rejected
```

See Also

sudo(8), sudoers(5).

5.9 Prohibiting Command Arguments with sudo

Problem

You want to permit a command to be run via sudo, but only without command-line arguments.

Solution

Follow the program name with the single argument "" in */etc/sudoers*:

```
/etc/sudoers:
smith  ALL = (root) /usr/local/bin/mycommand ""

smith$ sudo -u root mycommand a b c          Rejected
smith$ sudo -u root mycommand                Authorized
```

Discussion

If you specify no arguments to a command in */etc/sudoers*, then by default any arguments are permitted.

```
/etc/sudoers:
smith  ALL = (root) /usr/local/bin/mycommand

smith$ sudo -u root mycommand a b c          Authorized
```

Use "" to prevent any runtime arguments from being authorized.

See Also

sudo(8), sudoers(5).

5.10 Sharing Files Using Groups

Problem

Two or more users want to share files, both with write privileges.

Solution

Create a group containing only those users, say, smith, jones, and ling:

```
/etc/group:
friends:x:200:smith,jones,ling
```

Create the shared file in a directory writable by this group:

```
jones$ cd
jones$ mkdir share
jones$ chmod 2770 share
jones$ chgrp friends share
jones$ ls -ld share
drwxrws---   2 jones    friends    4096 Apr 18 20:17 share/
jones$ cd share
jones$ touch myfile
jones$ chmod 660 myfile
jones$ ls -l myfile
-rw-rw----   1 jones    friends       0 Apr 18 20:18 myfile
```

Users smith and ling can now enter the directory and modify jones's file:

```
smith$ cd ~jones/share
smith$ emacs myfile
```

Discussion

smith, jones, and ling should consider setting their umasks so files they create are group writable, e.g.:

```
$ umask 007
$ touch newfile
$ ls -l newfile
-rw-rw----   1 smith          0 Jul 17 23:09 newfile
```

The setgid bit on the directory (indicated by mode 2000 for chmod, or "s" in the output from ls -l) means that newly created files in the directory will be assigned the group of the directory. The applies to newly created subdirectories as well.

To enable this behavior for an entire filesystem, use the grpid mount option. This option can appear on the command line:

```
# mount -o grpid ...
```

or in */etc/fstab*:

```
/dev/hdd3   /home   ext2   rw,grpid   1 2
```

See Also

group(5), chmod(1), chgrp(1), umask(1).

5.11   Permitting Read-Only Access to a Shared File via sudo

Problem

Two or more users want to share a file, some read/write and the others read-only.

Solution

Create two Linux groups, one for read/write and one for read-only users:

```
/etc/group:
readers:x:300:r1,r2,r3,r4
writers:x:301:w1,w2,w3
```

Permit the writers group to write the file via group permissions:

```
$ chmod 660 shared_file
$ chgrp writers shared_file
```

Permit the readers group to read the file via sudo:

```
/etc/sudoers:
%readers  ALL = (w1) /bin/cat /path/to/shared_file
```

Discussion

This situation could arise in a university setting, for example, if a file must be writable by a group of teaching assistants but read-only to a group of students.

If there were only two users—one reader and one writer—you could dispense with groups and simply let the reader access the file via sudo. If smith is the reader and jones the writer, and we give smith the following capability:

```
/etc/sudoers:
smith  ALL = (jones) NOPASSWD: /bin/cat /home/jones/private.stuff
```

then jones can protect her file:

```
jones$ chmod 600 $HOME/private.stuff
```

and smith can view it:

```
smith$ sudo -u jones cat /home/jones/private.stuff
```

See Also

sudo(8), sudoers(5), group(5), chmod(1), chgrp(1).

5.12 Authorizing Password Changes via sudo

Problem

You want to permit a user to change the passwords of certain other users.

Solution

To permit smith to change the passwords of jones, chu, and agarwal:

```
/etc/sudoers:
smith  ALL = NOPASSWD: \
```

```
/usr/bin/passwd jones, \
/usr/bin/passwd chu, \
/usr/bin/passwd agarwal
```

The NOPASSWD tag is optional, for convenience. [5.4]

Discussion

As another example, permit a professor to change passwords for her students, whose logins are student00, student01, student02,...up to student99.

/etc/sudoers:
```
prof  ALL = NOPASSWD: /usr/bin/passwd student[0-9][0-9]
```

Note that this uses shell-style wildcard expansion; see sudoers(5) for the full syntax.

See Also

sudo(8), sudoers(5).

5.13   Starting/Stopping Daemons via sudo

Problem

You want specific non-superusers to start and stop system daemons.

Solution

Here we let four different users start, stop, and restart web servers. The script for doing so is */etc/init.d/httpd* for Red Hat, or */etc/init.d/apache* for SuSE. We'll reference the Red Hat script in our solution.

/etc/sudoers:
```
User_Alias  FOLKS=barbara, l33t, jimmy, miroslav
Cmnd_Alias  DAEMONS=/etc/init.d/httpd start,\
    /etc/init.d/httpd stop,\
    /etc/init.d/httpd restart
FOLKS  ALL = (ALL) DAEMONS
```

Discussion

Note our use of sudo aliases for the users and commands. Read the sudoers(5) manpage to learn all kinds of fun capabilities like this.

See Also

sudo(8), sudoers(5).

5.14 Restricting root's Abilities via sudo

Problem

You want to let a user run all commands as root *except* for specific exceptions, such as su.

Solution

Don't.

Instead, list all the permissible commands explicitly in */etc/sudoers*. Don't try the reverse—letting the user run all commands as root "except these few"—which is prohibitively difficult to do securely.

Discussion

It's tempting to try excluding dangerous commands with the "!" syntax:

```
/etc/sudoers:
smith  ALL = (root) !/usr/bin/su ...
```

but this technique is fraught with problems. A savvy user can easily get around it by renaming the forbidden executables:

```
smith$ ln -s /usr/bin/su gimmeroot
smith$ sudo gimmeroot
```

Instead, we recommend listing all acceptable commands individually, making sure that none have shell escapes.

See Also

sudo(8), sudoers(5).

5.15 Killing Processes via sudo

Problem

Allow a user to kill a certain process but no others.

Solution

Create a script that kills the process by looking up its PID dynamically and safely. Add the script to */etc/sudoers*.

Discussion

Because we don't know a process's PID until runtime, we cannot solve this problem with */etc/sudoers* alone, which is written before runtime. You need a script to deduce the PID for killing.

For example, to let users restart sshd:

```
#!/bin/sh
pidfile=/var/run/sshd.pid
sshd=/usr/sbin/sshd

# sanity check that pid is numeric
pid=`/usr/bin/perl -ne 'print if /^\d+$/; last;' $pidfile`
if [ -z "$pid" ]
then
    echo "$0: error: non-numeric pid $pid found in $pidfile" 1>&2
    exit 1
fi

# sanity check that pid is a running process
if [ ! -d "/proc/$pid" ]
then
    echo "$0: no such process" 1>&2
    exit 1
fi

# sanity check that pid is sshd
if [ `readlink "/proc/$pid/exe"` != "$sshd" ]
then
    echo "$0: error: attempt to kill non-sshd process" 1>&2
    exit 1
fi

kill -HUP "$pid"
```

Call the script */usr/local/bin/sshd-restart* and let users invoke it via sudo:

```
# /etc/sudoers:
smith ALL = /usr/local/bin/sshd-restart ""
```

The empty double-quotes prevent arguments from being passed to the script. [5.9]

Our script carefully signals only the parent sshd process, not its child processes for SSH sessions already in progress. If you prefer to kill *all* processes with a given name, use the pidof command:

```
# kill -USR1 `pidof mycommand`
```

or the skill command:

```
# skill -USR1 mycommand
```

See Also

kill(1), proc(5), pidof(8), skill(1), readlink(1).

5.16 Listing sudo Invocations

Problem

See a report of all unauthorized sudo attempts.

Solution

Use logwatch: [9.36]

```
# logwatch --print --service sudo --range all
smith => root
-------------
/usr/bin/passwd root
/bin/rm -f /etc/group
/bin/chmod 4755 /bin/sh
```

Discussion

If logwatch complains that the script */etc/log.d/scripts/services/sudo* cannot be found, upgrade logwatch to the latest version.

You could also view the log entries directly without logwatch, extracting the relevant information from */var/log/secure*:

```
#!/bin/sh
LOGFILE=/var/log/secure
echo 'Unauthorized sudo attempts:'
egrep 'sudo: .* : command not allowed' $LOGFILE \
    | sed 's/^.* sudo: \([^ ][^ ]*\) .* ; USER=\([^ ][^ ]*\) ; COMMAND=\(.*\)$/\1 (\
2): \3/'
```

Output:

```
Unauthorized sudo attempts:
smith (root): /usr/bin/passwd root
smith (root): /bin/rm -f /etc/group
smith (root): /bin/chmod 4755 /bin/sh
```

See Also

logwatch(8). The logwatch home page is *http://www.logwatch.org*.

5.17   Logging sudo Remotely

Problem

You want your sudo logs kept off-host to prevent tampering or interference.

Solution

Use syslog's @otherhost syntax: [9.29]

> */etc/syslog.conf:*
> ```
> authpriv.*          @securehost
> ```

Discussion

Remember that the remote host's syslogd needs must be invoked with the -r flag to receive remote messages. Make sure your remote host doesn't share root privileges with the sudo host, or else this offhost logging is pointless.

See Also

syslog.conf(5), syslogd(8).

5.18   Sharing root Privileges via SSH

Problem

You want to share superuser privileges with other users but not reveal the root password.

Solution

Append users' public keys to *~root/.ssh/authorized_keys.** [6.4] Users may then run a root shell:

```
$ ssh -l root localhost
```

or execute commands as root:

```
$ ssh -l root localhost ...command...
```

---

* In older versions of OpenSSH, the file for SSH-2 protocol keys is *authorized_keys2*.

Discussion

As an alternative to su, you can use ssh to assign superuser privileges without giving out the root password. Users connect to *localhost* and authenticate by public key. (There's no sense using password authentication here: you'd have to give out the root password, which is exactly what we're trying to avoid.)

This method is more flexible than using su, since you can easily instate and revoke root privileges: simply add and remove users' keys from *~root/.ssh/authorized_keys*. However, it provides less logging than sudo: you can learn who became root (by log messages) but not what commands were run during the SSH session.

Some discussion points:

* Make sure */etc/ssh/sshd_config* has `PermitRootLogin yes` specified.
* ssh is built for networking, so of course you can extend the scope of these root privileges to remote machines the same way. Instead of connecting to *localhost*, users connect to the remote machine as root:

  ```
  $ ssh -l root remote_host
  ```
* Users can avoid passphrase prompts by running ssh-agent. [6.9] This feature must be balanced against your security policy, however. If no passphrase is required for root privileges, then the user's terminal becomes a target for attack.
* For more security on a single machine, consider extending the method in this way:

  a. Run a second sshd on an arbitrary port (say 22222) with an alternative configuration file (sshd -f).

  b. In the alternative configuration file, set `PermitRootLogin yes`, and let the *only* method of authentication be `PubkeyAuthentication`.

  c. Disable all unneeded options in authorized_keys; in particular, use `from="127.0.0.1"` or `from="your actual IP address"` to prevent connections from other hosts to your local root account.

  d. In your firewall, block port 22222 to prevent unwanted incoming network connections.

  e. For convenience and abstraction, create a script that runs the command:

  ```
  ssh -p 22222 -l root localhost $@
  ```

See Also

ssh(1), sshd(8), sshd_config(5).

5.19   Running root Commands via SSH

Problem

You want to grant root privileges to another user, but permit only certain commands to be run.

Solution

Share your root privileges via SSH [5.18] and add forced commands to *~root/.ssh/ authorized_keys*.

Discussion

Using SSH forced commands, you can limit which programs a user may run as root. For example, this key entry:

```
~root/.ssh/authorized_keys:
command="/sbin/dump -0 /local/data" ssh-dss key...
```

permits only the command /sbin/dump -0 /local/data to be run, on successful authentication.

Each key is limited to one forced command, but if you make the command a shell script, you can restrict users to a specific set of programs after authentication. Suppose you write a script */usr/local/bin/ssh-switch*:

```
#!/bin/sh
case "$1" in
    backups)
        # Perform level zero backups
        /sbin/dump -0 /local/data
        ;;
    messages)
        # View log messages
        /bin/cat /var/log/messages
        ;;
    settime)
        # Set the system time via ntp
        /usr/sbin/ntpdate timeserver.example.com
        ;;
    *)
        # Refuse anything else
        echo 'Permission denied' 1>&2
        exit 1
        ;;
esac
```

and make it a forced command:

```
~root/.ssh/authorized_keys:
command="/usr/local/bin/ssh-switch $SSH_ORIGINAL_COMMAND" ssh-dss key...
```

Then users can run selected commands as:

```
$ ssh -l root localhost backups          Runs dump
$ ssh -l root localhost settime          Runs ntpdate
$ ssh -l root localhost cat /etc/passwd  Not authorized: Permission denied
```

Take care that your forced commands use full paths and have no shell escapes, and do not let the user modify *authorized_keys*. Here's a bad idea:

```
~root/.ssh/authorized_keys: DON'T DO THIS!!!!
command="/usr/bin/less some_file" ssh-dss key...
```

since less has a shell escape.

See Also

ssh(1), sshd(8), sshd_config(5).

5.20   Sharing root Privileges via Kerberos su

Problem

You want to obtain root privileges in a Kerberos environment.

Solution

Use ksu.

To obtain a root shell:

```
$ ksu
```

To obtain a shell as user barney:

```
$ ksu barney
```

To use another Kerberos principal besides your default for authentication:

```
$ ksu [user] -n principal ...
```

To execute a specific command under the target uid, rather than get a login shell:

```
$ ksu [user] -e command
```

Discussion

Like the usual Unix su program, ksu allows one account to access another, if the first account is authorized to do so. Unlike su, ksu does authentication using Kerberos rather than plain passwords, and has many more options for authorization.

With su, one simply types su <target>. su prompts for the target account's password; if the user supplies the correct password, su starts a shell under the target account's uid (or executes another program supplied on the su command line). With ksu, both authentication and authorization are done differently.

Authentication

ksu performs authentication via Kerberos, so you must select a Kerberos principal to use. First, ksu tries the *default principal* indicated in your current Kerberos credentials cache (klist command). If you have no credentials, then it will be the default principal indicated by your Unix account name and the local Kerberos configuration. For example, if your Unix username is fred and the Kerberos realm of your host is *FOO.ORG*, then your default principal would normally be *fred@FOO.ORG* (note that Kerberos realm names are case-sensitive and by convention are in uppercase). If this principal is authorized to access the target account (explained later), then ksu proceeds with it. If not, then it proceeds with the default principal corresponding to the target account. The usual effect of this arrangement is that either your usual Kerberos credentials will allow you access, or you'll be prompted for the target account's Kerberos password, and thus gain access if you know it.

You may select a different principal to use with the -n option, e.g.:

```
$ ksu -n wilma@FOO.ORG ...
```

but let's suppose your selected principal is *fred@FOO.ORG*.

First, ksu authenticates you as *fred@FOO.ORG*; specifically, if this host is *bar.foo.org*, you need a service ticket granted to that principal for host/bar.foo.org@FOO.ORG. ksu first attempts to acquire this ticket automatically. If you don't have exactly that ticket, but you do have valid Kerberos credentials for this principal—that is, you have previously done a kinit and acquired a ticket-granting ticket (TGT)—then ksu simply uses it to obtain the required ticket. Failing that, ksu may prompt you for *fred@FOO.ORG*'s password. Note two things, however: first, be careful not to type the password over an insecure link (e.g., an unencrypted Telnet session). Second, ksu may be compiled with an option to forbid password authentication, in which case you must have previously acquired appropriate credentials, or the ksu attempt will fail.

Authorization

Having authenticated you via Kerberos as *fred@FOO.ORG*, ksu now verifies that this principal is authorized to access the target account, given as the argument to ksu (e.g., ksu barney; the default is the root account). Authorization can happen one of two ways:

1. User barney has allowed you access to his account by editing his Kerberos authorization files. The two authorization files are *~barney/.k5login* and *~barney/.k5users*. The first contains simply a list of principals allowed to access the account; the second contains the same, but may also restrict which commands

may be executed by each authorized principal. So, to allow Fred to access his account via ksu, Barney would create ~/.k5login containing the single line:

```
~/.k5login:
fred@FOO.ORG
```

To allow Fred access only to run ~/bin/myprogram, Barney could instead place this line in ~/.k5users:

```
~/.k5users:
fred@FOO.ORG /home/barney/bin/myprogram
```

2. Your Kerberos principal and the target account match according to the local Kerberos *lname->aname* rules. Normally, this is the simple correspondence of account barney and principal *barney@FOO.ORG*. This doesn't usually happen, since normally you would be accessing a different account than your own, and have Kerberos credentials for the principal corresponding to your account, not the target. However, you could arrange for this by first running kinit barney, if you happen to know the password for *barney@FOO.ORG*.

Some additional notes:

- If either authorization file for an account exists, then it must specify *all* principals allowed access—including the one corresponding to that account and otherwise allowed access by default. This means that if you create a ~/.k5login file to allow your friend access, you will likely want to list your *own* principal there as well, or you cannot ksu to your own account.

- By default, the Kerberos credentials cache for the created process, under the target uid, will contain not only the ticket(s) authorizing the session, but also valid tickets from the original user as well. If you want to avoid this, use the -z or -Z options.

See Also

ksu(1), and our Kerberos coverage in Chapter 4.

CHAPTER 6
Protecting Outgoing Network Connections

6.0 Introduction

In Chapter 3, we discussed how to protect your computer from unwanted *incoming* network connections. Now we'll turn our attention to *outgoing* connections: how to contact remote machines securely on a network. If you naively telnet, ftp, rlogin, rsh, rcp, or cvs to another machine, your password gets transmitted over the network, available to any snooper passing by. [9.19] Clearly a better alternative is needed.

Our recipes will primarily use SSH, the Secure Shell, a protocol for secure authentication and encryption of network connections. It's an appropriate technology for many secure networking tasks. OpenSSH, a free implementation of the SSH protocol, is included in most Linux distributions, so our recipes are tailored to work with it. Its important programs and files are listed in Table 6-1.

Table 6-1. Important OpenSSH programs and files for this chapter

Client programs	
ssh	Performs remote logins and remote command execution
scp	Copies files between computers
sftp	Copies files between computers with an interactive, FTP-like user interface
Server programs	
sshd	Server daemon
Programs for creating and using cryptographic keys	
ssh-keygen	Creates and modifies public and private keys
ssh-agent	Caches SSH private keys to avoid typing passphrases
ssh-add	Manipulates the key cache of ssh-agent
Important files and directories	
~/.ssh	Directory (per user) for keys and configuration files
/etc/ssh	Directory (systemwide) for keys and configuration files
~/.ssh/config	Client configuration file (per user)
/etc/ssh/ssh_config	Client configuration file (systemwide)

For outgoing connections, the client program ssh initiates remote logins and invokes remote commands:

Do a remote login:
```
$ ssh -l remoteuser remotehost
```

Invoke a remote command:
```
$ ssh -l remoteuser remotehost uptime
```

and the client scp securely copies files between computers:

Copy local file to remote machine:
```
$ scp myfile remotehost:remotefile
```

Copy remote file to local machine:
```
$ scp remotehost:remotefile myfile
```

Some of our recipes might work for other implementations of SSH, such as the original *SSH Secure Shell* from SSH Communication Security (*http://www.ssh.com*). For a broader discussion see the book *SSH, The Secure Shell: The Definitive Guide* (O'Reilly).

6.1   Logging into a Remote Host

Problem

You want to log into a remote host securely.

Solution

```
$ ssh -l remoteuser remotehost
```

For example:

```
$ ssh -l smith server.example.com
```

If your local and remote usernames are the same, omit the -l option:

```
$ ssh server.example.com
```

Discussion

The client program ssh establishes a secure network connection to a remote machine that's running an SSH server. It authenticates you to the remote machine without transmitting a plaintext password over the network. Data that flows across the connection is encrypted and decrypted transparently.

By default, your login password serves as proof of your identity to the remote machine. SSH supports other authentication methods as we'll see in other recipes. [6.4][6.8]

Avoid the insecure programs rsh, rlogin, and telnet when communicating with remote hosts.* They do not encrypt your connection, and they transmit your login password across the network in the clear. Even if the local and remote hosts are together behind a firewall, don't trust these programs for communication: do you really want your passwords flying around unencrypted even on your intranet? What if the firewall gets hacked? What if a disgruntled coworker behind the firewall installs a packet sniffer? [9.19] Stick with SSH.

See Also

ssh(1). We keep lots of SSH tips at *http://www.snailbook.com*. The official OpenSSH site is *http://www.openssh.com*.

6.2   Invoking Remote Programs

Problem

You want to invoke a program on a remote machine over a secure network connection.

Solution

For noninteractive commands:

```
$ ssh -l remoteuser remotehost uptime
```

For interactive programs, add the -t option:

```
$ ssh -t -l remoteuser remotehost vi
```

For X Window applications, add the -X option to enable X forwarding. Also add the -f option to background the program after authentication, and to redirect standard input from */dev/null* to avoid dangling connections.

```
$ ssh -X -f -l remoteuser remotehost xterm
```

Discussion

For noninteractive commands, simply append the remote program invocation to the end of the ssh command line. After authentication, ssh will run the program remotely and exit. It will not establish a login session.

For interactive commands that run in your existing terminal window, such as a terminal-based text editor or game, supply the -t option to force ssh to allocate a pseudo-tty. Otherwise the remote program can get confused or refuse to run:

---

* And avoid ftp in favor of scp or sftp for the same reasons. [6.3]

```
$ ssh server.example.com emacs -nw
emacs: standard input is not a tty
$ ssh server.example.com /usr/games/nethack
NetHack (gettty): Invalid argument
NetHack (settty): Invalid argument Terminal must backspace.
```

If your program is an X application, use the -X option to enable X forwarding. This forces the connection between the X client and X server—normally insecure—to pass through the SSH connection, protecting the data.

```
$ ssh -X -f server.example.com xterm
```

If X forwarding fails, make sure that your remote session is *not* manually setting the value of the DISPLAY environment variable. ssh sets it automatically to the correct value. Check your shell startup files (e.g., *.bash_profile* or *.bashrc*) and their system-wide equivalents (such as */etc/profile*) to ensure they are not setting DISPLAY. Alternatively, X forwarding might be disabled in the SSH server: check the remote */etc/ssh/sshd_config* for the setting X11Forwarding no.

See Also

ssh(1). We keep lots of SSH tips at *http://www.snailbook.com*. The official OpenSSH site is *http://www.openssh.com*.

6.3   Copying Files Remotely

Problem

You want to copy files securely from one computer to another.

Solution

For one file:

```
$ scp myfile remotehost:
$ scp remotehost:myfile .
```

For one file, renamed:

```
$ scp myfile remotehost:myfilecopy
$ scp remotehost:myfile myfilecopy
```

For multiple files:

```
$ scp myfile* remotehost:
$ scp remotehost:myfile\* .
```

To specify another directory:

```
$ scp myfile* remotehost:/name/of/directory
$ scp remotehost:/name/of/directory/myfile\* .
```

To specify an alternate username for authentication:

```
$ scp myfile smith@remotehost:
$ scp smith@remotehost:myfile .
```

To copy a directory recursively (-r):

```
$ scp -r mydir remotehost:
$ scp -r remotehost:mydir .
```

To preserve file attributes (-p):

```
$ scp -p myfile* remotehost:
$ scp -p remotehost:myfile .
```

Discussion

The scp command has syntax very similar to that of rcp or even cp:

```
scp name-of-source name-of-destination
```

A single file may be copied to a remote file or directory. In other words, if *name-of-source* is a file, *name-of-destination* may be a file (existing or not) or a directory (which must exist).

Multiple files and directories, however, may be copied only into a directory. So, if *name-of-source* is two or more files, one or more directories, or a combination, then specify *name-of-destination* as an existing directory into which the copy will take place.

Both *name-of-source* and *name-of-destination* may have the following form, in order:

1. The *username of the account containing the file or directory, followed by "@".* (Optional; permitted only if a hostname is specified.) If omitted, the value is the username of the user invoking scp.

2. The *hostname of the host containing the file or directory, followed by a colon.* (Optional if the path is present.) If omitted, the local host is assumed.

3. The *path to the file or directory.* Relative pathnames are assumed relative to the default directory, which is the current directory (for local paths) or the remote user's home directory (for remote paths). If omitted entirely, the path is assumed to be the default directory.

Although each of the fields is optional, you cannot omit them all at the same time, yielding the empty string. Either the hostname (item 2) or the directory path (item 3) must be present.

Whew! Once you get the hang of it, scp is pretty easy to use, and most scp commands you invoke will probably be pretty basic. If you prefer a more interactive interface, try sftp, which resembles ftp.

If you want to "mirror" a set of files securely between machines, you could use scp -pr, but it has disadvantages:

- scp follows symbolic links automatically, which you might not want.
- scp copies every file in its entirety, even if they already exist on the mirror machine, which is inefficient.

A better alternative is rsync with ssh, which optimizes the transfer in various ways and needn't follow symbolic links:

```
$ rsync -a -e ssh mydir remotehost:otherdir
```

Add -v and --progress for more verbose output:

```
$ rsync -a -e ssh -v --progress mydir remotehost:otherdir
```

See Also

scp(1), sftp(1), rcp(1), rsync(1).

6.4 Authenticating by Public Key (OpenSSH)

Problem

You want to set up public-key authentication between an OpenSSH client and an OpenSSH server.

Solution

1. Generate a key if necessary:

   ```
   $ mkdir -p ~/.ssh            If it doesn't already exist
   $ chmod 700 ~/.ssh
   $ cd ~/.ssh
   $ ssh-keygen -t dsa
   ```

2. Copy the public key to the remote host:

   ```
   $ scp -p id_dsa.pub remoteuser@remotehost:
   Password: ********
   ```

3. Log into the remote host and install the public key:

   ```
   $ ssh -l remoteuser remotehost
   Password: ********

   remotehost$ mkdir -p ~/.ssh                              If it doesn't already exist
   remotehost$ chmod 700 ~/.ssh
   remotehost$ cat id_dsa.pub >> ~/.ssh/authorized_keys     (Appending)
   remotehost$ chmod 600 ~/.ssh/authorized_keys
   remotehost$ mv id_dsa.pub ~/.ssh                         Optional, just to be organized
   remotehost$ logout
   ```

4. Log back in via public-key authentication:

```
$ ssh -l remoteuser remotehost
Enter passphrase for key '/home/smith/.ssh/id_dsa': *******
```

 OpenSSH public keys go into the file *~/.ssh/authorized_keys*. Older versions of OpenSSH, however, require SSH-2 protocol keys to be in *~/.ssh/authorized_keys2*.

Discussion

Public-key authentication lets you prove your identity to a remote host using a cryptographic key instead of a login password. SSH keys are more secure than passwords because keys are never transmitted over the network, whereas passwords are (albeit encrypted). Also, keys are stored encrypted, so if someone steals yours, it's useless without the passphrase for decrypting it. A stolen password, on the other hand, is immediately usable.

An SSH "key" is actually a matched pair of keys stored in two files. The private or secret key remains on the client machine, encrypted with a passphrase. The public key is copied to the remote (server) machine. When establishing a connection, the SSH client and server perform a complex negotiation based on the private and public key, and if they match (in a cryptographic sense), your identity is proven and the connection succeeds.

To set up public-key authentication, first create an OpenSSH key pair, if you don't already have one:

```
$ ssh-keygen -t dsa
Generating public/private dsa key pair.
Enter file in which to save the key (/home/smith/.ssh/id_dsa): <RETURN>
Enter passphrase (empty for no passphrase): *******
Enter same passphrase again: *******
Your identification has been saved in id_dsa
Your public key has been saved in id_dsa.pub.
The key fingerprint is: 76:00:b3:e8:99:1c:07:9b:84:af:67:69:b6:b4:12:17
smith@mymachine
```

Copy the public key to the remote host using password authentication:

```
$ scp ~/.ssh/id_dsa.pub remoteuser@remotehost:
Password: *********
id_dsa.pub        100% |***************************|   736    00:03
```

Log into the remote host using password authentication:

```
$ ssh -l remoteuser remotehost
Password: *******
```

If your local and remote usernames are the same, you can omit the -l remoteuser part and just type ssh remotehost.

On the remote host, create the ~/.ssh directory if it doesn't already exist and set its mode appropriately:

```
remotehost$ mkdir -p ~/.ssh
remotehost$ chmod 700 ~/.ssh
```

Then append the contents of *id_dsa.pub* to *~/.ssh/authorized_keys*:

```
remotehost$ cat id_dsa.pub >> ~/.ssh/authorized_keys        (Appending)
remotehost$ chmod 600 ~/.ssh/authorized_keys
```

Log out of the remote host and log back in. This time you'll be prompted for your key passphrase instead of your password:

```
$ ssh -l remoteuser remotehost
Enter passphrase for key '/home/smith/.ssh/id_dsa': *******
```

and you're done! If things aren't working, rerun ssh with the -v option (verbose) to help diagnose the problem.

The SSH server must be configured to permit public-key authentication, which is the default:

```
/etc/ssh/sshd_config:
PubkeyAuthentication yes              If no, change it and restart sshd
```

For more convenience, you can eliminate the passphrase prompt using ssh-agent [6.9] and create host aliases in *~/.ssh/config*. [6.12]

See Also

ssh(1), scp(1), ssh-keygen(1).

6.5   Authenticating by Public Key (OpenSSH Client, SSH2 Server, OpenSSH Key)

Problem

You want to authenticate between an OpenSSH client and an SSH2 server (i.e., *SSH Secure Shell* from SSH Communication Security) using an existing OpenSSH-format key.

Solution

1. Export your OpenSSH key to create an SSH2-format public key. If your OpenSSH private key is *~/.ssh/id_dsa*:

```
$ cd ~/.ssh
$ ssh-keygen -e -f id_dsa > mykey-ssh2.pub
```

SSH-2 Key File Formats

The two major implementations of SSH—OpenSSH and *SSH Secure Shell* ("SSH2")—use different file formats for SSH-2 protocol keys. (Their SSH-1 protocol keys are compatible.) OpenSSH public keys for the SSH-2 protocol begin like this:

```
ssh-dss A9AAB3NzaC1iGMqHpSCEliaouBun8FF9t8p...
```

or:

```
ssh-rsa AAAAB3NzaC1yc2EAAAABIwAAAIEA3DIqRox...
```

SSH Secure Shell public keys for the SSH-2 protocol look like this:

```
---- BEGIN SSH2 PUBLIC KEY ----
AAAAB3NzaC1kc3MAAACBAM4a2KKBE6zhPBgRx4q6Dbjxo5hXNKNWYIGkX/W/k5PqcCHOJ6 ...
---- END SSH2 PUBLIC KEY ----
```

These keys are installed differently too. For OpenSSH, you insert your public keys into the file *~/.ssh/authorized_keys*. For *SSH Secure Shell*, you copy your public key files into the directory *~/.ssh2* and reference them in the file *~/.ssh2/authorization* by name:

```
Key public_key_filename
```

As for private keys, OpenSSH has no special requirements for installation, but *SSH Secure Shell* does. You must reference them in the file *~/.ssh2/identification* by name:

```
IdKey private_key_filename
```

---

2. Copy the public key to the SSH2 server:

```
$ scp mykey-ssh2.pub remoteuser@remotehost:
```

3. Log into the SSH2 server and install the public key, then log out:

```
$ ssh -l remoteuser remotehost
Password: ********

remotehost$ mkdir -p ~/.ssh2                         If it doesn't already exist
remotehost$ chmod 700 ~/.ssh2
remotehost$ mv mykey-ssh2.pub ~/.ssh2/
remotehost$ cd ~/.ssh2
remotehost$ echo "Key mykey-ssh2.pub" >> authorization    (Appending)
remotehost$ chmod 600 mykey-ssh2.pub authorization
remotehost$ logout
```

4. Now log in via public-key authentication:

```
$ ssh -l remoteuser remotehost
Enter passphrase for key '/home/smith/.ssh/id_dsa': *******
```

Discussion

OpenSSH's ssh-keygen converts OpenSSH-style keys into SSH2-style using the -e (export) option. Recall that SSH2 uses the *authorization* file, as explained in the sidebar, "SSH-2 Key File Formats."

See Also

ssh-keygen(1).

6.6 Authenticating by Public Key (OpenSSH Client, SSH2 Server, SSH2 Key)

Problem

You want to authenticate between an OpenSSH client and an SSH2 server (i.e., *SSH Secure Shell* from SSH Communication Security) using an existing SSH2-format key.

Solution

Suppose your SSH2 private key is *id_dsa_1024_a*.

1. Make a copy of the SSH2 private key:

   ```
   $ cd ~/.ssh2
   $ cp -p id_dsa_1024_a newkey
   ```

2. Set its passphrase to the empty string, creating an unencrypted key:

   ```
   $ ssh-keygen2 -e newkey
   ...
   Do you want to edit passphrase (yes or no)? yes
   New passphrase :
   Again        :
   ```

3. Import the SSH2 private key to convert it into an OpenSSH private key, *imported-ssh2-key*:

   ```
   $ mkdir -p ~/.ssh              If it doesn't already exist
   $ chmod 700 ~/.ssh
   $ cd ~/.ssh
   $ mv ~/.ssh2/newkey .
   $ ssh-keygen -i -f newkey > imported-ssh2-key
   $ rm newkey
   $ chmod 600 imported-ssh2-key
   ```

4. Change the passphrase of the imported key:

   ```
   $ ssh-keygen -p imported-ssh2-key
   ```

5. Use your new key:

   ```
   $ ssh -l remoteuser -i ~/.ssh/imported-ssh2-key remotehost
   ```

To generate the OpenSSH public key from the OpenSSH private key *imported-ssh2-key*, run:

```
$ ssh-keygen -y -f imported-ssh2-key > imported-ssh2-key.pub
Enter passphrase: ********
```

Discussion

OpenSSH's ssh-keygen can convert an SSH2-style private key into an OpenSSH-style private key, using the -i (import) option; however, it works only for unencrypted SSH2 keys. So we decrypt the key (changing its passphrase to null), import it, and re-encrypt it.

This technique involves some risk, since your SSH2 private key will be unencrypted on disk for a few moments. If this concerns you, perform steps 2–3 on a secure machine with no network connection (say, a laptop). Then burn the laptop.

To make the newly imported key your default OpenSSH key, name it *~/.ssh/id_dsa* instead of *imported-ssh2-key*.

As an alternative solution, you could ignore your existing SSH2 private key, generate a brand new OpenSSH key pair, and convert its public key for SSH2 use. [6.5] But if your SSH2 public key is already installed on many remote sites, it might make sense to import and reuse the SSH2 private key.

See Also

ssh-keygen(1), ssh-keygen2(1).

6.7   Authenticating by Public Key (SSH2 Client, OpenSSH Server)

Problem

You want to authenticate between an SSH2 client (*SSH Secure Shell* from SSH Communication Security) and an OpenSSH server by public key.

Solution

1. Create an SSH2 private key on the client machine, if one doesn't already exist, and install it by appending a line to *~/.ssh2/identification*:

   ```
   $ mkdir -p ~/.ssh2                        If it doesn't already exist
   $ chmod 700 ~/.ssh2
   $ cd ~/.ssh2
   $ ssh-keygen2                                          Creates id_dsa_1024_a
   $ echo "IdKey id_dsa_1024_a" >> identification         (Appending)
   ```

2. Copy its public key to the OpenSSH server machine:

   ```
   $ scp2 id_dsa_1024_a.pub remoteuser@remotehost:.ssh/
   ```

3. Log into the OpenSSH server host and use OpenSSH's ssh-keygen to import the public key, creating an OpenSSH format key: [6.6]

```
$ ssh2 -l remoteuser remotehost
Password: ********

remotehost$ cd ~/.ssh
remotehost$ ssh-keygen -i > imported-ssh2-key.pub
Enter file in which the key is (/home/smith/.ssh/id_rsa): id_dsa_1024_a.pub
```

4. Install the new public key by appending a line to ~/.ssh/authorized_keys:

```
remotehost$ cat imported-ssh2-key.pub >> authorized_keys      (Appending)
```

5. Log out and log back in using the new key:

```
remotehost$ exit
$ ssh2 -l remoteuser remotehost
```

Description

Recall that SSH2 uses the *identification* file as explained in the sidebar, "SSH-2 Key File Formats."

See Also

ssh-keygen(1), ssh-keygen2(1).

6.8 Authenticating by Trusted Host

Problem

You want to authenticate between an OpenSSH client and server using hostbased or "trusted host" authentication.

Solution

Suppose you want to allow the account *nocnoc@supplicant.foo.net* access to *whosthere@server.foo.net*. Then:

1. Make sure hostbased authentication enabled in on *server.foo.net*:

```
/etc/ssh/sshd_config:
HostbasedAuthentication yes
IgnoreRhosts no
```

and optionally (see "Discussion"):

```
HostbasedUsesNameFromPacketOnly yes
```

and restart sshd.

2. Ensure that the ssh-keysign program is setuid root on the client machine. The file is usually located in */usr/libexec* or */usr/libexec/openssh*:

```
$ ls -lo /usr/libexec/openssh/ssh-keysign
-rwsr-xr-x  1 root   222936 Mar  7 16:09 /usr/libexec/openssh/ssh-keysign
```

3. Enable trusted host authentication in your system's client configuration file: [6.12]

```
/etc/ssh/ssh_config:
Host remotehost
     HostName remotehost
     HostbasedAuthentication yes
```

4. Insert the client machine's host keys, */etc/ssh/ssh_host_dsa_key.pub* and */etc/ssh/ssh_host_rsa_key.pub*, into the server's known hosts database, */etc/ssh/ssh_known_hosts*, using the client host's canonical name (*supplicant.foo.net* here; see "Discussion"):

```
/etc/ssh/ssh_known_hosts on server.foo.net:
supplicant.foo.net ssh-dss ...key...
```

5. Authorize the client account to log into the server, by creating the file *~/.shosts*:

```
~whosthere/.shosts on server.foo.net:
supplicant.foo.net nocnoc
```

If the account names on the client and server hosts happen to be the same, you can omit the username. (But in this case the usernames are different, *nocnoc* and *whosthere*.)

6. Make sure your home directory and *.shosts* files have acceptable permissions:

```
$ chmod go-w ~
$ chmod go-w ~/.shosts
```

7. Log in from *supplicant.foo.net*:

```
$ ssh -l whosthere server.foo.net
```

Discussion

This recipe applies only to SSH-2 protocol connections. OpenSSH does support an SSH-1 type of trusted-host authentication (keyword RhostsRSAAuthentication) but as we've said before, we strongly recommend the more secure SSH-2.

Before using hostbased authentication at all, decide if you truly need it. This technique has assumptions and implications unlike other SSH user-authentication mechanisms:

Strong trust of the client host
> The server must trust the client host to have effectively authenticated the user. In hostbased authentication, the server does not authenticate the user, but instead authenticates the client *host*, then simply trusts whatever the client says about the user. If the client host is compromised, *all* accounts on the server accessible via hostbased authentication are also immediately vulnerable.

Weak authorization controls

Individual users on the server can override hostbased restrictions placed by the sysadmin. This is why the server's IgnoreRhosts option exists.

If all you want is automatic authentication (without a password), there are other ways to do it, such as public-key authentication with ssh-agent [6.9] or Kerberos. [4.14]

If you decide to use hostbased authentication for an entire user population, read the relevant sections of *SSH, The Secure Shell: The Definitive Guide* (O'Reilly), which detail various subtleties and unexpected consequences of this mechanism.

Speaking of subtleties, the issue of the client's *canonical hostname* can be tricky. The SSH server will look up the client's host key by this name, which it gets from the client's IP address via the gethostbyname library function. This in turn depends on the naming service setup on the server side, which might consult any (or none) of */etc/hosts*, NIS, DNS, LDAP, and so on, as specified in */etc/nsswitch.conf*. In short, the client's idea of its hostname might not agree with the server's view.

To learn the client's canonical hostname as sshd will determine it, run this quick Perl script on the server:

```
#!/usr/bin/perl
use Socket;
print gethostbyaddr(inet_aton("192.168.0.29"), AF_INET) . "\n";
```

where 192.168.0.29 is the IP address of the client in question. You can also run this as a one-liner:

```
$ perl -MSocket -e 'print gethostbyaddr(inet_aton("192.168.0.29"),AF_INET)."\n"'
```

You might be tempted to run the host program instead (e.g., host -x 192.168.0.29) on the server, but the output may be misleading, since host consults only DNS, which the server's naming configuration might not use. If the SSH server cannot get any name for the client's address, then it will look up the client's host key in its known-hosts file by address instead.

And that's not all. The canonical hostname issue is further complicated, because the client independently identifies itself by name within the SSH hostbased authentication protocol. If that name does not match the one determined by the SSH server, the server will refuse the connection. There are many reasons why these names may not match:

- The client is behind a NAT gateway
- Names are simply not coordinated across the hosts
- Your SSH connection is going through a proxy server
- The SSH client host is multi-homed

If this problem occurs, you'll see this server error message in your syslog output:

```
userauth_hostbased mismatch: client sends name1.example.com,
but we resolve 192.168.0.72 to name2.example.com
```

The configuration keyword HostbasedUsesNameFromPacketOnly will relax this restriction in the SSH server:

```
/etc/ssh/sshd_config:
HostbasedUsesNameFromPacketOnly yes
```

This means that sshd uses only the self-identifying hostname supplied by the client in its hostbased authentication request, to look up the client's public host key for verification. It will not insist on any match between this name and the client's IP address.

The client-side, per-user configuration files in ~/.ssh may be used instead of the global ones, /etc/ssh/ssh_config and /etc/ssh/ssh_known_hosts. There is no harm in placing keys into the global list: it does not by itself authorize logins (an authorization task), but only enables authentication with the given client host.

You can authorize hostbased authentication globally on the server by placing the client hostname into /etc/shosts.equiv. This means that *all* users authenticated on the client host can log into accounts with matching usernames on the server. Think carefully before doing this: it implies a high level of inter-host trust and synchronized administration. You should probably customize the *shosts.equiv* file using netgroups to restrict hostbased authentication to user accounts; see the sshd manpage.

Lastly, note that earlier versions of OpenSSH required the ssh client program to be setuid for hostbased authentication, in order to access the client host's private key. But in the current version, this function has been moved into a separate program, ssh-keysign; the ssh program itself need no longer be setuid.

See Also

sshd(8), sshd_config(5), gethostbyname(3).

6.9   Authenticating Without a Password (Interactively)

Problem

You want to authenticate without typing a password or passphrase.

Solution

Use ssh-agent, invoking it within backticks as shown:

```
$ eval `ssh-agent`
```

Add your keys to the agent using ssh-add:

```
$ ssh-add
Enter passphrase for /home/smith/.ssh/id_dsa: ********
```

Then log in using public-key authentication and you won't be prompted for a passphrase: [6.4]

```
$ ssh -l remoteuser remotehost
```

Some Linux distributions automatically run ssh-agent when you log in under an X session manager. In this case just skip the ssh-agent invocation.

Discussion

The SSH agent, controlled by the programs ssh-agent and ssh-add, maintains a cache of private keys on your local (client) machine. You load keys into the agent, typing their passphrases to decrypt them. SSH clients (ssh, scp, sftp) then query the agent transparently about keys, rather than prompting you for a passphrase.

The invocation of ssh-agent might look a little odd with the eval and backticks:

```
$ eval `ssh-agent`
```

but it is necessary because ssh-agent prints several commands on the standard output that set environment variables when run. To view these commands for testing, run ssh-agent alone:

```
$ ssh-agent
SSH_AUTH_SOCK=/tmp/ssh-XXNe6NhE/agent.13583; export SSH_AUTH_SOCK;
SSH_AGENT_PID=13584; export SSH_AGENT_PID;
echo Agent pid 13584;
```

and then kill it manually (kill 13584).*

ssh-add, invoked with no command-line arguments, adds your default keys to the cache. To add a selected key, simply list it:

```
$ ssh-add ~/.ssh/other_key
```

Removing keys is done like this:

Remove one key:
```
$ ssh-add -d ~/.ssh/other_key
```

Remove all keys:
```
$ ssh-add -D
```

A tempting but naive alternative to ssh-agent is a key with an empty passphrase, called a *plaintext key*. If you authenticate with this key, indeed, no passphrase is needed...but this is risky! If a cracker steals your plaintext key, he can immediately impersonate you on every machine that contains the corresponding public key.

For interactive use, there is *no reason* to use a plaintext key. It's like putting your login password into a file named *password.here.please.steal.me*. Don't do it. Use ssh-agent instead.

---

* In this case, you cannot kill the agent with ssh-agent -k because the environment variables aren't set.

Another way to avoid passphrases is to use hostbased (trusted host) authentication [6.8], but for interactive use we recommend public-key authentication with ssh-agent as inherently more secure.

See Also

ssh-agent(1), ssh-add(1).

6.10 Authenticating in cron Jobs

Problem

You want to invoke unattended remote commands, i.e., as cron or batch jobs, and do it securely without any prompting for passwords.

Solution

Use a plaintext key and a forced command.

1. Create a plaintext key:

   ```
   $ cd ~/.ssh
   $ ssh-keygen -t dsa -f batchkey -N ""
   ```

2. Install the public key (*batchkey.pub*) on the server machine. [6.4]

3. Associate a forced command with the public key on the server machine, to limit its capabilities:

   ~/.ssh/authorized_keys:
   ```
   command="/usr/local/bin/my_restricted_command" ssh-dss AAAAB3NzaC1kc3MAA ...
   ```

   Disable other capabilities for this key as well, such as forwarding and pseudo-ttys, and if feasible, restrict use of the key to a particular source address or set of addresses. (This is a single line in *authorized_keys*, though it's split on our page.)

   ~/.ssh/authorized_keys:
   ```
   no-port-forwarding,no-X11-forwarding,no-agent-forwarding,no-pty, from="myclient.
   example.com", command="/usr/local/bin/my_restricted_command" ssh-dss
   AAAAB3NzaC1kc3MAA ...
   ```

4. Use the plaintext key in batch scripts on the client machine:

   ```
   $ ssh -i ~/.ssh/batchkey remotehost ...
   ```

Alternatively, use hostbased authentication [6.8] instead of public-key authentication.

Discussion

A *plaintext key* is a cryptographic key with no passphrase. Usually it's not appropriate to omit the passphrase, since a thief who steals the key could immediately use it to impersonate you. But for batch jobs, plaintext keys are a reasonable approach, especially if the key's scope can be restricted to specific remote commands. You create a plaintext key by supplying an empty password to the -N option:

```
$ ssh-keygen -t dsa -f batchkey -N ""
```

A *forced command* is a server-side restriction on a given public key listed in *~/.ssh/authorized_keys*. When someone authenticates by that key, the forced command is automatically invoked in place of any command supplied by the client. So, if you associate a forced command with a key (say, *batchkey*) with the following public component:

```
~/.ssh/authorized_keys:
command="/bin/who" ssh-dss key...
```

and a client tries to invoke (say) /bin/ls via this key:

```
$ ssh -i batchkey remotehost /bin/ls
```

the forced command /bin/who is invoked instead. Therefore, you prevent the key from being used for unplanned purposes. You can further restrict use of this key by source address using the from keyword:

```
~/.ssh/authorized_keys:
command="/bin/who",from="client.example.com" ssh-dss key...
```

Additionally, disable any unneeded capabilities for this key, such as port forwarding, X forwarding, agent forwarding, and the allocation of pseudo-ttys for interactive sessions. The key options no-port-forwarding, no-X11-forwarding, no-agent-forwarding, and no-pty, respectively, perform these jobs.

Make sure you edit *authorized_keys* with an appropriate text editor that does not blindly insert newlines. Your key and all its options must remain on a single line of text, with no whitespace around the commas.

Carefully consider whether to include plaintext keys in your regular system backups. If you do include them, a thief need only steal a backup tape to obtain them. If you don't, then you risk losing them, but if new keys can easily be generated and installed, perhaps this is an acceptable tradeoff.

Finally, store plaintext keys only on local disks, not insecurely shared volumes such as NFS partitions. Otherwise their unencrypted contents will travel over the network and risk interception. [9.19]

See Also

ssh-keygen(1), sshd(1).

6.11 Terminating an SSH Agent on Logout

Problem

When you log out, you want the ssh-agent process to be terminated automatically.

Solution

For bash:

```
~/.bash_profile:
trap 'test -n "$SSH_AGENT_PID" && eval `/usr/bin/ssh-agent -k`' 0
```

For csh or tcsh:

```
~/.logout:
if ( "$SSH_AGENT_PID" != "" ) then
    eval `/usr/bin/ssh-agent -k`
endif
```

Discussion

SSH agents you invoke yourself don't die automatically when you log out: you must kill them explicitly. When you run an agent, it defines the environment variable SSH_AGENT_PID. [6.9] Simply test for its existence and kill the agent with the -k option.

See Also

ssh-agent(1).

6.12   Tailoring SSH per Host

Problem

You want to simplify a complicated SSH command line, or tailor SSH clients to operate differently per remote host.

Solution

Create a host alias in *~/.ssh/config*:

```
~/.ssh/config:
Host mybox
    HostName mybox.whatever.example.com
    User smith
    ...other options...
```

Then connect via the alias:

```
$ ssh mybox
```

Discussion

OpenSSH clients obey configurations found in *~/.ssh/config*. Each configuration begins with the word Host followed by an hostname alias of your invention.

```
Host work
```

Immediately following this line, and continuing until the next Host keyword or end of file, place configuration keywords and values documented on the ssh(1) manpage. In this recipe we include the real name of the remote machine (HostName), and the remote username (User):

```
Host work
    HostName mybox.whatever.example.com
    User smith
```

Other useful keywords (there are dozens) are:

```
IdentityFile ~/.ssh/my_alternate_key_dsa      Choose a private key file
Port 12345                                    Connect on an alternative port
Protocol 2                                     Use only the SSH-2 protocol
```

See Also

ssh_config(5) defines the client configuration keywords.

6.13 Changing SSH Client Defaults

Problem

You want to change the default behavior of ssh.

Solution

Create a host alias named "*" in ~/.ssh/config:

```
Host *
    keyword value
    keyword value
    ...
```

If this is the *first* entry in the file, these values will override all others. If the *last* entry in the file, they are fallback values, i.e., defaults if nobody else has set them. You can make Host * both the first and last entry to achieve both behaviors.

Discussion

We are just taking advantage of a few facts about host aliases in the configuration file:

- Earlier values take precedence
- The aliases may be patterns, and "*" matches anything
- *All* matching aliases apply, not just the first one to match your ssh command

So if this is your ~/.ssh/config file:

```
Host *
    User smith
Host server.example.com
    User jones
    PasswordAuthentication yes
Host *
    PasswordAuthentication no
```

then your remote username will always be smith (even for *server.example.com*!), and password authentication will be disabled by default (except for *server.example.com*).

You can still override host aliases using command-line options:

```
$ ssh -l jane server.example.com
```
The -l option overrides the User keyword

See Also

ssh_config(5) documents the client configuration keywords.

6.14   Tunneling Another TCP Session Through SSH

Problem

You want to secure a client/server TCP connection such as POP, IMAP, NNTP (Usenet news), IRC, VNC, etc. Both the client and server must reside on computers that run SSH.

Solution

Tunnel (forward) the TCP connection through SSH. To secure port 119, the NNTP protocol for Usenet news, which you read remotely from *news.example.com*:

```
$ ssh -f -N -L12345:localhost:119 news.example.com
```

While this tunnel is open, read news via local port 12345, e.g.:

```
$ export NNTPSERVER=localhost
$ tin -r -p 12345
```

Discussion

Tunneling or port forwarding uses SSH to secure another TCP/IP connection, such as an NNTP or IMAP connection. You first create a tunnel, a secure connection between an SSH client and server. Then you make your TCP/IP applications (client and server) communicate over the tunnel, as in Figure 6-1. SSH makes this process mostly transparent.

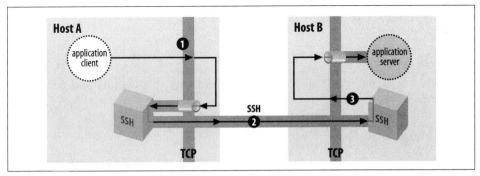

Figure 6-1. SSH forwarding or tunneling

The SSH command:

```
$ ssh -f -N -L12345:localhost:119 news.example.com
```

establishes a tunnel between *localhost* and *news.example.com*. The tunnel has three segments:

1. The newsreader on your local machine sends data to local port 12345. This occurs entirely on your local machine, not over the network.

2. The local SSH client reads port 12345, encrypts the data, and sends it through the tunnel to the remote SSH server on *news.example.com*.

3. The remote SSH server on *news.example.com* decrypts the data and passes it to the news server running on port 119. This runs entirely on *news.example.com*, not over the network.

Therefore, when your local news client connects to *localhost* port 12345:

```
$ tin -r -p 12345
```

the connection operates through the tunnel to the remote news server on *news. example.com*. Data is sent back from the news server to the news client by the same process in reverse.

The general syntax for this forwarding command is:

```
$ ssh -f -N -Llocal_port_number:localhost:remote_port_number remote_host
```

local_port_number is arbitrary: select an unused port number higher than 1024. The -N option keeps the tunnel open without the need to run a remote command.

See Also

ssh(1) and sshd(8) discuss port forwarding and its configuration keywords briefly.

The target host of the forwarding need not be *localhost*, but this topic is beyond the scope of our cookbook. For more depth, try Chapter 9 of *SSH, The Secure Shell: The Definitive Guide* (O'Reilly).

6.15 Keeping Track of Passwords

Problem

You have to remember a zillion different usernames, passwords, and SSH pass-phrases for various remote hosts and web sites.

Solution

Store them in a file encrypted with GnuPG. Maintain it with Emacs and *crypt++.el* [7.23] or with vim. [7.24] Create handy scripts to extract and print passwords as you need them.

Discussion

A possible file format is:

```
login<tab>password<tab>comment
```

Protect the file from access by other users:

```
$ chmod 600 $HOME/lib/passwords.gpg
```

Then create a script, say, $HOME/bin/mypass, to extract passwords based on grep patterns:

```
#!/bin/bash
PWFILE=$HOME/lib/passwords.gpg
/usr/bin/gpg -d $PWFILE | /bin/grep -i $@

$ mypass yahoo
Enter passphrase: ********
karma24    s3kr1TT    My Yahoo password
billybob   4J%ich3!UKMr  Bill's Yahoo password
```

Now you can type or copy/paste the username and password as needed. When finished, clear your window scroll history (or close the window entirely) and clear your clipboard if it contained the password.

Admittedly, this technique will not satisfy every security expert. If the password file gets stolen, it could conceivably be cracked and all your passwords compromised *en masse*. Nevertheless, the method is convenient and in use at major corporations. If you are concerned about higher security, keep the password file on a computer that has no network connection. If this is not possible, at least keep the computer behind a firewall. For very high security installations, also physically isolate the computer in a locked room and distribute door keys only to trusted individuals.

See Also

gpg(1).

## CHAPTER 7

Protecting Files

7.0 Introduction

So far we've been concerned mainly with securing your computer system. Now we turn to securing your data, specifically, your files. At a basic level, *file permissions*, enforced by the operating system, can protect your files from other legitimate users on your system. (But not from the superuser.) We'll provide a few recipes based on the chmod (change mode) command.

File permissions only go so far, however—your file data are still readable if an attacker masquerades as you (e.g., by stealing your login password) or breaks other aspects the system, perhaps using some security exploit to gain root access on the host, or simply stealing a backup tape.

To guard against these possibilities, use *encryption* to scramble your data, so that a secret password or key is required to unscramble and make it intelligible again. Thus, merely gaining the ability to *read* your file is not enough; an attacker must also have your secret password in order to make any sense out of the data. We'll focus on the excellent encryption software included with most Linux systems: the *Gnu Privacy Guard*, also known as GnuPG or GPG. If you've used PGP (Pretty Good Privacy), you'll find GnuPG quite similar but far more configurable. While the pgp command has around 35 command-line flags, its GnuPG equivalent gpg has a whopping 140 at press time.

GnuPG supports two types of encryption: *symmetric* (or *secret-key*) and *asymmetric* (or *public-key*). In symmetric encryption, the same key is used for encrypting and decrypting. Typically this key is a password. Public-key encryption, on the other hand, uses two related keys (a "key pair") known as the public and private (a.k.a. secret) keys. They are related in a mathematically clever way: data encrypted with the public key can be decrypted with the private one, but it is not feasible to discover the private key from the public. In daily use, you keep your private key, well... private, and distribute the public key freely to anyone who wants it, without worrying about disclosure. Ideally, you publish it in a directory next to your name, as in a telephone book. When someone wants to send you a secret message, she encrypts it with your public key. Decryption requires your corresponding private key, however, which is your closely guarded secret. Although other people may have your public key, it won't allow them to decrypt the message.

Symmetric encryption is GnuPG's simplest operating mode: just provide the same password for encrypting and decrypting. [7.4] Public-key encryption requires setup, at the very least generating a key pair [7.6], but it is more flexible: it allows others to send you confidential messages without the hassle of first agreeing on a shared secret key.

Before using a public key to encrypt sensitive data to send to someone, make sure that the key actually belongs to that person! GnuPG allows keys to be *signed*, indicating that the signer vouches for the key. It also lets you control how much you trust others to vouch for keys (called "trust management"). When you consider the interconnections between keys and signatures, as users vouch for keys of users who vouch for keys, this interconnected graph is called a *web of trust*. To participate in this web, try to collect signatures on your GnuPG key from widely trusted people within particular communities of interest, thereby enabling your key to be trusted automatically by others.

Public-key methods are also the basis for *digital signatures*: extra information attached to a digital document as evidence that a particular person created it, or has seen and agreed to it, much as a pen-and-ink signature does with a paper document. When we speak of "signing" a file in this chapter, we mean adding a digital signature to a file to certify that it has not been modified since the signature was created.

Once you're comfortable with encryption, check out Chapter 8 to integrate encryption into your preferred mail program.

7.1   Using File Permissions

Problem

You want to prevent other users on your machine from reading your files.

Solution

To protect existing files and directories:

```
$ chmod 600 file_name
$ chmod 700 directory_name
```

To protect future files and directories:

```
$ umask 077
```

Discussion

chmod and umask are the most basic file-protection commands available for Linux. Protected in this manner, the affected files and directories are accessible only to you and the superuser. (Not likely to be helpful against an intruder, however.)

The two chmod commands set the protection bits on a file and directory, respectively, to limit access to their owner. This protection is enforced by the filesystem. The umask command informs your shell that newly created files and directories should be accessible only to their owner.

See Also

chmod(1). See your shell documentation for umask: bash(1), tcsh(1), etc.

7.2   Securing a Shared Directory

Problem

You want a directory in which anybody can create files, but only the file owners can delete or rename them. (For example, */tmp*, or an ftp upload directory.)

Solution

Set the sticky bit on a world-writable directory:

```
$ chmod 1777 dirname
```

Discussion

Normally, anyone can delete or rename files in a world-writable directory, mode 0777. The sticky bit prevents this, permitting only the file owner, the directory owner, and the superuser to delete or rename the files.*

The sticky bit has a completely different meaning for files, particularly executable files. It specifies that the file should be retained in swap space after execution. This feature was most useful back in the days when RAM was scarce, but you'll hardly see it nowadays. This has nothing to do with our recipe, just a note of historical interest.

See Also

chmod(1).

---

* Directories with the sticky bit set are often called, somewhat inaccurately, "append-only" directories.

7.3 Prohibiting Directory Listings

Problem

You want to prohibit directory listings for a particular directory, yet still permit the files within to be accessed by name.

Solution

Use a directory that has read permission disabled, but execute permission enabled:

```
$ mkdir dir
$ chmod 0111 dir
$ ls -ld dir
d--x--x--x   2 smith    smith    4096 Apr  2 22:04 dir/
$ ls dir
/bin/ls: dir: Permission denied

$ echo hello world > dir/secretfile
$ cd dir
$ cat secretfile
hello world
```

More practically, to permit only yourself to list a directory owned by you:

```
$ chmod 0711 dir
$ ls -ld dir
drwx--x--x   2 smith    smith    4096 Apr  2 22:04 dir/
```

Discussion

A directory's read permission controls whether it can be listed (e.g., via ls), and the execute permission controls whether it can be entered (e.g., via cd). Of course the superuser can still access your directory any way she likes.

This technique is useful for web sites. If your web pages are contained in a readable, non-listable directory, then they can be retrieved directly by their URLs (as you would want), but other files in the containing directory cannot be discovered via HTTP. This is one way to prevent web robots from crawling a directory.

FTP servers also use non-listable directories as private rendezvous points. Users can transfer files to and from such directories, but third parties cannot eavesdrop as long as they cannot guess the filenames. The directories need to be writable for users to create files, and you might want to restrict deletions or renaming via the sticky bit. [7.2]

See Also

chmod(1).

7.4   Encrypting Files with a Password

Problem

You want to encrypt a file so only you can decrypt it with a password.

Solution

```
$ gpg -c filename
```

Discussion

Symmetric encryption (-c) is the simplest way to encrypt a file with gpg: just provide a password at encryption time. To decrypt, provide the password again.

By default, encrypted files are binary. To produce an ASCII text file instead, add the -a (armor) option:

```
$ gpg -c -a filename
```

Binary encrypted files are created with the suffix *.gpg*, whereas ASCII encrypted files have the suffix *.asc*.

Though simple, symmetric encryption has some gotchas:

- It's not practical for handling multiple files at once, as in scripts:

  ```
  A bad idea:
  #!/bin/sh
  for file in file1 file2 file3 ...
  do
        gpg -c "$file"
  done
  ```

  GnuPG will prompt for the password for *each* file during encryption and decryption. This is tedious and error-prone. Public-key encryption does not have this limitation, since no passphrase is needed to encrypt a file. [7.6] Another strategy is to bundle the files into a single file using tar, then encrypt the tarball. [7.18]

- If you mistype the password during encryption and don't realize it, kiss your data goodbye. You can't decrypt the file without the mistyped (and therefore unknown) password. gpg prompts you for the password twice, so there's less chance you'll mistype it, but GnuPG's public-key encryption leaves less opportunity to mistype a password unknowingly.

- It's not much good for sharing files securely, since you'd also have to share the secret password. Again, this is not true of public-key encryption.

See Also

gpg(1).

7.5   Decrypting Files

Problem

You want to decrypt a file that was encrypted with GnuPG.

Solution

Assuming the file is *myfile.gpg*, decrypt it in place with:

```
$ gpg myfile.gpg                          creates myfile
```

Decrypt to standard output:

```
$ gpg --decrypt myfile.gpg
```

Decrypt to a named plaintext file:

```
$ gpg --decrypt --output new_file_name myfile.gpg
```

Discussion

These commands work for both symmetric and public-key encrypted files. You'll be prompted for a password (symmetric) or passphrase (public-key), which you must enter correctly to decrypt the file.

ASCII encrypted files (with the suffix *.asc*) are decrypted in the same way as binary encrypted files (with the suffix *.gpg*).

See Also

gpg(1).

7.6   Setting Up GnuPG for Public-Key Encryption

Problem

You want to start using GnuPG for more sophisticated operations, such as encrypting and signing files for other parties to decrypt.

Solution

Generate a GnuPG keypair:

```
$ gpg --gen-key
```

then set a default key if you like [7.8] and you're ready to use public-key encryption.

We strongly recommend you also create a *revocation certificate* at this time, in case you ever lose the key and need to tell the world to stop using it. [7.22]

Discussion

Public-key encryption lets you encrypt a file that only a designated recipient can decrypt, without sharing any secrets like an encryption password. This recipe discusses just the initial setup.

First you need to generate your very own GnuPG keypair, which consists of a secret (private) key and a public key. This is accomplished by:

```
$ gpg --gen-key
```

You'll be asked various questions, such as the key size in bits, key expiration date if any, an ID for the key, and a passphrase to protect the key from snoopers.

First you'll be asked to choose the type of key. For most purposes simply choose the default by pressing RETURN:

```
Please select what kind of key you want:
     (1) DSA and ElGamal (default)
     (2) DSA (sign only)
     (4) ElGamal (sign and encrypt)
Your selection? <return>
```

Next, choose how many bits long the key should be. Longer keys are less like to be cracked. They also slow down encryption and decryption performance, but on a fast processor you aren't likely to notice. Choose at least 1024 bits.

```
DSA keypair will have 1024 bits.
About to generate a new ELG-E keypair.
            minimum keysize is   768 bits
            default keysize is  1024 bits
    highest suggested keysize is 2048 bits
What keysize do you want? (1024) 2048
```

Next specify when the key should expire. For average use, a permanent key is best:

```
Please specify how long the key should be valid.
     0 = key does not expire
   <n>  = key expires in n days
   <n>w = key expires in n weeks
   <n>m = key expires in n months
   <n>y = key expires in n years
Key is valid for? (0) <return>

Key does not expire at all
Is this correct (y/n)? y
```

But if your key should expire, choose a lifetime and you'll see:

```
Key expires at Fri 19 Apr 2002 08:32:24 PM EDT
Is this correct (y/n)?
```

Next, choose a unique identifier for your key. gpg constructs an ID by combining your name, email address, and a comment.

```
You need a User-ID to identify your key; the software constructs the user id
from Real Name, Comment and Email Address in this form:
    "Heinrich Heine (Der Dichter) <heinrichh@duesseldorf.de>"

Real name: Shawn Smith
Email address: smith@example.com
Comment: My work key
You selected this USER-ID:
    "Shawn Smith (My work key) <smith@example.com>"

Change (N)ame, (C)omment, (E)mail or (O)kay/(Q)uit? o
```

Next, choose a secret passphrase. Your key will be stored encrypted, and only this passphrase can unlock it for use.

```
You need a Passphrase to protect your secret key.
Enter passphrase: ******
Repeat passphrase: ******
```

Eventually, you will see:

```
public and secret key created and signed.
```

which means your key is ready for use. Now you can encrypt [7.11], decrypt [7.5], sign [7.12], and verify [7.15] files by public-key encryption.

See Also

gpg(1).

7.7   Listing Your Keyring

Problem

You want to view the keys on your keyring.

Solution

To list your secret keys:

```
$ gpg --list-secret-keys
```

To list your public keys:

```
$ gpg --list-public-keys
```

Discussion

Here's a sample listing of a key on a keyring:

```
pub  1024D/83FA91C6 2000-07-21 Shawn Smith <smith@example.com>
```

It lists the following information:

- Whether the key is secret (sec) or public (pub).[*]
- The number of bits in the key (1024)
- The encryption algorithm (D means DSA)
- The key ID (83FA91C6)
- The key creation date (2000-07-21)
- The user ID (Shawn Smith <smith@example.com>)

See Also

gpg(1).

7.8   Setting a Default Key

Problem

You want a designated secret key to be your default for gpg operations.

Solution

List your keys: [7.7]

```
$ gpg --list-secret-keys
```

Then locate the desired secret (sec) key, and specify its ID in your ~/.gnupg/options file:

~/.gnupg/options:
```
default-key ID_goes_here
```

Discussion

Most often, people have only a single secret key that GnuPG uses by default. This recipe applies if you have generated multiple secret keys for particular purposes. For

---

[*] Actually, the key types are secret master signing key (sec), secret subordinate key (ssb), public master signing key (pub), and public subordinate key (sub). Subordinate keys are beyond the scope of this book and you might never need them. Just remember "sec" for secret and "pub" for public.

example, if you're a software developer, you might a have a separate key for signing software releases, in addition to a personal key.

gpg places keys into *keyring* files held in your account. View your default keyring with:

```
$ gpg --list-secret-keys
/home/smith/.gnupg/secring.gpg
--------------------------------
sec  1024D/967D108B 2001-02-21 Shawn Smith (My work key) <smith@example.com>
ssb  2048g/6EA5084A 2001-02-21
sec  1024D/2987358A 2000-06-04 S. Smith (other key) <smith@example.com>
ssb  2048g/FC9274C2 2000-06-04
```

Normally the first secret (sec) key listed is the default for GnuPG operations. To change this, edit the GnuPG options file, *~/.gnupg/options*, which is automatically created by gpg with default values. Modify the default-key line, setting its value to the ID of your desired secret key:

```
~/.gnupg/options:
default-key 2987358A
```

See Also

Key IDs can also be specified by email address or other identifying information: see the gpg(1) manpage. We find using key IDs to be easy and unambiguous.

7.9   Sharing Public Keys

Problem

You want to obtain a friend's public key securely but conveniently.

Solution

Most securely, get the public key on disk directly from your friend in person. Barring that:

1. Obtain the public key by any means (e.g., email, keyserver [7.19]).
2. Add the key to your keyring. [7.10]
3. Before using the key, telephone its owner and ask him to read the key fingerprint aloud. View the fingerprint with:

   ```
   $ gpg --fingerprint key_id
   ```

   If they match, you're done. If not, consider the key suspect, delete it from your keyring, and don't use it.

4. If you trust the key, indicate this to GnuPG:

```
$ gpg --edit-key key_id
Command> trust
```

and follow the prompts.

Discussion

Public keys are not secret, but they do require trust: the trust that a given key actually belongs to its alleged owner. A fingerprint can provide that trust in a convenient form, easy to read aloud over a telephone.

Always verify the fingerprint before trusting a public key. If you don't, consider this scenario:

1. You email your friend, asking for his public key.
2. A snooper intercepts your email and sends you *his* public key instead of your friend's.
3. You blindly add the snooper's public key to your keyring, believing it to be your friend's.
4. You encrypt sensitive mail using the snooper's key and send it to your friend.
5. The snooper intercepts your mail and decrypts it.

See Also

gpg(1).

7.10 Adding Keys to Your Keyring

Problem

You want to add a public or secret key to your keyring.

Solution

If the public key is in the file *keyfile*:

```
$ gpg --import keyfile
```

If the secret key is in the file *keyfile*:

```
$ gpg --import --allow-secret-key-import keyfile
```

Discussion

Importing the secret key implicitly imports the public key as well, since the public key is derivable from the secret one.

See Also

gpg(1).

7.11 Encrypting Files for Others

Problem

You want to encrypt a file so only particular recipients can decrypt it.

Solution

1. Obtain a recipient's GnuPG public key. [7.9]
2. Add it to your GnuPG key ring. [7.10]
3. Encrypt the file using your private key and the recipient's public key:

```
$ gpg -e -r recipient_public_key_ID myfile
```

To make the file decryptable by multiple recipients, repeat the -r option:

```
$ gpg -e -r key1 -r key2 -r key3 myfile
```

 When you encrypt a file for a recipient other than yourself, *you* can't decrypt it! To make a file decryptable by yourself as well, include your own public key at encryption time (-r your_key_id).

Discussion

This is a classic use of GnuPG: encrypting a file to be read only by an intended recipient, say, Barbara Bitflipper. To decrypt the file, Barbara will need her private key (corresponding to the public one used for encryption) and its passphrase, both of which only Barbara has (presumably). Even if Barbara's private key gets stolen, the thief would still need Barbara's passphrase to decrypt the file.

By default, encrypted files are binary. To produce an ASCII file instead, suitable for including in a text message (email, Usenet post, etc.), add the -a (armor) option:

```
$ gpg -e -r Barbara's_public_key_ID -a filename
```

See Also

gpg(1).

7.12   Signing a Text File

Problem

You want to attach a digital signature to a text file to verify its authenticity, leaving the file human-readable.

Solution

```
$ gpg --clearsign myfile
```

You'll be prompted for your passphrase.

Discussion

If your original file has this content:

```
Hello world!
```

then the signed file will look something like this:

```
-----BEGIN PGP SIGNED MESSAGE-----
Hash: SHA1

Hello world!
-----BEGIN PGP SIGNATURE-----
Version: GnuPG v1.0.6 (GNU/Linux)
Comment: For info see http://www.gnupg.org

iD8DBQE9WFNU5UoZSgD1tx8RAkAmAJ4wWTKWSy6C3OraF2RWfQ6Eh8ZXAQCePUW3
N9JVeHSgYuSFu6XPLKW+2XU=
=5XaU
-----END PGP SIGNATURE-----
```

Anyone who has your public key can check the signature in this file using gpg, thereby confirming that the file is from you. [7.15]

See Also

gpg(1).

7.13   Signing and Encrypting Files

Problem

You want to sign and encrypt a file, with the results not human-readable.

Solution

To sign *myfile*:

```
$ gpg -s myfile
```

To sign and encrypt *myfile*:

```
gpg -e -s myfile
```

In either case you must provide your passphrase. Add the -r option to encrypt the file with an intended recipient's public key, so only he or she can decrypt it. [7.11]

If you want the result to be an ASCII text file—say, for mailing—add the -a (armor) option.

Discussion

This signature confirms to a recipient that the file is authentic: that the claimed signer really signed it.

See Also

gpg(1).

7.14   Creating a Detached Signature File

Problem

You want to sign a file digitally, but have the signature reside in a separate file.

Solution

To create a binary-format detached signature, *myfile.sig*:

```
$ gpg --detach-sign myfile
```

To create an ASCII-format detached signature, *myfile.asc*:

```
$ gpg --detach-sign -a myfile
```

In either case, you'll be prompted for your passphrase.

Discussion

A detached signature is placed into a file by itself, not inside the file it represents. Detached signatures are commonly used to validate software distributed in compressed tar files, e.g., *myprogram.tar.gz*. You can't sign such a file internally without altering its contents, so the signature is created in a separate file such as *myprogram. tar.gz.sig*.

See Also

gpg(1).

7.15   Checking a Signature

Problem

You want to verify that a GnuPG-signed file has not been altered.

Solution

To check a signed file, *myfile*:

```
$ gpg --verify myfile
```

To check *myfile* against a detached signature in *myfile.sig*: [7.15]

```
$ gpg --verify myfile.sig myfile
```

Decrypting a signed file [7.5] also checks its signature, e.g.:

```
$ gpg myfile
```

Discussion

When GnuPG detects a signature, it lets you know:

```
gpg: Signature made Wed 15 May 2002 10:19:20 PM EDT using DSA key ID 00F5B71F
```

If the signed file has not been altered, you'll see a result like:

```
gpg: Good signature from "Shawn Smith <smith@example.com>"
```

Otherwise:

```
gpg: BAD signature from "Shawn Smith <smith@example.com>"
```

indicates that the file is not to be trusted.

If you don't have the public key needed to check the signature, contact the key owner or check keyservers [7.21] to obtain it, then import it. [7.10]

See Also

gpg(1).

7.16 Printing Public Keys

Problem

You want to display your default public key in ASCII to share with other users.

Solution

Display in ASCII on standard output:

```
$ gpg -a --export keyname [keyname...]
```

Discussion

Try finding this combination in gpg's massive manpage. Whew!

Now you can distribute your public key to others [7.9], and they can check its finger-print and add it to their keyrings. [7.10] An ASCII public key looks like:

```
-----BEGIN PGP PUBLIC KEY BLOCK-----
Version: GnuPG v1.0.6 (GNU/Linux)
Comment: For info see http://www.gnupg.org

mQGiBDqTFZ8RBACuT1xDXPKORUFBgcGKx7gk85v4r3tt98qWq+kCyWA1XuRqROyq
aj4OufqiabWm2QYjYrLSBx+BrAE5t84Fi4AR23M1dNOy2gUm2R6IvjwneL4erppk
...more...
2WEACgkQ5UoZSgD1tx9A3XYbBLpbNBVOw25TnqiUy/vOWZcxJEAoMz4ertAFAAO
=j962
-----END PGP PUBLIC KEY BLOCK-----
```

To write the results to a file, add the option `--output` *pubkeyfile*. You can also cre-ate binary output by omitting the `-a` option.

See Also

gpg(1).

7.17 Backing Up a Private Key

Problem

You want to protect against losing your private key or forgetting your passphrase. (And thereby losing the ability to decrypt your files.)

Solution

Store your key pair in an offline, physically secure location, together with a throw-away passphrase. First change the passphrase temporarily to something you do not use for any other purpose. This will be your "throwaway" passphrase.

```
$ gpg --edit mykey_id ...
Command> passwd
...follow the prompts...
```

Then make a copy of your key pair that uses this throwaway passphrase, storing it in the file *mykey.asc*:

```
$ gpg -a -o mykey.asc --export mykey_id
$ gpg -a --export-secret-keys mykey_id >> mykey.asc
```

Finally, restore the original passphrase to your key on your keyring:

```
$ gpg --edit mykey_id ...
Command> passwd
...follow the prompts...
```

You now have a file called *mykey.asc* that contains your key pair, in which the private key is protected by the throwaway passphrase, not your real passphrase. Now, store this file in a safe place, such as a safety deposit box in a bank. Together with the key, store the passphrase, either on disk or on paper.

To guard against media deterioration or obsolescence, you can even print *mykey.asc* on acid-free paper and store the printout with the media. Or maybe have the key laser-engraved on a gold plate? Whatever makes you feel comfortable.

Discussion

Imagine what would happen if you forgot your passphrase or lost your secret key. All your important encrypted files would become useless junk. Even if you are *sure* you could *never* forget your passphrase, what if you become injured and suffer amnesia? Or what about when you die? Could your family and business associates ever decrypt your files, or are they lost forever? This isn't just morbid, it's realistic: your encrypted data may outlive you. So plan ahead.

If gpg could output your secret key to a file unencrypted, we would do so, but it has no such option. You could get the same effect by temporarily changing to a null passphrase and then doing the export, but that's dangerous and awkward to describe, so we recommend a throwaway passphrase instead.

Storing your plaintext key anywhere is, of course, a tradeoff. If your passphrase exists only inside your head, then your encrypted data are more secure—but not necessarily "safer" in the general sense. If losing access to your encrypted data is more worrisome than someone breaking into your safety deposit box to steal your key, then use this procedure.

Other cryptographic techniques can address these issues, such as secret-sharing, or simply encrypting documents with multiple keys, but they require extra software support and effort. A secure, plaintext, backup copy of your private key ensures that your data will not be irretrievably lost in these situations. You can, of course, create multiple keys for use with different kinds of data, some keys backed up in this way and others not.

While you're visiting your safety deposit box, drop off a copy of your global password list as well. [6.15] Your heirs may need it someday.

See Also

gpg(1).

7.18   Encrypting Directories

Problem

You want to encrypt an entire directory tree.

Solution

To produce a single encrypted file containing all files in the directory, with symmetric encryption:

```
$ tar cf - name_of_directory | gpg -c > files.tar.gpg
```

or key-based encryption:

```
$ tar cf - name_of_directory | gpg -e > files.tar.gpg
```

To encrypt each file separately:

```
$ find name_of_directory -type f -exec gpg -e '{}' \;
```

Discussion

Notice the find method uses public-key encryption, not symmetric. If you need a symmetric cipher [7.4] or to sign the files [7.13], avoid this method, as you'd be prompted for your password/passphrase for each file processed.

See Also

gpg(1), find(1), tar(1).

7.19   Adding Your Key to a Keyserver

Problem

You have generated a new GnuPG key, and you want to make your public key available to others via a keyserver.

Solution

Send the key to the keyserver:

```
$ gpg --keyserver server_name_or_IP_address --send-keys key_ID
```

Some well-known PGP/GnuPG keyservers are:

wwwkeys.pgp.net
www.keyserver.net
pgp.mit.edu

Additionally, most keyservers have a web-based interface for adding and locating keys.

Discussion

A *keyserver* is a resource for storing and retrieving public keys, often accessible via the Web. Most widely-used GnuPG keyservers share keys automatically amongst themselves, so it is not necessary to send your key to all of them. Your key should be available on many keyservers within a day or two.

See Also

gpg(1), and the keyservers mentioned herein.

7.20   Uploading New Signatures to a Keyserver

Problem

You have collected some new signatures on your public key, and want to update your key on a keyserver with those signatures.

Solution

Simply re-send your key to the keyserver [7.19]; it will merge in the new signatures with your existing entry on the keyserver.

7.21   Obtaining Keys from a Keyserver

Problem

You want to obtain a public key from a keyserver.

Solution

If you have the key ID, you can import it immediately:

```
$ gpg --keyserver keyserver --recv-keys key_ID
```

Otherwise, to search for a key by the owner's name or email address, and match keys before importing them, use:

```
$ gpg --keyserver keyserver --search-keys string_to_match
```

To specify a default keyserver, so you need not use the --keyserver option above:

```
~/.gnupg/options:
keyserver keyserver_DNS_name_or_IP_address
```

To have GnuPG automatically contact a keyserver and import keys whenever needed:

```
~/.gnupg/options:
keyserver keyserver_DNS_name_or_IP_address
keyserver-options auto-key-retrieve
```

With this configuration, for example, if you were to verify the signature on some downloaded software signed with a key you didn't have (gpg --verify foo.tar.gz.sig), GnuPG would automatically download and import that key from your keyserver, if available.

Additionally, most keyservers have a web-based interface for adding and locating keys.

Remember to check the key fingerprint with the owner before trusting it. [7.9]

Discussion

Importing a key does not verify its validity—it does not verify that the claimed binding between a user identity (name, email address, etc.) and the public key is legitimate. For example, if you use gpg --verify to check the signature of a key imported from a keyserver, GnuPG may still produce the following warning, even if the signature itself is good:

```
gpg: WARNING: This key is not certified with a trusted signature!
gpg:          There is no indication that the signature belongs to the owner.
```

A keyserver does *absolutely nothing* to assure the ownership of keys. Anyone can add a key to a keyserver, at any time, with any name whatsoever. A keyserver is only a convenient way to share keys and their associated certificates; all responsibility for checking keys against identities rests with you, the GnuPG user, employing the normal GnuPG web-of-trust techniques. To trust a given key *K*, either you must trust *K* directly, or you must trust another key which has signed *K*, and thus whose owner (recursively) trusts *K*.

The ultimate way to verify a key is to check its fingerprint with the key owner directly. [7.9] If you need to verify a key and do not have a chain of previously verified and trusted keys leading to it, then anything you do to verify it involving only computers has some degree of uncertainty; it's just a question of how paranoid you are and how sure you want to be.

This situation comes up often when verifying signatures on downloaded software. [7.15] You should *always* verify such signatures, since servers do get hacked and Trojan horses do get planted in commonly-used software packages. A server that contains some software (*foo.tar.gz*) and a signature (commonly *foo.tar.gz.asc* or *foo.tar.gz.sig*) should also have somewhere on it the public key used to generate the signature. If you have not previously obtained and verified this key, download it now and add it to your keyring. [7.10] If the key is signed by other keys you already trust, you're set. If not, don't trust it simply because it came from the same server as the software! If the server were compromised and software modified, a savvy attacker would also have replaced the public key and generated new, valid signatures using that key. In this case, it is wise to check the key against as many other sources as possible. For instance:

- Check the key fingerprint against copies of the key stored elsewhere. [7.9]
- Look who signed the key in question:

    $ gpg --list-sigs *keyname*

    Obtain those public keys, and verify these signatures. Try to pick well-known people or organizations.

- For both these operations, obtain the keys not only from keyservers, but also from web sites or other repositories belonging to the key owners. Use secure web sites if available (HTTPS/SSL), and verify the certificates and DNS names involved.

Try several of the above avenues together. None of them provides absolute assurance. But the more smartly selected checks you make, the more independent servers and systems an attacker would have to subvert in order to trick you—and thus the less likely it is that such an attack has actually occurred.

 This process will also merge new signatures into an existing key on your key ring, if any are available from the keyserver.

See Also

For more information on the web of trust, visit *http://webber.dewinter.com/gnupg_howto/english/GPGMiniHowto-1.html.*

7.22 Revoking a Key

Problem

You want to inform a keyserver that a particular public key (of yours) is no longer valid.

Solution

1. Create a revocation certificate:

    ```
    $ gpg --gen-revoke --output certificate.asc key_id
    ```

2. Import the certificate:

    ```
    $ gpg --import certificate.asc
    ```

3. Revoke the key at the keyserver:

    ```
    $ gpg --keyserver server_name --send-keys key_id
    ```

4. Delete the key (optional)

    ```
    $ gpg --delete-secret-and-public-key key_id
    ```

 THINK CAREFULLY BEFORE DELETING A KEY. Once you delete a key, any files that remain encrypted with this key CANNOT BE DECRYPTED. EVER.

Discussion

At times it becomes necessary to stop using a particular key. For example:

- Your private key has been lost.
- Your private key has been stolen, or you suspect it may have been.
- You have forgotten your private key passphrase.
- You replace your keys periodically (say, every two years) to enhance security, and this key has expired.

Whatever the reason, it's time to inform others to stop using the corresponding public key to communicate with you. Otherwise, if the key is lost, you might receive encrypted messages that you can no longer decrypt. Worse, if the key has been stolen or compromised, the thief can read messages encrypted for you.

To tell the world to cease using your key, distribute a revocation certificate for that key: a cryptographically secure digital object that says, "Hey, don't use this public key anymore!" Once you create the certificate, send it directly to your communication partners or to a keyserver [7.19] for general distribution.

For security reasons, the revocation certificate is digitally signed by you, or more specifically, with the private key that it revokes. This proves (cryptographically speaking) that the person who generated the certificate (you) is actually authorized to make this decision.

But wait: how can you create and sign a revocation certificate if you've lost the original private key necessary for signing it? Well, you can't.* Instead, you should create the certificate in advance, just in case you ever lose the key. As standard practice, you should create a revocation certificate immediately each time you generate a new key. [7.6]

Guard your revocation certificate as carefully as your private key. If a thief obtains it, he can publish it (anonymously) and immediately invalidate your keys, causing you a big headache.

See Also

http://www.keyserver.net/en/info.html and *http://www.keyserver.net/en/about.html*.

7.23 Maintaining Encrypted Files with Emacs

Problem

You want to edit encrypted files in place with GNU Emacs, without decrypting them to disk.

Solution

Use the Emacs package *crypt++.el*:

```
~/.emacs:
(if (load "crypt++" t)
    (progn
       (setq crypt-encryption-type 'gpg)
       (setq crypt-confirm-password t)
       (crypt-rebuild-tables)))
```

---

* And this is a good thing. Otherwise, *anybody* could create a revocation certificate for your keys.

Discussion

crypt++ provides a transparent editing mode for encrypted files. Once the package is installed and loaded, simply edit any GnuPG-encrypted file. You'll be prompted for the passphrase within Emacs, and the file will be decrypted and inserted into an Emacs buffer. When you save the file, it will be re-encrypted automatically.

See Also

Crypt++ is available from *http://freshmeat.net/projects/crypt* and *http://www.cs.umb.edu/~karl/crypt++/crypt++.el*.

7.24   Maintaining Encrypted Files with vim

Problem

You want to edit encrypted files in place with vim, without decrypting them to disk.

Solution

Add the following lines to your *~/.vimrc* file:

```
" Transparent editing of GnuPG-encrypted files
" Based on a solution by Wouter Hanegraaff
augroup encrypted
    au!

    " First make sure nothing is written to ~/.viminfo while editing
    " an encrypted file.
    autocmd BufReadPre,FileReadPre      *.gpg,*.asc set viminfo=
    " We don't want a swap file, as it writes unencrypted data to disk.
    autocmd BufReadPre,FileReadPre      *.gpg,*.asc set noswapfile
    " Switch to binary mode to read the encrypted file.
    autocmd BufReadPre,FileReadPre      *.gpg        set bin
    autocmd BufReadPre,FileReadPre      *.gpg,*.asc let ch_save = &ch|set ch=2
    autocmd BufReadPost,FileReadPost    *.gpg,*.asc
        \ '[,']!sh -c 'gpg --decrypt 2> /dev/null'
    " Switch to normal mode for editing
    autocmd BufReadPost,FileReadPost    *.gpg        set nobin
    autocmd BufReadPost,FileReadPost    *.gpg,*.asc let &ch = ch_save|unlet ch_save
    autocmd BufReadPost,FileReadPost    *.gpg,*.asc
            \ execute ":doautocmd BufReadPost " . expand("%:r")

    " Convert all text to encrypted text before writing
    autocmd BufWritePre,FileWritePre    *.gpg
            \ '[,']!sh -c 'gpg --default-recipient-self -e 2>/dev/null'
    autocmd BufWritePre,FileWritePre    *.asc
            \ '[,']!sh -c 'gpg --default-recipient-self -e -a 2>/dev/null'
    " Undo the encryption so we are back in the normal text, directly
```

```
    " after the file has been written.
    autocmd BufWritePost,FileWritePost  *.gpg,*.asc u
augroup END
```

Discussion

vim can edit GnuPG-encrypted files transparently, provided they were encrypted for your key of course! If the stanza in our recipe has been added to your *~/.vimrc* file, simply edit an encrypted file. You'll be prompted for your passphrase, and the decrypted file will be loaded into the current buffer for editing. When you save the file, it will be re-encrypted automatically.

vim will recognize encrypted file types by their suffixes, *.gpg* for binary and *.asc* for ASCII-armored. The recipe carefully disables viminfo and swap file functionality, to avoid storing any decrypted text on the disk.

The gpg commands in the recipe use public-key encryption. Tailor the command-line options to reflect your needs.

Incidentally, vim provides its own encryption mechanism, if vim was built with encryption support: you can tell by running vim --version or using the :version command within vim, and looking for +cryptv in the list of features. To use this feature when creating a new file, run vim -x. For existing files, vim will recognize encrypted ones automatically, so -x is optional.

We don't recommend vim -x, however, because it has some significant disadvantages compared to GnuPG:

- It's nonstandard: you can encrypt and decrypt these files only with vim.
- It's weaker cryptographically than GnuPG.
- It doesn't automatically disable viminfo or swap files. You can do this manually by setting the viminfo and swapfile variables, but it's easy to forget and leave decrypted data on the disk as a consequence.

See Also

Wouter Hanegraaff's original solution can be found at *http://qref.sourceforge.net/ Debian/reference/examples/vimgpg*.

7.25   Encrypting Backups

Problem

You want to create an encrypted backup.

Solution

Method 1: Pipe through gpg.

- To write a tape:

    ```
    $ tar cf - mydir | gpg -c | dd of=/dev/tape bs=10k
    ```

- To read a tape:

    ```
    $ dd if=/dev/tape bs=10k | gpg --decrypt | tar xf -
    ```

- To write an encrypted backup of directory *mydir* onto a CD-ROM:

    ```
    #!/bin/sh
    mkdir destdir
    tar cf - mydir | gpg -c > destdir/myfile.tar.gpg
    mkisofs -R -l destdir | cdrecord speed=${SPEED} dev=${SCSIDEVICE} -
    ```

    where SPEED and SCSIDEVICE are specific to your system; see cdrecord(1).

Method 2: Encrypt files separately.

1. Make a new directory containing links to your original files:

    ```
    $ cp -lr mydir newdir
    ```

2. In the new directory, encrypt each file, and remove the links to the unencrypted files:

    ```
    $ find newdir -type f -exec gpg -e '{}' \; -exec rm '{}' \;
    ```

3. Back up the new directory with the encrypted data:

    ```
    $ tar c newdir
    ```

Discussion

Method 1 produces a backup that may be considered fragile: one big encrypted file. If part of the backup gets corrupted, you might be unable to decrypt any of it.

Method 2 avoids this problem. The cp -l option creates hard links, which can only be used within a single filesystem. If you want the encrypted files on a separate filesystem, use symbolic links instead:

```
$ cp -sr /full/path/to/mydir newdir
$ find newdir -type l -exec gpg -e '{}' \; -exec rm '{}' \;
```

Note that a full, absolute pathname must be used for the original directory in this case.

gpg does not preserve the owner, group, permissions, or modification times of the files. To retain this information in your backups, copy the attributes from the original files to the encrypted files, before the links to the original files are deleted:

```
# find newdir -type f -exec gpg -e '{}' \; \
                -exec chown --reference='{}' '{}.gpg' \;
                -exec chmod --reference='{}' '{}.gpg' \;
                -exec touch --reference='{}' '{}.gpg' \;
                -exec rm '{}' \;
```

Method 2 and the CD-ROM variant of method 1 use disk space (at least temporarily) for the encrypted files.

See Also

gpg(1), tar(1), find(1), cdrecord(1).

7.26   Using PGP Keys with GnuPG

Problem

You want to use PGP keys in GnuPG operations.

Solution

Using PGP, export your key to a file called *pgpkey.asc*. For example, using freeware PGP 6.5.8, you export a public key with:

```
$ pgp -kxa my_key pgpkey.asc
```

or a private key with:

```
$ pgp -kxa my_key pgpkey.asc my_secret_keyring.skr
```

Then import the key into your GnuPG keyring. For public keys:

```
$ gpg --import pgpkey.asc
```

For private keys:

```
$ gpg --import --allow-secret-key-import pgpkey.asc
```

Now you can use the key in normal GnuPG operations.

Discussion

Keys are really abstract mathematical objects; this recipe simply converts a key from one representation to another so that GnuPG can use it. It's similar to converting an SSH key between the SSH2 and OpenSSH formats. [6.6]

Once you've imported a PGP key into your GPG keyring, this doesn't mean you can interoperate with PGP in all ways using this key. Many versions of PGP have appeared over the years, before and after the emergence of the OpenPGP standard, and GPG does not interoperate with every one. Suppose you convert your friend's old PGP public key for use with GPG via this recipe. Now you can encrypt a message to her, using her public key... but can she read it? Only if her version of PGP is capable of reading and decrypting GPG messages, and not all can. Conversely, you may not be able to read old messages encrypted with the PGP software—for example, some versions of PGP use the IDEA cipher for data encryption, which GPG does not use because it is patented. Make sure you share a few test messages with your friend before encrypting something truly important for her.

See Also

gpg(1), pgp(1).

## CHAPTER 8

Protecting Email

8.0   Introduction

Email is a terrific medium for communication, but it's neither private nor secure. For example, did you know that:

- Each message you send may pass through many other machines en route to its intended recipient?
- Even on the recipient's computer, other users (particularly superusers) can conceivably read your messages as they sit on disk?
- Messages traveling over a traditional POP or IMAP connection can be captured and read in transit by third parties?

In this chapter, we provide recipes to secure different segments of the email trail:

From sender to recipient
Secure your email messages, using encryption and signing

Between mail client and mail server
Protect your mail session, using secure IMAP, secure POP, or tunneling

At the mail server
Avoid exposing a public mail server, using `fetchmail` or SMTP authentication

We assume that you have already created a GnuPG key pair (private and public) on your GnuPG keyring, a prerequisite for many recipes in this chapter. [7.6]

8.1   Encrypted Mail with Emacs

Problem

You use an Emacs mailer (`vm`, `rmail`, etc.) and want to send and receive encrypted email messages.

Solution

Use *mailcrypt.el* with GnuPG:

```
~/.emacs:
(load-library "mailcrypt")
(mc-setversion "gpg")
```

Then open a mail buffer, and use any Mailcrypt functions or variables as desired:

mc-encrypt
> Encrypt the mail message in the current buffer

mc-decrypt
> Decrypt the mail message in the current buffer

mc-sign
> Sign the mail message in the current buffer

mc-verify
> Verify the signature of the mail message in the current buffer

mc-insert-public-key
> Insert your public key, in ASCII format, into the current buffer

...and many more.

Discussion

Mailcrypt is an Emacs package for encrypting, decrypting, and cryptographically signing email messages. Once you have installed *mailcrypt.el* in your Emacs load path, e.g., by installing it in */usr/share/emacs/site-lisp,* and loaded and configured it in your *~/.emacs* file:

```
(load-library "mailcrypt")
(mc-setversion "gpg")
```

compose a mail message in your favorite Emacs-based mailer. When done writing the message, invoke:

```
M-x mc-encrypt
```

(or select the Encrypt function from the Mailcrypt menu). You'll be prompted for the recipient, whose public key must be on your GnuPG keyring:

```
Recipients: jones@example.com
```

and then asked whether you want to sign the message, which is an optional step and requires your GnuPG passphrase.

```
Sign the message? (y or n)
```

Then *voilà*, your message becomes GnuPG-encrypted for that recipient:

```
-----BEGIN PGP MESSAGE-----
Version: GnuPG v1.0.6 (GNU/Linux)
```

```
Comment: Processed by Mailcrypt 3.5.8 and Gnu Privacy Guard
hQEOAxpFbNGB4CNMEAP/SeAEOPP6XW+uMrkHZ5b2kuYPE5BLO6brHNL2Dae6uIjK
sMBhvKGcS3THpCcXzjCRRAJLsquUaazakXdLveyTRPMa9J7GhRUAJvd8n7ZZ8iRn
...
-----END PGP MESSAGE-----
```

Finally, send the message normally.

If you receive an encrypted message, and you already have the sender's key (indexed by her email address) on your GnuPG public keyring, simply invoke:

```
M-x mc-decrypt
```

for the buffer containing the message. If you receive a signed message, check the signature by invoking: [7.15]

```
M-x mc-verify
```

Mailcrypt can be finicky about the buffer contents. If all else fails, save the encrypted message to a file and decrypt it with gpg manually. [7.5]

By default, Mailcrypt will remember your GnuPG passphrase once entered—but only for the duration of the current Emacs session. You can run mc-deactivate-passwd to force Mailcrypt to erase your passphrase from its memory immediately.

The load-library code given earlier will cause your startup file to abort if Emacs cannot find Mailcrypt. To have it load conditionally, use this instead:

```
(if (load-library "mailcrypt") t)
    (mc-setversion "gpg"))
```

See Also

The official web site for Mailcrypt is *http://mailcrypt.sourceforge.net*. To list all Mailcrypt functions and variables in Emacs, try:

```
M-x apropos mc-
```

8.2   Encrypted Mail with vim

Problem

You want to compose an encrypted mail message, and your mail editor is vim.

Solution

~/.vimrc:
```
map ^E :1,$!gpg --armor --encrypt 2>/dev/null^M^L
map ^G :1,$!gpg --armor --encrypt --sign 2>/dev/null^M^L
map ^Y :1,$!gpg --clearsign 2>/dev/null^M^L
```

The ^X symbols are actual control characters inserted into the file, not a caret followed by a letter. In vim, this is accomplished by pressing ctrl-V followed by the desired key, for example, ctrl-V ctrl-E to insert a ctrl-E.

Discussion

These macros filter the entire edit buffer (1,$) through gpg. The first macro merely encrypts the buffer, the second encrypts and signs, and the third only signs. You'll be prompted for your passphrase for any signing.

See Also

gpg(1), vim(1). Credit goes to Rick van Rein for this tip: *http://rick.vanrein.org/linux/tricks/elmPGP.html.*

8.3   Encrypted Mail with Pine

Problem

You want to send and receive encrypted email conveniently with the Pine mailer.

Solution

Use PinePGP.

Description

Before using PinePGP, make sure you have previously used Pine on your local computer, so you have a *~/.pinerc* configuration file. Then download PinePGP from *http://www.megaloman.com/~hany/software/pinepgp*, build, and install it. (As root if you prefer.)

When installing PinePGP, you must make a choice: Should messages you encrypt be decryptable only by their intended recipients, or by yourself as well? If the former, which is the default behavior, run:

```
$ pinegpg-install
```

Alternatively, if you want to change this default, making your messages decryptable by you (with your public key) in addition to the recipient, instead invoke:

```
$ pinegpg-install your@email.address.com
```

where *your@email.address.com* is the email address associated with your intended GnuPG key. [7.7]

Now let's send an encrypted message to our friend *buddy@example.com*, whose GnuPG public key is already on our keyring. Run pine and compose a message. Press ctrl-X to send the message normally, and you will receive this prompt, asking if you want the message filtered before sending:

```
Send message (unfiltered)?
```

Press ctrl-N repeatedly to display the filters, which will appear like this:

```
Send message (filtered thru "gpg-sign")?
Send message (filtered thru "gpg-encrypt")?
Send message (filtered thru "gpg-sign+encrypt")?
```

Select the filter you want and press Return to send the message. If you're signing the message, you'll be prompted for your key passphrase first.

That's sending, but what about receiving? When an encrypted message arrives in your mailbox and you attempt to view it, pine will automatically prompt for your passphrase. If entered correctly, the message will be displayed. The beginning and end of the decrypted text will be surrounded by [PinePGP] markers:

```
Date: Tue, 22 Oct 2002 21:08:32 -0400 (EDT)
From: Some Buddy <buddy@example.com>
To: You <smith@example.com>
Subject: Test message

--[PinePGP]--------------------------------------------------[begin]--
Hey, d0od, this encryption stuff rocks!
--[PinePGP]-----------------------------------------------------------
gpg: encrypted with 1024-bit ELG-E key, ID 61E9334C, created 2001-02-21
      "Some W. Buddy (The d0od) <buddy@example.com>"
--[PinePGP]---------------------------------------------------[end]--
```

How does this all work? PinePGP filters your sent and displayed email via the sending-filters and display-filters variables in *~/.pinerc*.

See Also

pine(1). The Pine home page is *http://www.washington.edu/pine*. PinePGP is found at *http://www.megaloman.com/~hany/software/pinepgp*.

8.4   Encrypted Mail with Mozilla

Problem

You want to send and receive encrypted email conveniently with Mozilla's Mail & Newsgroups application.

Solution

Use Enigmail from *enigmail.mozdev.org* for GnuPG encryption support. S/MIME is also supported natively within Mozilla.

Discussion

Once you have downloaded and installed Enigmail, compose a message normally, addressing it to someone whose public key is in your GnuPG keyring. Instead of clicking the Send button, notice that your message window has a new menu, Enigmail. From this menu, you choose to encrypt or sign your message, or both, and it is immediately sent.

To decrypt a message you receive, simply view it and Mozilla will prompt for your GnuPG passphrase.

Your Mail & Newsgroups window also has a new Enigmail menu. Explore both menus where you'll find numerous useful options and utilities: generating new GnuPG keys, setting default behavior, viewing the actual gpg commands invoked, and more.

See Also

The Enigmail home page is *http://enigmail.mozdev.org*, and Mozilla's is *http://www.mozilla.org*.

8.5   Encrypted Mail with Evolution

Problem

You want to send and receive encrypted email conveniently with the Evolution mailer from Ximian.

Solution

During setup:

1. Under *Inbox/Tools/Mail Settings/Other*, make sure "PGP binary path" refers to your encryption program, usually */usr/bin/gpg*.

2. In the Evolution Account Editor, set your Security preferences, including your default GnuPG key, whether you want all messages signed by default, etc.

In use:

1. Compose an email message to someone whose key is in your GnuPG public keyring. You must trust their public key [7.9] or encryption will fail.

---

2. From the Security menu, select PGP Sign, PGP Encrypt, or both. (Or do nothing, and the defaults you set in the Evolution Account Editor will be used.)

3. Click Send. Your message will be sent encrypted or signed as you requested. (You'll be prompted for your passphrase before signing.)

Discussion

Evolution supports PGP, GnuPG, and S/MIME out of the box.

See Also

The home page for Ximian, makers of Evolution, is *http://www.ximian.com*.

8.6   Encrypted Mail with mutt

Problem

You want to send and receive encrypted email conveniently with the mutt mailer.

Solution

mutt comes with configuration files *pgp2.rc*, *pgp5.rc*, and *gpg.rc*, ready to use with pgp2, pgp5, and gpg, respectively. Include one of these files inside your *~/.muttrc*. (For GnuPG support, obviously include *gpg.rc*.)

Discussion

Compose a message normally. Notice the headers include a setting called PGP:

```
From: Daniel Barrett <dbarrett@oreilly.com>
To: Shawn Smith <smith@example.com>
Cc:
Bcc:
Subject: Test message
Reply-To:
Fcc:
PGP: Clear
```

By default, encryption is disabled (Clear). To change this, type **p** to display the PGP options, and choose to encrypt, sign, or both. When you send the message (press **y**), you'll be presented with the available private keys for encrypting or signing. Select one and the message will be sent.

To decrypt a message you receive, simply view it. mutt will prompt for your GnuPG passphrase and display the decrypted message.

See Also

mutt(1), and Mutt's supplied documentation in *usr/share/doc/mutt**, in particular the file *PGP-Notes.txt*. The home page for Mutt is *http://www.mutt.org*.

8.7 Encrypted Mail with elm

Problem

You want to send and receive encrypted email conveniently with the `elm` mailer.

Solution

While viewing an encrypted message, type:

```
| gpg --decrypt | less
```

to display the decrypted text page by page. To send an encrypted message, encrypt it in your text editor. [8.1][8.2]

Discussion

We take advantage of `elm`'s pipe feature, which sends the body of a mail message to another Linux command, in this case gpg. We further pipe it to a pager (we chose `less`) for convenient display. For encryption, we handle it in the text editor invoked by `elm` to compose messages. [8.1][8.2]

There are alternatives. A patched version of `elm`, known as `ELMME+`, supports GnuPG directly. (The author, Michael Elkins, went on to create `mutt`, [8.6] which also supports GnuPG.)

You might also try the pair of scripts `morepgp` (for decrypting and reading) and `mailpgp` (for encrypting and sending), available at *http://www.math.fu-berlin.de/~guckes/elm/scripts/elm.pgp.scripts.html*. These scripts are for PGP, but modification for GnuPG should not be difficult.

See Also

The elm home page is *http://www.instinct.org/elm*. Read more about the scripts `morepgp` and `mailpgp` at *http://www.math.fu-berlin.de/~guckes/elm/scripts/elm.pgp.scripts.html* and *http://www.math.fu-berlin.de/~guckes/elm/elm.index.html#security*.

8.8   Encrypted Mail with MH

Problem

You want to send and receive encrypted email conveniently with the MH mail handler.

Solution

To view an encrypted message:

```
show | gpg --decrypt | less
```

To encrypt and send a message, use the encryption features of your text editor, such as emacs [8.1] or vim [8.2]. Care must be taken so that only the message body, not the header, gets encrypted.

Discussion

MH (or more likely found on Linux, nmh) differs from most mailers in that each mail-handling command is invoked from the shell prompt and reads/writes standard input/output. Therefore, to decrypt a message normally displayed by the show command, pipe show through gpg, then optionally through a pager such as less.

See Also

Further instructions for integrating MH and GnuPG (and PGP) are at *http://www.tac.nyc.ny.us/mail/mh* and *http://www.faqs.org/faqs/mail/mh-faq/part1/section-68.html*.

8.9   Running a POP/IMAP Mail Server with SSL

Problem

You want to allow secure, remote mail access that protects passwords and prevents session eavesdropping or tampering.

Solution

Use imapd with SSL. Out of the box, imapd can negotiate SSL protection on mail sessions via the STARTTLS (IMAP) and STLS (POP) mechanisms. (See the sidebar "SSL for Securing Mail.") Simply set your client to require SSL on the same port as the normal protocol (143 for IMAP, 110 for POP), and verify that it works. If so, you're done.

SSL for Securing Mail

Most major mail clients (pine, mutt, etc.) support *secure* POP and IMAP using the *Secure Sockets Layer* (SSL) protocol (also known by its later, IETF-standards name, *Transport Layer Security* or TLS). Most commercial mail servers and ISPs, however, do not support SSL, which is highly annoying. But if you're lucky enough to find a mail server that does support it, or if you run your own server [8.9], here's a brief introduction to how it works.

A mail server may support SSL in two ways, to protect your session against eavesdroppers:

STARTTLS
> The mail server listens on the *normal service port* for unsecured connections, such as 110 for POP3 or 143 for IMAP, and permits a client to "turn on" SSL *after the fact*. The IMAP command for this is STARTTLS; the POP command, STLS; we will refer to this approach generically as STARTTLS.

SSL-port
> The mail server listens on a *separate port*, such as 995 for POP3 or 993 for IMAP, and requires that SSL be negotiated on that port *before* speaking to the mail protocol.

STARTTLS is the more modern, preferred method (see RFC 2595 for reasoning), but both are common. Our recipes suggest that you try STARTTLS first, and if it's unsupported, fall back to SSL-port.

The most critical thing to protect in email sessions is, of course, your mail server password. The *strong session protection* provided by SSL is one approach, which protects not only the password but also all other data in the session. Another approach is *strong authentication*, which focuses on protecting the password (or other credential), as found in Kerberos [4.16] for example.[a] These two classes of protection are orthogonal: they can be used separately or together, as shown in Table 8-1.

Whatever happens, you don't want your password flying unprotected over the network, where hordes of dsniff-wielding script kiddies can snarf it up while barely lifting a finger. [9.19] In most cases, protecting the content of the email over POP or IMAP is less critical, since it has already traversed the public network as plain text before delivery. (If this concerns you, encrypt your mail messages.)

Finally, as with any use of SSL, check your certificates; otherwise server authentication is meaningless. [4.4]

---

[a] SSL can also perform user authentication, but we do not address it. Our recipes employ SSL to protect an interior protocol that performs its own user authentication.

Otherwise, if your client insists on using alternate ports, it is probably using the older convention of connecting to those ports with SSL first. In that case, use the following recipe:

1. Enable the IMAP daemon within xinetd:

```
/etc/xinetd.d/imaps:
service imaps
{
    ...
    disabled = no
}
```

or within inetd (add or uncomment the line below):

```
/etc/inetd.conf:
imaps   stream  tcp     nowait  root    /usr/sbin/tcpd  imapd
```

whichever your system supports.

2. Signal xinetd or inetd, whichever the case may be, to re-read its configuration and therefore begin accepting imapd connections. [3.3][3.4]

3. Test the SSL connection locally on the mail server, port 993: [8.10]

```
$ openssl s_client -quiet -connect localhost:993
```

(Type **0 LOGOUT** to end the test.)

Alternatively, use POP with SSL, following an analogous procedure:

1. Enable the POP daemon within xinetd:

```
/etc/xinetd.d/pop3s:
service pop3s
{
    ...
    disabled = no
}
```

or inetd (add or uncomment the line below):

```
/etc/inetd.conf:
pop3s   stream  tcp     nowait  root    /usr/sbin/tcpd  ipop3d
```

whichever your system supports.

2. Signal xinetd or inetd, whichever the case may be, to reread its configuration and therefore begin accepting ipop3d connections. [3.3][3.4]

3. Test the SSL connection locally on the mail server, port 995: [8.10]

```
$ openssl s_client -quiet -connect localhost:995
```

(Type **QUIT** to end the test.)

Table 8-1. Authentication and session protection are independent

	Strong session protection	Weak session protection
Strong authentication	Protects all	Protects password, but session is still vulnerable to eavesdropping, corruption, hijacking, server spoofing, or man-in-the-middle attack
Weak authentication	Protects all	No protection: avoid this combination

Discussion

Many mail clients can run POP or IMAP over SSL to protect email sessions from eavesdropping or attack. [8.11][8.12][8.13] In particular they protect your mail server passwords, which may otherwise be transmitted over the network unencrypted. Red Hat 8.0 and SuSE 8.0 come preconfigured with SSL support in the POP/IMAP server, */usr/sbin/imapd*.

First, enable imapd within xinetd or inetd as shown, then signal the server to re-read its configuration. Examine */var/log/messages* to verify that the daemon reconfigured correctly, and then test the connection using the openssl command. [8.10] A successful connection will look like this:

```
$ openssl s_client -quiet -connect localhost:993
depth=0 /C=--/ST=SomeState/L=SomeCity/...
verify error:num=18:self signed certificate
verify return:1
depth=0 /C=--/ST=SomeState/L=SomeCity/...
verify return:1
* OK [CAPABILITY IMAP4REV1 LOGIN-REFERRALS AUTH=PLAIN AUTH=LOGIN] localhost ...
```

The first few lines indicate a problem verifying the server's SSL certificate, discussed later. The last line is the initial IMAP protocol statement from the server. Type **0 LOGOUT** or just Ctrl-C to disconnect from the server.

Next, test the connection from your mail client, following its documentation for connecting to a mail server over SSL. This is usually an option when specifying the mail server, or sometimes in a separate configuration section or GUI panel for "advanced" settings, labeled "secure connection" or "Use SSL." Use any existing user account on the server for authentication; by default, imapd uses the same PAM-based password authentication scheme as most other services like Telnet and SSH. (We discuss PAM in Chapter 4.)

Examine */var/log/debug* for information on your test; a successful connection would produce entries like this:

```
Mar  3 00:28:38 server xinetd[844]: START: imaps pid=2061 from=10.1.1.5
Mar  3 00:28:38 server imapd[2061]: imaps SSL service init from 10.1.1.5
Mar  3 00:28:43 server imapd[2061]: Login user=res host=client [10.1.1.5]
Mar  3 00:28:54 server imapd[2061]: Logout user=res host=client [10.1.1.5]
Mar  3 00:28:54 server xinetd[844]: EXIT: imaps pid=2061 duration=16(sec)
```

If you don't see the expected entries, be sure that the system logger is configured to send debug priority messages to this file. [9.27]

You might see warning messages that imapd is unable to verify the server's SSL certificate; for testing purposes you may ignore these, but for production systems beware! Some Linux systems have dummy keypairs and corresponding certificates installed for use by imapd and pop3d; for instance, Red Hat 8.0 has */usr/share/ssl/certs/imapd.pem* and */usr/share/ssl/certs/ipop3d.pem*, respectively. This setup is fine for testing, but do *not* use these certificates for a production system. These keys are distributed with every Red Hat system: they are public knowledge. If you deploy a service using default, dummy keys, you are vulnerable to a man-in-the-middle (MITM) attack, in which the attacker impersonates your system using the well-known dummy private keys. Furthermore, the name in the certificate does not match your server's hostname, and the certificate is not issued by a recognized Certifying Authority; both of these conditions will be flagged as warnings by your mail client. [4.4]

To preserve the server authentication and MITM resistance features of SSL, generate a new key for your mail server, and obtain an appropriate certificate binding the key to your server's name. [4.7][4.8]

You can control how imapd performs password validation by means of PAM. The configuration file */etc/pam.d/imap* directs imapd to use general system authentication, so it will be controlled by that setting, either through authconfig or by direct customization of */etc/pam.d/imap* yourself.

Note also that the "common name" field of the SSL server's certificate must match the name you configure clients with, or they will complain during certificate validation. Even if the two names are aliases for one another in DNS, they must match in this usage. [4.7]

Our described configuration absolutely requires SSL for all IMAP connections. However, you may also want to permit unsecured sessions from *localhost* only, if:

- You also provide mail access on the same server via a Web-based package such as SquirrelMail or IMP. Such packages often require an unsecured back-end connection to the mail server. Perhaps you could hack them to use SSL, but there's little point if they are on the same machine.

- You sometimes access your mail by port-forwarding when logged into the mail server via SSH. [6.14][8.15]

You can permit unsecured IMAP connections by editing */etc/xinetd.d/imap* (note "imap" and not "imaps") to read:

```
/etc/xinetd.d/imap:
service imap
{
    ...
    disabled = no
    bind = localhost
}
```

This accepts unsecured IMAP connections to port 143, but *only* from the same host.

See Also

imapd(8C), ipopd(8C). SquirrelMail is found at *http://www.squirrelmail.org*, and IMP at *http://www.horde.org/imp*.

8.10 Testing an SSL Mail Connection

Problem

You want to verify an SSL connection to a secure POP or IMAP server.

Solution

For secure POP:

```
$ openssl s_client -quiet -connect server:995
[messages about server certificate validation]
+OK POP3 server.net v2001.78rh server ready
```

Type **QUIT** to exit.

For secure **IMAP**:

```
$ openssl s_client -quiet -connect server:993
[messages about server certificate validation]
* OK [CAPABILITY ...] server.net IMAP4rev1 2001.315rh at Mon, 3 Mar 2003 20:01:43 -
0500 (EST)
```

Type **0 LOGOUT** to exit.

Discussion

If you omit the -quiet switch, openssl will print specifics about the SSL protocol negotiation, including the server's X.509 public-key certificate.

The openssl command can verify the server certificate only if that certificate, or one in its issuer chain, is listed in the system trusted certificate cache. [4.4]

See Also

openssl(1).

8.11 Securing POP/IMAP with SSL and Pine

Problem

You want to secure your POP or IMAP email session. Your mail client is pine, and your mail server supports SSL.

Solution

Test whether you can use STARTTLS, as explained in the sidebar "SSL for Securing Mail:"

```
$ pine -inbox-path='{mail.server.net/user=fred/protocol}'
```

replacing *protocol* with either pop or imap as desired. One of three outcomes will occur:

1. You get no connection. In this case, you cannot use STARTTLS; move on and try SSL-port, below.

2. You get a connection, but the login prompt includes the word INSECURE:

   ```
   HOST: mail.server.net (INSECURE)  ENTER LOGIN NAME [fred] :
   ```

   In this case, you again cannot use STARTTLS; move on and try SSL-port, below.

3. You get a connection and the login prompt does *not* say INSECURE. In this case, congratulations, you have a secure mail connection. You are done.

If you could not use STARTTLS as shown, try the SSL-port method:

```
$ pine -inbox-path='{mail.server.net/user=fred/protocol/ssl}'
```

again replacing *protocol* with either pop or imap as appropriate.

To ensure you have a secure connection (i.e., to forbid pine to engage in weak authentication, unless it's over a secure connection), add /secure to your inbox-path. For example:

```
$ pine -inbox-path='{mail.server.net/user=fred/imap/secure}'
```

If none of this works, your ISP does not appear to support IMAP over SSL in any form; try SSH instead. [8.16]

Discussion

You might be able to simplify the mailbox specifications; for instance:

```
{mail.server.net/user=fred/imap}
```

could be simply {mail} instead: IMAP is the default, the usernames on both sides are assumed to be the same if unspecified, and your DNS search path may allow using the short hostname.

See Also

pine(1).

SSL Connection Problems: Server-Side Debugging

If you have access to the system logs on the mail server, you can examine them to debug SSL connection problems, or just to verify what's happening. In */var/log/maillog*, successful SSL-port–style connections look like this:

```
Mar  7 16:26:13 mail imapd[20091]: imaps SSL service init from 209.225.172.154
Mar  7 16:24:17 mail ipop3d[20079]: pop3s SSL service init from 209.225.172.154
```

as opposed to these, indicating no initial use of SSL:

```
Mar  7 16:26:44 mail imapd[20099]: imap service init from 209.225.172.154
Mar  7 16:15:47 mail ipop3d[20018]: pop3 service init from 209.225.172.154
```

Note, however, that you cannot distinguish the success of STARTTLS-style security this way.

Another way of verifying the secure operation is to watch the mail protocol traffic directly using tcpdump [9.16] or Ethereal [9.17]. Ethereal is especially good, as it understands all the protocols involved here and will show exactly what's happening in a reasonably obvious fashion.

8.12   Securing POP/IMAP with SSL and mutt

Problem

You want to secure your POP or IMAP email session. Your mail client is mutt, and your mail server supports SSL.

Solution

If you want a POP connection, use SSL-port, since mutt does not support START-TLS over POP. (See the sidebar "SSL for Securing Mail" for definitions.)

```
$ MAIL=pops://fred@mail.server.net/   mutt
```

For an IMAP connection, test whether you can use STARTTLS:

```
$ MAIL=imap://fred@mail.server.net/   mutt
```

If this works, mutt will flash a message about setting up a "TLS/SSL" connection, confirming your success. If not, then try SSL-port:

```
$ MAIL=imaps://fred@mail.server.net/   mutt
```

If none of this works, your ISP does not appear to support IMAP over SSL in any form; try SSH instead. [8.15]

Discussion

Many SSL-related configuration variables in mutt affect its behavior; we are assuming the defaults here.

Mutt uses the systemwide trusted certificate list in */usr/share/ssl/cert.pem*, which contains certificates from widely recognized Certifying Authorities, such as Verisign, Equifax, and Thawte. If this file does not contain a certificate chain sufficient to validate your mail server's SSL certificate, mutt will complain about the certificate. It will then prompt you to accept or reject the connection. You can alter this behavior by setting:

```
~/.muttrc:
set certificate_file=~/.mutt/certificates
```

Now mutt will further offer to accept the connection either "once" or "always." If you choose "always," mutt will store the certificate in *~/.mutt/certificates* and accept it automatically from then on. Be cautious before doing this, however: it allows a man-in-the-middle attack on the first connection. A far better solution is to add the appropriate, trusted issuer certificates to *cert.pem*.

See Also

mutt(1).

8.13   Securing POP/IMAP with SSL and Evolution

Problem

You want to read mail on a POP or IMAP mail server securely, using Evolution. The mail server supports SSL.

Solution

In the Evolution menu *Tools/Mail Settings/Edit/Receiving Mail*, check "Use secure connection (SSL)".

The default ports for IMAP and POP over SSL are 993 and 995, respectively. If your server uses a non-standard port, specify it.

If you're having problems establishing the connection, you can test it. [8.10]

Discussion

Evolution on Red Hat 8.0 does not appear to check any pre-installed trusted certificates automatically. As it encounters certificates, it will store them in *~/evolution/cert7.db*. This file is not ASCII text, so adding certificates is not easy; you'll need the program certutil.

See Also

certutil is found at *http://www.mozilla.org/projects/security/pki/nss/tools/certutil.html*. Additional discussion is found at *http://lists.ximian.com/archives/public/evolution/2001-November/014351.html*.

8.14   Securing POP/IMAP with stunnel and SSL

Problem

You want to read mail on a POP or IMAP mail server securely. Your mail client supports SSL, but the mail server does not.

Solution

Use stunnel, installed on the mail server machine. Suppose your client host is *myclient*, the mail server host is *mailhost*, and the mail server listens on standard port numbers (110 for POP, 143 for IMAP).

1. Generate a self-signed X.509 certificate *foo.crt*, with private key in *foo.key*. [4.8]

2. Place the certificate and key into a single file:

   ```
   $ cat foo.crt foo.key > foo.pem
   $ chmod 600 foo.pem
   ```

3. Choose an arbitrary, unused TCP port number on *mailhost*, such as 12345.

4. Run this stunnel process on *mailhost* for a POP server, supplying the certificate's private-key passphrase when prompted:

   ```
   mailhost$ /usr/sbin/stunnel -p foo.pem -d 12345 -r localhost:110 -P none -f
   2003.03.27 15:07:08 LOG5[621:8192]: Using 'localhost.110' as tcpwrapper service
   name
   Enter PEM pass phrase: ********
   2003.03.27 15:07:10 LOG5[621:8192]: stunnel 3.22 on i386-redhat-linux-gnu
   PTHREAD+LIBWRAP with OpenSSL 0.9.6b [engine] 9 Jul 2001
   2003.03.27 15:07:10 LOG5[621:8192]: FD_SETSIZE=1024, file ulimit=1024->500
   clients allowed
   ```

   For an IMAP server, use port 143 instead of 110.

5. Add *foo.crt* to the client's list of trusted certificates, in whatever way is appropriate for the client software and OS. You may need to convert the certificate format from PEM to DER: [4.10]

   ```
   $ openssl x509 -in foo.crt -out foo.der -outform der
   ```

6. Configure your mail client on myclient to connect to port 12345 of mailhost using SSL.

Discussion

This recipe assumes you are not a system administrator on *mailhost*, and need to get this working just for yourself. If you have root privileges, just configure your mail server to support SSL directly.

We create two secure connections to *mailhost*'s port 12345. The stunnel command connects this arbitrary port to the mail server, all locally on *mailhost*. Then the mail client crosses the network via SSL to connect to port 12345. These two segments together form a complete, secure connection between mail client and mail server.

If you remove the -f option, stunnel will fork into the background and log messages to syslog, instead of remaining on the terminal and printing status messages to stderr.

See Also

The directory */usr/share/doc/stunnel-* contains stunnel documentation. The stunnel home page is *http://www.stunnel.org*.

8.15 Securing POP/IMAP with SSH

Problem

You want to read mail on a POP or IMAP mail server securely. The mail server machine runs an SSH daemon.

Solution

Use SSH port forwarding. [6.14]

1. Choose an arbitrary, unused TCP port number on your client machine, such as 12345.

2. Assuming your client is *myclient* and your mail server is *mailhost*, open a tunnel to its POP server (TCP port 110):

   ```
   myclient$ ssh -f -N -L 12345:localhost:110 mailhost
   ```

   or IMAP server (port 143):

   ```
   myclient$ ssh -f -N -L 12345:localhost:143 mailhost
   ```

   or whatever other port your mail server listens on.

3. Configure your mail client to connect to the mail server on port 12345 of *localhost*, instead of the POP or IMAP port on *mailhost*.

Discussion

As we discussed in our recipe on general port forwarding [6.14], ssh -L opens a secure connection from the SSH client to the SSH server, tunneling the data from TCP-based protocol (in this case POP or IMAP) across the connection. We add -N so ssh keeps the tunnel open without requiring a remote command to do so.

Be aware that our recipe uses *localhost* in two subtly different ways. When we specify the tunnel:

```
12345:localhost:143
```

the name "localhost" is interpreted on the SSH server side. But when your mail client connects to *localhost*, the name is interpreted on the SSH client side. This is normally the behavior you want. However, if the server machine is not listening on the loopback address for some reason, you may need to specify the server name explicitly instead:

```
12345:mailhost:143
```

In addition, if the server machine is multihomed (has multiple real network interfaces), the situation may be more complicated. Find out which socket the mail server is listening on by asking your systems staff, or by looking yourself: [9.14]

```
mailhost$ netstat --inet --listening
```

If your mail client and SSH client are on different hosts, consider adding the -g option of ssh to permit connections to the forwarded port from other hosts. Be careful, however, as this option allows anyone with connectivity to the client machine to use your tunnel.

If your SSH server and mail server are on different hosts, say *sshhost* and *mailhost*, then use this tunnel instead:

```
myclient$ ssh -f -N -L 12345:mailhost:143 sshhost
```

sshhost could be an SSH login gateway for a corporate network, while *mailhost* is an internal mail server on which you have a mailbox but no SSH login. *sshhost* must have connectivity to *mailhost*, and your client machine to *sshhost*, but your client machine cannot reach *mailhost* directly (that's the point of the gateway).

See Also

ssh(1) and sshd(8) discuss port forwarding and its configuration keywords briefly. For more depth, try Chapter 9 of our previous book, *SSH, The Secure Shell: The Definitive Guide* (O'Reilly), which goes into great detail on the subject.

8.16 Securing POP/IMAP with SSH and Pine

Problem

You want to read mail on a POP or IMAP mail server securely using Pine, with automatic authentication. The mail server machine runs an SSH daemon.

Solution

Use Pine's built-in SSH subprocess feature, together with SSH public-key authentication and ssh-agent.

1. Set up SSH public-key authentication with the mail server machine. [6.4]

2. Set up the SSH agent. [6.9]

3. Set up the SSH authentication in your ~/.pinerc file:

   ```
   inbox-path={mailserver/imap/user=username}inbox
   ssh-path=/usr/bin/ssh
   ```

4. Simply run pine, and it should automatically open your remote mailbox without prompting for a password or any other authentication credentials.

Discussion

Suppose your mail server is *mail.server.net*, and your account there is joe. First, arrange for public-key authentication to your login account on the server [6.4] using ssh-agent. [6.9] Verify that this works smoothly, e.g., you have all the necessary user and host keys in place, so that you can execute a command like this:

```
$ ssh -l joe mail.server.net echo FOO
FOO
```

If you see any password or passphrase prompts, doublecheck your public key and ssh-agent setup. If you are prompted to accept the mail server's SSH host key, get this out of the way as well. The preceding ssh command must succeed uninterrupted for Pine/SSH integration to work.

Next, log into the mail server machine and locate the mail server program.* Pine assumes its location is */etc/rimapd*. If it's not there, other likely locations are:

/usr/sbin/imapd
/usr/local/sbin/imapd

---

* We will assume here that it's an IMAP server. For a POP server, simply substitute "POP" for "IMAP"—and "pop" for "imap"—in the subsequent discussion.

Test the IMAP server by running it; you should see something similar to this:

```
$ /usr/sbin/imapd
* PREAUTH [CAPABILITY IMAP4REV1 IDLE NAMESPACE]
Pre-authenticated user joe client.bar.org ...
```

To stop the program, type:

```
0 logout
```

or ctrl-D, or ctrl-C.

Now, edit your ~/.*pinerc* file and make the following setting:

```
inbox-path={mail.server.net/imap/user=joe}inbox
ssh-path=/usr/bin/ssh
```

(or whatever the path to your SSH client is; run `which ssh` on your client machine if you're not sure).

If your server program was not in the default location (*/etc/rimapd*), point to it with the `ssh-command` setting:

```
ssh-command="%s %s -l %s exec /usr/sbin/%sd"
```

The final argument, `/usr/sbin/%sd`, must expand to the path to the IMAP daemon when the final "%s" expands to "imap". (So in this case your path is */usr/sbin/imapd*.)

Note that you may need to find the existing settings in ~/.*pinerc* and change them, rather than add new ones. Also make sure the `ssh-timeout` parameter has not been set to 0, which disables Pine's use of SSH.

Now you're all set; simply run Pine:

```
$ pine
```

and it should automatically open your remote mailbox without prompting for further authentication. If it doesn't work, run the following command manually on the client machine:

```
$ /usr/bin/ssh mail.server.net -l joe exec /usr/sbin/imapd
```

(modified to match the settings you made above), and verify that this starts the remote server program. If not, you have further debugging to do.

Now, why does automatic authentication work? Because your `ssh` command starts the server *as yourself* in *your account* on the mail server machine, rather than as root by the system. This runs the IMAP server in pre-authenticated mode, and simply accesses the mail of the account under which it runs. So, the `ssh` subprocess gets you single-signon for your mail. That is, once you have SSH authorization to log into the mail server, you don't need to authenticate again via password to access your mail.

This method of mail access can be slow. If you're using IMAP and have multiple mail folders, each time you change folders Pine will create a new IMAP connection, which now involves setting up a complete SSH connection. However, this is a matter of implementation—ideally we'd establish a single SSH connection to the server, and then have a command that quickly establishes a new SSH channel to the server via the existing connection. The free SSH implementation lsh in fact has this capability; see its lsh -G and lshg commands.

Notes:

- For concreteness we suggested SSH public-key authentication with ssh-agent, but any form of automatic SSH authentication will work, such as Kerberos [4.14], hostbased [6.8], etc.

- Although this recipe is written for Pine, you can adapt the same technique for any mail client that can connect to its server via an arbitrary external program.

See Also

pine(1). The LSH home page is *http://www.lysator.liu.se/~nisse/lsh*.

8.17 Receiving Mail Without a Visible Server

Problem

You want to receive Internet email without running a publicly accessible mail server or daemon.

Solution

Don't run a mail daemon. Queue your mail on another ISP and use fetchmail to download it. Authenticate to the ISP via SSH, and transfer the email messages over an SSH tunnel. Then have fetchmail invoke your local mail delivery agent directly to deliver the mail.

```
~/.fetchmailrc:
poll imap.example.com with proto IMAP:
preauth ssh
plugin "ssh %h /usr/sbin/imapd";
user 'shawn' there is smith here;
mda "/usr/sbin/sendmail -oem -f %F %T"
fetchall;
no keep;

~/.bash_profile:
if [ -z "$SSH_AGENT_PID" ]
then
    eval `/usr/bin/ssh-agent` > /dev/null 2> /dev/null
fi
```

~/.bashrc:
```
(/usr/bin/ssh-add -l | /bin/grep -q 'no identities') \
    && /usr/bin/ssh-add \
    && /usr/bin/fetchmail -d 600
```

Discussion

`fetchmail` is the Swiss army knife of mail delivery. Using a powerful configuration mechanism (*~/.fetchmailrc*), `fetchmail` can poll remote IMAP and POP servers, retrieve messages, and forward them through `sendmail` and other mail delivery systems.

For security reasons, you might not want a `sendmail` daemon visible to the outside world, and yet you want mail delivered locally. For example, the machine where you read mail could be behind a firewall.

This recipe is run by user smith on the local machine. When he logs in, the given commands in his *.bash_profile* and *.bashrc* make sure an SSH agent [6.9] is running and is loaded with the necessary keys. Also `fetchmail` is launched, polling a remote IMAP server, *imap.example.com*, every 10 minutes (600 seconds). `fetchmail` authenticates via SSH as user *shawn@imap.example.com* and downloads all messages (`fetchall`) in shawn's mailbox. These messages are delivered to smith's local mailbox by invoking `sendmail` directly (`mda`). Our recipe also deletes the messages from the IMAP server (`no keep`) but this is optional: you might skip this until you're sure things are working correctly.

While smith is not logged in, `fetchmail` doesn't run. Mail will arrive normally on *imap.example.com*, awaiting retrieval.

If you prefer to run a mail daemon (`sendmail -bd`) on the machine receiving your email messages, simply delete the `mda` line.

`fetchmail` is tremendously useful and has tons of options. The manpage is well worth reading in full.

See Also

fetchmail(1).

8.18 Using an SMTP Server from Arbitrary Clients

Problem

You want your SMTP server to relay mail from arbitrary places, without creating an open relay.

Solution

Use SMTP authentication. To set up the server:

1. Find this line in */etc/mail/sendmail.mc*:

   ```
   DAEMON_OPTIONS(`Port=smtp,Addr=127.0.0.1, Name=MTA')
   ```

   and change it to:

   ```
   DAEMON_OPTIONS(`Port=smtp, Name=MTA')
   ```

   The default setting restricts sendmail to accepting connections only from the same host, for security; now it will accept connections from elsewhere.

2. Make sure this line in */etc/mail/sendmail.mc* appears uncommented (i.e., it is not preceded by the comment symbol dnl):

   ```
   TRUST_AUTH_MECH(`EXTERNAL DIGEST-MD5 CRAM-MD5 LOGIN PLAIN')
   ```

3. If you have changed */etc/mail/sendmail.mc*, rebuild your sendmail configuration file[*] and restart sendmail.

   Rebuild the configuration:

   ```
   # m4 /etc/mail/sendmail.mc > /etc/sendmail.cf
   ```

   Restart sendmail:

   ```
   # /etc/init.d/sendmail restart
   ```

4. Establish an account for SMTP authentication, say, with username mailman:

   ```
   # /usr/sbin/saslpasswd -c mailman
   Password: ********
   Again (for verification): ********
   ```

Your mail server should now be ready to do SMTP authentication. To set up the email client:

1. Configure your mail client to use SMTP authentication for outbound email, using either the DIGEST-MD5 (preferred) or CRAM-MD5 authentication types.

   Your client might also have an option nearby for a "secure connection" using SSL. Do *not* turn it on; that is a separate feature.

2. Try sending a test message via relay: address it to a domain considered non-local to your server. Instead of replying with a "relay denied" error (which you should have gotten previous to this setup), you should be prompted for a username and password. Use the mailman account you established previously. The mail message should get sent.

---

[*] You'll need the RPM package sendmail-cf installed to do this. Note also that some Linux distributions put *sendmail.cf* in the */etc/mail* directory.

Discussion

An SMTP server accepts Internet email. There are two kinds of email messages it may receive:

Local mail
> Intended to be delivered to a local user on that host. This mail usually arrives from other mail servers.

Non-local mail
> Intended to be forwarded to another host for delivery. This mail usually comes from email programs, such as Pine and Ximian Evolution, configured to use your SMTP server to send mail.

A mail server that forwards non-local mail is called a *relay*. Normally, you'll want your SMTP server to accept local mail from anywhere, but restrict who may use your server as a relay for non-local mail. If you don't restrict it, your SMTP server is called an *open relay*. Open relays invite trouble: spammers seek them out as convenient drop-off points; your machine could be co-opted to send unwanted email to thousands of people. Say goodbye to your good Internet karma... and you will shortly find your mail server blacklisted by spam-control services, and hence useless. In fact, you might come home one day to find your ISP has shut down your Net access, due to complaints of mail abuse! You really don't want an open relay.

ISP mail servers normally accept relay mail only from addresses on their network, restricting them to use by their customers. This makes good business sense, but is inconvenient for mobile users who connect to various ISPs for Net access at different times. It's a pain to keep switching email program settings to use the different required relays (or even to find out what they are).

Our recipe demonstrates how to set up your SMTP server to get around this inconvenience, by requiring *authentication* before relaying mail. Thus, a single SMTP server can accept non-local mail no matter where the client is connected, while still avoiding an open relay. One caveat: the email clients must support SMTP authentication, as do Evolution, Pine, the Mail program of Macintosh OS X, and others.

Our recipe depends on two lines in */etc/mail/sendmail.mc*. The first, once you disable it, allows `sendmail` to accept mail from other hosts; by default, it only listens on the network loopback interface and accepts mail only from local processes. The second line, once enabled, tells `sendmail` which authentication mechanisms to accept as trusted: that is, if a client authenticates using one of these methods, it will be allowed to relay mail.

When you send your test message, if your mail client claims the server does not support SMTP authentication, try this on the server:

```
# sendmail -O LogLevel=14 -bs -Am
EHLO foo
```

```
QUIT
```

```
# tail /var/log/maillog
```

and look for any enlightening error messages.

This configuration by itself does not secure the entire SMTP session, which is still a plaintext TCP connection. So don't use simple password authentication, as your passwords can then be stolen by network eavesdropping. By default, `sendmail` accepts only the `DIGEST-MD5` and `CRAM-MD5` authentication methods, which do not send the password in plaintext.

It is also possible to configure `sendmail` to use SSL to protect the entire SMTP session. If you understand the security properties and limitations of the authentication mechanisms mentioned above, and consider them inadequate for your application, this might be a necessary step to take. However, don't do it out of some notion to "protect" the *content* of your email. Unless you have a closed system, your email will be further relayed across other networks on the way to its destination, so securing this one hop is of little value. For more security, use an end-to-end approach, encrypting messages with GnuPG, PGP, or S/MIME (see [8.1] through [8.8]).

See Also

Learn more about SMTP authentication at *ftp://ftp.isi.edu/in-notes/rfc2554.txt*, and sendmail's particular implementation at *http://www.sendmail.org/~ca/email/auth.html*. The SASL RFC is at *ftp://ftp.isi.edu/in-notes/rfc2222.txt*.

CHAPTER 9
Testing and Monitoring

9.0   Introduction

To keep your system secure, be proactive: test for security holes and monitor for unusual activity. If you don't keep watch for break-ins, you may wake up one day to find your systems totally hacked and owned, which is no party.

In this chapter we cover useful tools and techniques for testing and monitoring your system, in the following areas:

Logins and passwords
> Testing password strength, locating accounts with no password, and tracking suspicious login activity

Filesystems
> Searching them for weak security, and looking for rootkits

Networking
> Looking for open ports, observing local network use, packet-sniffing, tracing network processes, and detecting intrusions

Logging
> Reading your system logs, writing log entries from various languages, configuring syslogd, and rotating log files

We must emphasize that our discussion of network monitoring and intrusion detection is fairly basic. Our recipes will get you started, but these important topics are complex, with no easy, turnkey solutions. You may wish to investigate additional resources for these purposes, such as:

- Computer Incident Advisory Capability (CIAC) Network Monitoring Tools page: *http://ciac.llnl.gov/ciac/ToolsUnixNetMon.html*

- Stanford Linear Accelerator (SLAC) Network Monitoring Tools page: *http://www.slac.stanford.edu/xorg/nmtf/nmtf-tools.html*

- National Institutes of Health "Network and Network Monitoring Software" page: *http://www.alw.nih.gov/Security/prog-network.html*
- Setting Up a Network Monitoring Console: *http://com.pp.asu.edu/support/nmc/nmcdocs/nmc.html*
- Insecure.org's top 50 security tools: *http://www.insecure.org/tools.html*

9.1   Testing Login Passwords (John the Ripper)

Problem

You want to check that all login passwords in your system password database are strong.

Solution

Use John the Ripper, a password-cracking utility from the Openwall Project (*http://www.openwall.com*). After the software is installed, run:

```
# cd /var/lib/john
# umask 077
# unshadow /etc/passwd /etc/shadow > mypasswords
# john mypasswords
```

Cracked passwords will be written into the file *john.pot*. Cracked username/password pairs can be shown after the fact (or during cracking) with the -show option:

```
# john -show mypasswords
```

You can instruct john to crack the passwords of only certain users or groups with the options -users:u1,u2,... or -groups:g1,g2,..., e.g.:

```
# john -users:smith,jones,akhmed mypasswords
```

Running john with no options will print usage information.

Discussion

SuSE distributes John the Ripper, but Red Hat does not. If you need it, download the software in source form for Unix from *http://www.openwall.com/john*, together with its signature, and check the signature before proceeding. [7.15]

Unpack the source:

```
$ tar xvzpf john-*.tar.gz
```

Prepare to compile:

```
$ cd `ls -d john-* | head -1`/src
$ make
```

This will print out a list of targets for various systems; choose the appropriate one for your host, e.g.:

```
linux-x86-any-elf        Linux, x86, ELF binaries
```

and run make to build your desired target, e.g.:

```
$ make linux-x86-any-elf
```

Install the software, as root:

```
# cd ../run
# mkdir -p /usr/local/sbin
# umask 077
# cp -d john un* /usr/local/sbin
# mkdir -p /var/lib/john
# cp *.* mailer /var/lib/john
```

Then use the recipe we've provided.

By default, Red Hat 8.0 uses MD5-hashed passwords stored in *letc/shadow*, rather than the traditional DES-based crypt( ) hashes stored in *letc/passwd*; this is effected by the md5 and shadow directives in *letc/pam.d/system-auth*:

```
password    sufficient    /lib/security/pam_unix.so nullok use_authtok md5 shadow
```

The unshadow command gathers the account and hash information together again for cracking. This information should not be publicly available for security reasons— that's why it is split up in the first place—so be careful with this re-integrated file. If your passwords change, you will have to re-run the unshadow command to build an up-to-date password file for cracking.

In general, cracking programs use dictionaries of common words when attempting to crack a password, trying not only the words themselves but also permutations, mis-spellings, alternate capitalizations, and so forth. The default dictionary (*/var/lib/john/password.lst*) is small, so obtain larger ones for effective cracking. Also, add words appropriate to your environment, such as the names of local projects, machines, companies, and people. Some available dictionaries are:

ftp://ftp.ox.ac.uk/pub/wordlists/
ftp://ftp.cerias.purdue.edu/pub/dict/wordlists

Concatenate your desired word lists into a single file, and point to it with the wordlist directive in */var/lib/john/john.ini*.

john operates on a file of account records, so you can gather the password data from many machines and process them in one spot. You must ensure, however, that they all use the same hashing algorithms compiled into the version you built on your cracking host. For security, it might be wise to gather your account databases, then perform the cracking on a box off the network, in a secure location.

There are other crackers available, notably Crack by Alec Muffet. [9.2] We feature John the Ripper here not because it's necessarily better, but because it's simpler to use on Red Hat 8.0, automatically detecting and supporting the default MD5 hashes.

See Also

See the *doc* directory of the John the Ripper distribution for full documentation and examples.

Learn about Alec Muffet's Crack utility at *http://www.users.dircon.co.uk/~crypto/ download/c50-faq.HTML.*

The Red Hat Guide to Password Security is at *http://www.redhat.com/docs/manuals/ linux/RHL-8.0-Manual/security-guide/s1-wstation-pass.html.*

9.2   Testing Login Passwords (CrackLib)

Problem

You want assurance that your login passwords are secure.

Solution

Write a little program that calls the FascistCheck function from CrackLib:

```
#include <stdlib.h>
#include <unistd.h>
#include <stdio.h>
#include <crack.h>
#define DICTIONARY "/usr/lib/cracklib_dict"
int main(int argc, char *argv[]) {
    char *password;
    char *problem;
    int status = 0;
    printf("\nEnter an empty password or Ctrl-D to quit.\n");
    while ((password = getpass("\nPassword: ")) != NULL && *password ) {
        if ((problem = FascistCheck(password, DICTIONARY)) != NULL) {
            printf("Bad password: %s.\n", problem);
            status = 1;
        } else {
            printf("Good password!\n");
        }
    }
    exit(status);
}
```

Compile and link it thusly:

```
$ gcc cracktest.c -lcrack -o cracktest
```

Run it (the passwords you type will not appear on the screen):

```
$ ./cracktest
Enter an empty password or Ctrl-D to quit.
Password: xyz
Bad password: it's WAY too short.
Password: elephant
Bad password: it is based on a dictionary word.
Password: kLu%ziF7
Good password!
```

Discussion

CrackLib is an offshoot of Alec Muffet's password cracker, Crack. It is designed to be embedded in other programs, and hence is provided only as a library (and dictionary). The FascistCheck function subjects a password to a variety of tests, to ensure that it is not vulnerable to guessing.

See Also

Learn more about CrackLib at *http://www.crypticide.org/users/alecm*.

Perl for System Administration (O'Reilly), section 10.5, shows how to make a Perl module to use CrackLib.

PAM can use CrackLib to force users to choose good passwords. [4.2]

9.3   Finding Accounts with No Password

Problem

You want to detect local login accounts that can be accessed without a password.

Solution

```
# awk -F: '$2 == "" { print $1, "has no password!" }' /etc/shadow
```

Discussion

The worst kind of password is no password at all, so you want to make sure every account has one. Any good password-cracking program can be employed here—they often try to find completely unprotected accounts first—but you can also look for missing passwords directly.

Encrypted passwords are stored in the second field of each entry in the shadow password database, just after the username. Fields are separated by colons.

Note that the *shadow* password file is readable only by superusers.

See Also

shadow(5).

9.4 Finding Superuser Accounts

Problem

You want to list all accounts with superuser access.

Solution

```
$ awk -F: '$3 == 0 { print $1, "is a superuser!" }' /etc/passwd
```

Discussion

A superuser, by definition, has a numerical user ID of zero. Be sure your system has only one superuser account: root. Multiple superuser accounts are a very bad idea because they are harder to control and track. (See Chapter 5 for better ways to share root privileges.)

Numerical user IDs are stored in the third field of each entry in the *passwd* database. The username is stored in the first field. Fields are separated by colons.

See Also

passwd(5).

9.5 Checking for Suspicious Account Use

Problem

You want to discover unusual or dangerous usage of accounts on your system: dormant user accounts, recent logins to system accounts, etc.

Solution

To print information about the last login for each user:

```
$ lastlog [-u username]
```

To print the entire login history:

```
$ last [username]
```

To print failed login attempts:

```
$ lastb [username]
```

To enable recording of bad logins:

```
# touch /var/log/btmp
# chown --reference=/var/log/wtmp /var/log/btmp
# chmod --reference=/var/log/wtmp /var/log/btmp
```

Discussion

Attackers look for inactive accounts that are still enabled, in the hope that intrusions will escape detection for long periods of time. If Joe retired and left the organization last year, will anyone notice if his account becomes compromised? Certainly not Joe! To avoid problems like this, examine all accounts on your system for unexpected usage patterns.

Linux systems record each user's last login time in the database */var/log/lastlog*. The terminal (or X Window System display name) and remote system name, if any, are also noted. The `lastlog` command prints this information in a convenient, human-readable format.

 /var/log/lastlog is a database, not a log file. It does not grow continuously, and therefore should not be rotated. The apparent size of the file (e.g., as displayed by `ls -l`) is often much larger than the actual size, because the file contains "holes" for ranges of unassigned user IDs.

Access is restricted to the superuser by recent versions of Red Hat (8.0 or later). If this seems too paranoid for your system, it is safe to make the file world-readable:

```
# chmod a+r /var/log/lastlog
```

In contrast, the *btmp* log file will grow slowly (unless you are under attack!), but it should be rotated like other log files. You can either add *btmp* to the *wtmp* entry in */etc/logrotate.conf*, or add a similar entry in a separate file in the */etc/logrotate.d* directory. [9.30]

A history of all logins and logouts (interspersed with system events like shutdowns, reboots, runlevel changes, etc.) is recorded in the log file */var/log/wtmp*. The `last` command scans this log file to produce a report of all login sessions, in reverse chronological order, sorted by login time.

Failed login attempts can also be recorded in the log file */var/log/btmp*, but this is not done by default. To enable recording of bad logins, create the *btmp* file manually, using the same owner, group, and permissions as for the *wtmp* file. The `lastb` command prints a history of bad logins.

The preceding methods do not scale well to multiple systems, so see our more general solution. [9.6]

See Also

lastlog(1), last(1), lastb(1).

9.6 Checking for Suspicious Account Use, Multiple Systems

Problem

You want to scan multiple computers for unusual or dangerous usage of accounts.

Solution

Merge the *lastlog* databases from several systems, using Perl:

```
use DB_File;
use Sys::Lastlog;
use Sys::Hostname;
my %omnilastlog;
tie(%omnilastlog, "DB_File", "/share/omnilastlog");
my $ll = Sys::Lastlog->new();
while (my ($user, $uid) = (getpwent())[0, 2]) {
    if (my $llent = $ll->getlluid($uid)) {
        $omnilastlog{$user} = pack("Na*", $llent->ll_time(),
                                    join("\0", $llent->ll_line(),
                                               $llent->ll_host(),
                                               hostname))
              if $llent->ll_time() >
                  (exists($omnilastlog{$user}) ?
                      unpack("N", $omnilastlog{$user}) : -1);
    }
}
untie(%omnilastlog);
exit(0);
```

To read the merged *lastlog* database, *omnilastlog*, use another Perl script:

```
use DB_File;
my %omnilastlog;
tie(%omnilastlog, "DB_File", "/share/omnilastlog");
while (my ($user, $record) = each(%omnilastlog)) {
    my ($time, $rest) = unpack("Na*", $record);
    my ($line, $host_from, $host_to) = split("\0", $rest, -1);
    printf("%-8s %-16.16s -> %-16.16s %-8s %s\n",
        $user, $host_from, $host_to, $line,
        $time ? scalar(localtime($time)) : "**Never logged in**");
}
untie(%omnilastlog);
exit(0);
```

Discussion

Perusing the output from the `lastlog`, `last`, and `lastb` commands [9.5] might be sufficient to monitor activity on a single system with a small number of users, but the technique doesn't scale well in the following cases:

- If accounts are shared among many systems, you probably want to know a user's most recent login on *any* of your systems.

- Some system accounts intended for special purposes, such as bin or daemon, should *never* be used for routine logins.

- Disabled accounts should be monitored to make sure they have no login activity.

Legitimate usage patterns vary, and your goal should be to notice deviations from the norm. We need more flexibility than the preceding tools provide.

We can solve this dilemma through automation. The Perl modules `Sys::Lastlog` and `Sys::Utmp`, which are available from CPAN, can parse and display a system's last-login data. Despite its name, `Sys::Utmp` can process the *wtmp* and *btmp* files; they have the same format as */var/log/utmp*, the database containing a snapshot of currently logged-in users.

Our recipe merges *lastlog* databases from several systems into a single database, which we call *omnilastlog*, using Perl. The script steps through each entry in the password database on each system, looks up the corresponding entry in the *lastlog* database using the `Sys::Lastlog` module, and updates the entry in the merged *omnilastlog* database if the last login time is more recent than any other we have previously seen.

The merged *omnilastlog* database is tied to a hash for easy access. We use the Berkeley DB format because it is byte-order–independent and therefore portable: this would be important if your Linux systems run on different architectures. If all of your Linux systems are of the same type (e.g., Intel x86 systems), then any other Perl database module could be used in place of `DB_File`.

Our hash is indexed by usernames rather than numeric user IDs, in case the user IDs are not standardized among the systems (a bad practice that, alas, does happen). The record for each user contains the time, terminal (`ll_line`), and remote and local host-names. The time is packed as an integer in network byte order (another nod to portability: for homogeneous systems, using the native "L" packing template instead of "N" would work as well). The last three values are glued together with null characters, which is safe because the strings never contain nulls.

Run the merge script on all of your systems, as often as desired, to update the merged *omnilastlog* database. Our recipe assumes a shared filesystem location, */share/omnilastlog*; if this is not convenient, copy the file to each system, update it, and then copy it back to a central repository. The merged database is compact, often smaller than the individual *lastlog* databases.

An even simpler Perl script reads and analyzes the merged *omnilastlog* database. Our recipe steps through and unpacks each record in the database, and then prints all of the information, like the `lastlog` command.

This script can serve as a template for checking account usage patterns, according to your own conventions. For example, you might notice dormant accounts by insisting that users with valid shells (as listed in the file */etc/shells*, with the exception of */sbin/nologin*) must have logged in somewhere during the last month. Conversely, you might require that system accounts (recognized by their low numeric user IDs) with invalid shells must never login, anywhere. Finally, you could maintain a database of the dates when accounts are disabled (e.g., as part of a standard procedure when people leave your organization), and demand that no logins occur for such accounts after the termination date for each.

Run a script frequently to verify your assumptions about legitimate account usage patterns. This way, you will be reminded promptly after Joe's retirement party that his account should be disabled, hopefully before crackers start guessing his password.

See Also

The Sys::Lastlog and Sys::Utmp Perl modules are found at *http://www.cpan.org*.

Perl for System Administration (section 9.2) from O'Reilly shows how to unpack the *utmp* records used for *wtmp* and *btmp* files. O'Reilly's *Perl Cookbook* also has sample programs for reading records from *lastlog* and *wtmp* files: see the `laston` and `tailwtmp` scripts in Chapter 8 of that book.

9.7   Testing Your Search Path

Problem

You want to avoid invoking the wrong program of a given name.

Solution

Ensure that your search path contains no relative directories:

```
$ perl -e 'print "PATH contains insecure relative directory \"$_\"\n"
           foreach grep ! m[^/], split /:/, $ENV{"PATH"}, -1;'
```

Discussion

Imagine you innocently type `ls` while your current working directory is */tmp*, and you discover to your chagrin that you have just run a malicious program, */tmp/ls*, instead of the expected */bin/ls*. Worse, you might not notice at all, if the rogue program behaves like the real version while performing other nefarious activities silently.

This can happen if your search path contains a period ("."), meaning the current working directory. The possibility of unexpected behavior is higher if "." is early in your search path, but even the last position is not safe: consider the possibility of misspellings. A cracker could create a malicious */tmp/hwo*, a misspelling of the common who command, and hope you type "hwo" sometime while you're in */tmp*. As there is no earlier "hwo" in your search path, you'll unintentionally run the cracker's *./hwo* program. (Which no doubt prints, `basename $SHELL`: hwo: command not found to stderr while secretly demolishing your filesystem.) Play it safe and keep "." out of your search path.

An empty search path element—two adjacent colons, or a leading or trailing colon— also refers to the current working directory. These are sometimes created inadvertently by scripts that paste together the PATH environment variable with ":" separators, adding one too many, or adding an extra separator at the beginning or end.

In fact, any relative directories in your search path are dangerous, as they implicitly refer to the current working directory. Remove all of these relative directories: you can still run programs (securely!) by explicitly typing their relative directory, as in:

```
./myprogram
```

Our recipe uses a short Perl script to split the PATH environment variable, complaining about any directory that is not absolute (i.e., that does not start with a "/" character). The negative limit (-1) for split is important for noticing troublesome empty directories at the end of the search path.

See Also

environ(5).

9.8   Searching Filesystems Effectively

Problem

You want to locate files of interest to detect security risks.

Solution

Use find and xargs, but be knowledgeable of their important options and limitations.

Discussion

Are security risks lurking within your filesystems? If so, they can be hard to detect, especially if you must search through mountains of data. Fortunately, Linux provides the powerful tools find and xargs to help with the task. These tools have so many options, however, that their flexibility can make them seem daunting to use. We recommend the following good practices:

Know your filesystems

Linux supports a wide range of filesystem types. To see the ones configured in your kernel, read the file */proc/filesystems*. To see which filesystems are currently mounted (and their types), run:

```
$ mount
/dev/hda1 on / type ext2 (rw)
/dev/hda2 on /mnt/windows type vfat (rw)
remotesys:/export/spool/mail on /var/spool/mail type nfs
(rw,hard,intr,noac,addr=192.168.10.13)
//MyPC/C$ on /mnt/remote type smbfs (0)
none on /proc type proc (rw)
...
```

with no options or arguments. We see a traditional Linux ext2 filesystem (*/dev/hda1*), a Windows FAT32 filesystem (*/dev/hda2*), a remotely mounted NFS filesystem (*remotesys:/export/spool/mail*), a Samba filesystem (*//MyPC/C$*) mounted remotely, and the *proc* filesystem provided by the kernel. See mount(8) for more details.

Know which filesystems are local and which are remote

Searching network filesystems like NFS partitions can be quite slow. Furthermore, NFS typically maps your local root account to an unprivileged user on the mounted filesystem, so some files or directories might be inaccessible even to root. To avoid these problems when searching a filesystem, run find locally on the server that physically contains it.

Be aware that some filesystem types (e.g., for Microsoft Windows) use different models for owners, groups, and permissions, while other filesystems (notably some for CD-ROMs) do not support these file attributes at all. Consider scanning "foreign" filesystems on servers that recognize them natively, and just skip read-only filesystems like CD-ROMs (assuming you know and trust the source).

The standard Linux filesystem type is ext2. If your local filesystems are of this type only,* you can scan them all with a command like:

```
# find / ! -fstype ext2 -prune -o ... (other find options) ...
```

This can be readily extended to multiple local filesystem types (e.g., ext2 and ext3):

```
# find / ! \( -fstype ext2 -o -fstype ext3 \) -prune -o ...
```

---

* And if they are not mounted on filesystems of other types, which would be an unusual configuration.

The find -prune option causes directories to be skipped, so we prune any filesystems that do *not* match our desired types (ext2 or ext3). The following -o ("or") operator causes the filesystems that survive the pruning to be scanned.

The find -xdev option prevents crossing filesystem boundaries, and can be useful for avoiding uninteresting filesystems that might be mounted. Our recipes use this option as a reminder to be conscious of filesystem types.

Carefully examine permissions

The find -perm option can conveniently select a subset of the permissions, optionally ignoring the rest. In the most common case, we are interested in testing for *any* of the permissions in the subset: use a "+" prefix with the permission argument to specify this. Occasionally, we want to test *all* of the permissions: use a "-" prefix instead.* If no prefix is used, then the entire set of permissions is tested; this is rarely useful.

Handle filenames safely

If you scan enough filesystems, you will eventually encounter filenames with embedded spaces or unusual characters like newlines, quotation marks, etc. The null character, however, *never* appears in filenames, and is therefore the only safe separator to use for lists of filenames that are passed between programs.

The find -print0 option produces null-terminated filenames; xargs and perl both support a -0 (zero) option to read them. Useful filters like sort and grep also understand a -z option to use null separators when they read and write data, and grep has a separate -Z option that produces null-terminated filenames (with the -l or -L options). Use these options whenever possible to avoid misinterpreting filenames, which can be disastrous when modifying filesystems as root!

Avoid long command lines

The Linux kernel imposes a 128 KB limit on the combined size of command-line arguments and the environment. This limit can be exceeded by using shell command substitution, e.g.:

```
$ mycommand `find ...`
```

Use the xargs program instead to collect filename arguments and run commands repeatedly, without exceeding this limit:

```
$ find ... -print0 | xargs -0 -r mycommand
```

The xargs -r option avoids running the command if the output of find is empty, i.e., no filenames were found. This is usually desirable, to prevent errors like:

```
$ find ... -print0 | xargs -0 rm
rm: too few arguments
```

---

* Of course, if the subset contains only a single permission, then there is no difference between "any" and "all," so either prefix can be used.

It can occasionally be useful to connect multiple xargs invocations in a pipeline, e.g.:

```
$ find ... -print0 | xargs -0 -r grep -lZ pattern | xargs -0 -r mycommand
```

The first xargs collects filenames from find and passes them to grep, as command-line arguments. grep then searches the file contents (which find cannot do) for the pattern, and writes another list of filenames to stdout. This list is then used by the second xargs to collect command-line arguments for mycommand.

If you want grep to select filenames (instead of contents), insert it directly into the pipe:

```
$ find ... -print0 | grep -z pattern | xargs -0 -r mycommand
```

In most cases, however, find -regex *pattern* is a more direct way to select filenames using a regular expression.

Note how grep -Z refers to writing filenames, while grep -z refers to reading and writing data.

xargs is typically much faster than find -exec, which runs the command separately for each file and therefore incurs greater start-up costs. However, if you need to run a command that can process only one file at a time, use either find -exec or xargs -n 1:

```
$ find ... -exec mycommand '{}' \;
$ find ... -print0 | xargs -0 -r -n 1 mycommand
```

These two forms have a subtle difference, however: a command run by find -exec uses the standard input inherited from find, while a command run by xargs uses the pipe as its standard input (which is not typically useful).

See Also

find(1), xargs(1), mount(8).

9.9   Finding setuid (or setgid) Programs

Problem

You want to check for potentially insecure setuid (or setgid) programs.

Solution

To list all setuid or setgid files (programs and scripts):

```
$ find /dir -xdev -type f -perm +ug=s -print
```

To list only setuid or setgid scripts:

```
$ find /dir -xdev -type f -perm +ug=s -print0 | \
perl -0ne 'chomp;
           open(FILE, $_);
           read(FILE, $magic, 2);
           print $_, "\n" if $magic eq "#!";
           close(FILE)'
```

To remove setuid or setgid bits from a file:

```
$ chmod u-s file        Remove the setuid bit
$ chmod g-s file        Remove the setgid bit
```

To find and interactively fix setuid and setgid programs:

```
$ find /dir -xdev -type f \
    \( -perm +u=s -printf "setuid: %p\n" -ok chmod -v u-s {} \; , \
       -perm +g=s -printf "setgid: %p\n" -ok chmod -v g-s {} \;    \)
```

To ignore the setuid or setgid attributes for executables in a filesystem, mount it with the nosuid option. To prohibit executables entirely, use the noexec mount option. These options can appear on the command line:

```
# mount -o nosuid ...
# mount -o noexec ...
```

or in */etc/fstab*:

```
/dev/hdd3   /home   ext2    rw,nosuid   1 2
/dev/hdd7   /data   ext2    rw,noexec   1 3
```

Be aware of the important options and limitations of find, so you don't inadvertently overlook important files. [9.8]

Discussion

If your system has been compromised, it is quite likely that an intruder has installed backdoors. A common ploy is to hide a setuid root program in one of your filesystems.

The setuid permission bit changes the effective user ID to the owner of the file (even root) when a program is executed; the setgid bit performs the same function for the group. These two attributes are independent: either or both may be set.

Programs (and especially scripts) that use setuid or setgid bits must be written very carefully to avoid security holes. Whether you are searching for backdoors or auditing your own programs, be aware of any activity that involves these bits.

Many setuid and setgid programs are legitimately included in standard Linux distributions, so do not panic if you detect them while searching directories like */usr*. You can maintain a list of known setuid and setgid programs, and then compare the list with results from more recent filesystem scans. Tripwire (Chapter 1) is an even better tool for keeping track of such changes.

Our recipe uses find to detect the setuid and setgid bits. By restricting attention to regular files (with -type f), we avoid false matches for directories, which use the setgid bit for an unrelated purpose. In addition, our short Perl program identifies scripts, which contain "#!" in the first two bytes (the magic number).

The chmod command removes setuid or setgid bits (or both) for individual files. We can also combine detection with interactive repair using find: our recipe tests each bit separately, prints a message if it is found, asks (using -ok) if a chmod command should be run to remove the bit, and finally confirms each repair with chmod -v. Commands run by find -ok (or -exec) must be terminated with a "\;" argument, and the "{}" argument is replaced by the filename for each invocation. The separate "," (comma) argument causes find to perform the tests and actions for the setuid and setgid bits independently.

Finally, mount options can offer some protection against misuse of setuid or setgid programs. The nosuid option prevents recognition of either bit, which might be appropriate for network filesystems mounted from a less trusted server, or for local filesystems like /home or /tmp.* The even more restrictive noexec option prevents execution of any programs on the filesystem, which might be useful for filesystems that should contain only data files.

See Also

find(1), xargs(1), chmod(1), perlsec(1).

9.10 Securing Device Special Files

Problem

You want to check for potentially insecure device special files.

Solution

To list all device special files (block or character):

```
$ find /dir -xdev \( -type b -o -type c \) -ls
```

To list any regular files in /dev (except the MAKEDEV program):

```
$ find /dev -type f ! -name MAKEDEV -print
```

To prohibit device special files on a filesystem, use mount -o nodev or add the nodev option to entries in /etc/fstab.

---

* Note that Perl's suidperl program does not honor the nosuid option for filesystems that contain setuid Perl scripts.

Be aware of the important options and limitations of find, so you don't inadvertently overlook important files. [9.8]

Discussion

Device special files are objects that allow direct access to devices (either real or virtual) via the filesystem. For the security of your system, you must carefully control this access by maintaining appropriate permissions on these special files. An intruder who hides extra copies of important device special files can use them as backdoors to read—or even modify—kernel memory, disk drives, and other critical devices.

Conventionally, device special files are installed only in the */dev* directory, but they can live anywhere in the filesystem, so don't limit your searches to */dev*. Our recipe looks for the two flavors of device special files: block and character (using -type b and -type c, respectively). We use the more verbose -ls (instead of -print) to list the major and minor device numbers for any that are found: these can be compared to the output from ls -l /dev to determine the actual device (the filename is irrelevant).

It is also worthwhile to monitor the */dev* directory, to ensure that no regular files have been hidden there, either as replacements for device special files, or as rogue (perhaps setuid) programs. An exception is made for the */dev/MAKEDEV* program, which creates new entries in */dev*.

The mount option nodev prevents recognition of device special files. It is a good idea to use this for any filesystem that does not contain */dev*, especially network filesystems mounted from less trusted servers.

See Also

find(1).

9.11   Finding Writable Files

Problem

You want to locate world-writable files and directories on your machine.

Solution

To find world-writable files:

```
$ find /dir -xdev -perm +o=w ! \( -type d -perm +o=t \) ! -type l -print
```

To disable world write access to a file:

```
$ chmod o-w file
```

To find and interactively fix world-writable files:

```
$ find /dir -xdev -perm +o=w ! \( -type d -perm +o=t \) ! -type l -ok chmod -v o-w {} \;
```

To prevent newly created files from being world-writable:

```
$ umask 002
```

Be aware of the important options and limitations of find, so you don't inadvertently overlook important files. [9.8]

Discussion

Think your system is free of world-writable files? Check anyway: you might be surprised. For example, files extracted from Windows Zip archives are notorious for having insecure or screwed-up permissions.

Our recipe skips directories that have the sticky bit set (e.g., */tmp*). Such directories are often world-writable, but this is safe because of restrictions on removing and renaming files. [7.2]

We also skip symbolic links, since their permission bits are ignored (and are usually all set). Only the permissions of the targets of symbolic links are relevant for access control.

The chmod command can disable world-write access. Combine it with find -ok and you can interactively detect and repair world-writable files.

You can avoid creating world-writable files by setting a bit in your umask. You also can set other bits for further restrictions. [7.1] Note that programs like unzip are free to override the umask, however, so you still need to check.

See Also

find(1), chmod(1). See your shell documentation for information on umask: bash(1), tcsh(1), etc.

9.12 Looking for Rootkits

Problem

You want to check for evidence that a rootkit—a program to create or exploit security holes—has been run on your system.

Solution

Use chkrootkit. Download the tarfile from *http://www.chkrootkit.org*, verify its checksum:

```
$ md5sum chkrootkit.tar.gz
```

unpack it:

```
$ tar xvzpf chkrootkit.tar.gz
```

build it:

```
$ cd chkrootkit-*
$ make sense
```

and run it as root:

```
# ./chkrootkit
```

More securely, run it using known, good binaries you have previously copied to a secure medium, such as CD-ROM, e.g.:

```
# ./chkrootkit -p /mnt/cdrom
```

Discussion

chkrootkit tests for the presence of certain rootkits, worms, and trojans on your system. If you suspect you've been hacked, this is a good first step toward confirmation and diagnosis.

chkrootkit invokes a handful of standard Linux commands. At press time they are awk, cut, egrep, find, head, id, ls, netstat, ps, strings, sed, and uname. If these programs have been compromised on your system, chkrootkit's output cannot be trusted. So ideally, you should keep around a CD-ROM or write-protected floppy disk with these programs, and run chkrootkit with the -p option to use these known good binaries.

Be sure to use the latest version of chkrootkit, which will be aware of the most recently discovered threats.

See Also

The *README* file included with chkrootkit explains the tests conducted, and lists the full usage information.

9.13   Testing for Open Ports

Problem

You want a listing of open network ports on your system.

Solution

Probe your ports from a remote system.

To test a specific TCP port (e.g., SSH):

```
$ telnet target.example.com ssh
$ nc -v -z target.example.com ssh
```

To scan most of the interesting TCP ports:

```
# nmap -v target.example.com
```

To test a specific UDP port (e.g., 1024):

```
$ nc -v -z -u target.example.com 1024
```

To scan most of the interesting UDP ports (slowly!):

```
# nmap -v -sU target.example.com
```

To do host discovery (only) for a range of addresses, without port scanning:

```
# nmap -v -sP 10.12.104.200-222
```

To do operating system fingerprinting:

```
# nmap -v -O target.example.com
```

For a handy (but less flexible) GUI, run nmapfe instead of nmap.

Discussion

When attackers observe your systems from the outside, what do they see? Obviously, you want to present an image of an impenetrable fortress, not a vulnerable target. You've designed your defenses accordingly: a carefully constructed firewall, secure network services, etc. But how can you really be sure?

You don't need to wait passively to see what will happen next. Instead, actively test your own armor with the same tools the attackers will use.

Your vulnerability to attack is influenced by several interacting factors:

The vantage point of the attacker
Firewalls sometimes make decisions based on the source IP address (or the source port).

All intervening firewalls
You have your own, of course, but your ISP might impose additional restrictions on incoming or even outgoing traffic from your site.

The network configuration of your systems
Which servers listen for incoming connections and are willing to accept them?

Start by testing the last two subsystems in isolation. Verify your firewall operation by simulating the traversal of packets through ipchains. [2.21] Examine the network state on your machines with netstat. [9.14]

Next, the acid test is to probe from the outside. Use your own accounts on distant systems, if you have them (and if you have permission to do this kind of testing, of course). Alternatively, set up a temporary test system immediately outside your firewall, which might require cooperation from your ISP.

The nmap command is a powerful and widely used tool for network security testing. It gathers information about target systems in three distinct phases, in order:

Host discovery
Initial probes to determine which machines are responding within an address range

Port scanning
More exhaustive tests to find open ports that are not protected by firewalls, and are accepting connections

Operating system fingerprinting
An analysis of network behavioral idiosyncrasies can reveal a surprising amount of detailed information about the targets

 Use nmap to test only systems that you maintain. Many system administrators consider port scanning to be hostile and antisocial. If you intend to use nmap's stealth features, obtain permission from third parties that you employ as decoys or proxies.

Inform your colleagues about your test plans, so they will not be alarmed by unexpected messages in system logs. Use the logger command [9.31] to record the beginning and end of your tests.

Use caution when probing mission-critical, production systems. You *should* test these important systems, but nmap deliberately violates network protocols, and this behavior can occasionally confuse or even crash target applications and kernels.

To probe a single target, specify the hostname or address:

```
# nmap -v target.example.com
# nmap -v 10.12.104.200
```

We highly recommend the -v option, which provides a more informative report. Repeat the option (-v -v...) for even more details.

You can also scan a range of addresses, e.g., those protected by your firewall. For a class C network, which uses the first three bytes (24 bits) for the network part of each address, the following commands are all equivalent:

```
# nmap -v target.example.com/24
# nmap -v 10.12.104.0/24
# nmap -v 10.12.104.0-255
# nmap -v "10.12.104.*"
```

Lists of addresses (or address ranges) can be scanned as well:

```
# nmap -v 10.12.104.10,33,200-222,250
```

nmapfe is a graphical front end that runs nmap with appropriate command-line options and displays the results. nmapfe is designed to be easy to use, though it does not provide the full flexibility of all the nmap options.

By default, nmap uses both TCP and ICMP pings for host discovery. If these are blocked by an intervening firewall, the nmap -P options provide alternate ping strategies. Try these options when evaluating your firewall's policies for TCP or ICMP. The goal of host discovery is to avoid wasting time performing port scans for unused addresses (or machines that are down). If you know that your targets are up, you can disable host discovery with the -P0 (that's a zero) option.

The simplest way to test an individual TCP port is to try to connect with telnet. The port might be open:

```
$ telnet target.example.com ssh
Trying 10.12.104.200...
Connected to target.example.com.
Escape character is '^]'.
SSH-1.99-OpenSSH_3.1p1
```

or closed (i.e., passed by the firewall, but having no server accepting connections on the target):

```
$ telnet target.example.com 33333
Trying 10.12.104.200...
telnet: connect to address 10.12.104.200: Connection refused
```

or blocked (filtered) by a firewall:

```
$ telnet target.example.com 137
Trying 10.12.104.200...
telnet: connect to address 10.12.104.200: Connection timed out
```

Although telnet's primary purpose is to implement the Telnet protocol, it is also a simple, generic TCP client that connects to arbitrary ports.

The nc command is an even better way to probe ports:

```
$ nc -z -vv target.example.com ssh 33333 137
target.example.com [10.12.104.200] 22 (ssh) open
target.example.com [10.12.104.200] 33333 (?) : Connection refused
target.example.com [10.12.104.200] 137 (netbios-ns) : Connection timed out
```

The -z option requests a probe, without transferring any data. The repeated -v options control the level of detail, as for nmap.

Port scans are a *tour de force* for nmap:

```
# nmap -v target.example.com
Starting nmap V. 3.00 ( www.insecure.org/nmap/ )
No tcp,udp, or ICMP scantype specified, assuming SYN Stealth scan.
Use -sP if you really don't want to portscan (and just want to see what hosts are
up).
```

```
Host target.example.com (10.12.104.200) appears to be up ... good.
Initiating SYN Stealth Scan against target.example.com (10.12.104.200)
Adding open port 53/tcp
Adding open port 22/tcp
The SYN Stealth Scan took 21 seconds to scan 1601 ports.
Interesting ports on target.example.com (10.12.104.200):
(The 1595 ports scanned but not shown below are in state: closed)
Port        State       Service
22/tcp      open        ssh
53/tcp      open        domain
137/tcp     filtered    netbios-ns
138/tcp     filtered    netbios-dgm
139/tcp     filtered    netbios-ssn
1080/tcp    filtered    socks
Nmap run completed -- 1 IP address (1 host up) scanned in 24 seconds
```

In all of these cases, be aware that intervening firewalls can be configured to return TCP RST packets for blocked ports, which makes them appear closed rather than filtered. *Caveat prober.*

nmap can perform more sophisticated (and efficient) TCP probes than ordinary connection attempts, such as the SYN or "half-open" probes in the previous example, which don't bother to do the full initial TCP handshake for each connection. Different probe strategies can be selected with the -s options: these might be interesting if you are reviewing your firewall's TCP policies, or you want to see how your firewall logs different kinds of probes.

> Run nmap as root if possible. Some of its more advanced tests intentionally violate IP protocols, and require raw sockets that only the superuser is allowed to access.
>
> If nmap can't be run as root, it will still work, but it may run more slowly, and the results may be less informative.

UDP ports are harder to probe than TCP ports, because packet delivery is not guaranteed, so blocked ports can't be reliably distinguished from lost packets. Closed ports can be detected by ICMP responses, but scanning is often very slow because many systems limit the rate of ICMP messages. Nevertheless, your firewall's UDP policies are important, so testing is worthwhile. The nc -u and nmap -sU options perform UDP probes, typically by sending a zero-byte UDP packet and noting any responses.

By default, nmap scans all ports up to 1024, plus well-known ports in its extensive collection of services (used in place of the more limited */etc/services*). Use the -F option to quickly scan only the well-known ports, or the -p option to select different, specific, numeric ranges of ports. If you want to exhaustively scan *all* ports, use -p 0-65535.

If you are interested only in host discovery, disable port scanning entirely with the nmap -sP option. This might be useful to determine which occasionally-connected laptops are up and running on an internal network.

Finally, the nmap -O option enables operating system fingerprinting and related tests that reveal information about the target:

```
# nmap -v -O target.example.com
...
For OSScan assuming that port 22 is open and port 1 is closed and neither are
firewalled
...
Remote operating system guess: Linux Kernel 2.4.0 - 2.5.20
Uptime 3.167 days (since Mon Feb 21 12:22:21 2003)
TCP Sequence Prediction: Class=random positive increments
                         Difficulty=4917321 (Good luck!)
IPID Sequence Generation: All zeros

Nmap run completed -- 1 IP address (1 host up) scanned in 31 seconds
```

Fingerprinting requires an open and a closed port, which are chosen automatically (so a port scan is required). nmap then determines the operating system of the target by noticing details of its IP protocol implementation: Linux is readily recognized (even the version!). It guesses the uptime using the TCP timestamp option. The TCP and IPID Sequence tests measure vulnerability to forged connections and other advanced attacks, and Linux performs well here.

It is sobering to see how many details nmap can learn about a system, particularly by attackers with no authorized access. Expect that attacks on your Linux systems will focus on known Linux-specific vulnerabilities, especially if you are using an out-dated kernel. To protect yourself, keep up to date with security patches.

nmap can test for other vulnerabilities of specific network services. If you run an open FTP server, try nmap -b to see if it can be exploited as a proxy. Similarly, if you allow access to an IDENT server, use nmap -I to determine if attackers can learn the user-name (especially root!) that owns other open ports. The -sR option displays information about open RPC services, even without direct access to your portmapper.

If your firewall makes decisions based on source addresses, run nmap on different remote machines to test variations in behavior. Similarly, if the source port is consulted by your firewall policies, use the nmap -g option to pick specific source ports.

The nmap -o options save results to log files in a variety of formats. The XML format (-oX) is ideal for parsing by scripts: try the XML::Simple Perl module for an especially easy way to read the structured data. Alternately, the -oG option produces results in a simplified format that is designed for searches using grep. The -oN option uses the same human-readable format that is printed to stdout, and -oA writes all three formats to separate files.

nmap supports several stealth options that attempt to disguise the source of attacks by using third-parties as proxies or decoys, or to escape detection by fragmenting packets, altering timing parameters, etc. These can occasionally be useful for testing your logging and intrusion detection mechanisms, like Snort. [9.20]

See Also

nmap(1), nmapfe(1), nc(1), telnet(1). The nmap home page is *http://www.insecure. org/nmap.*The XML::Simple Perl module is found on CPAN, *http://www.cpan.org.*

9.14   Examining Local Network Activities

Problem

You want to examine network use occurring on your local machine.

Solution

To print a summary of network use:

```
$ netstat --inet                 Connected sockets
$ netstat --inet --listening     Server sockets
$ netstat --inet --all           Both
# netstat --inet ... -p          Identify processes
```

To print dynamically assigned ports for RPC services:

```
$ rpcinfo -p [host]
```

To list network connections for all processes:

```
# lsof -i[TCP|UDP][@host][:port]
```

To list all open files for specific processes:

```
# lsof -p pid
# lsof -c command
# lsof -u username
```

To list all open files (and network connections) for all processes:

```
# lsof
```

To trace network system calls, use strace. [9.15]

Discussion

Suppose you see a process with an unfamiliar name running on your system. Should you be concerned? What is it doing? Could it be surreptitiously transmitting data to some other machine on a distant continent?

The /proc Filesystem

Programs like ps, netstat, and lsof obtain information from the Linux kernel via the */proc* filesystem. Although */proc* looks like an ordinary file hierarchy (e.g., you can run */bin/ls* for a directory listing), it actually contains simulated files. These files are like windows into the kernel, presenting its data structures in an easy-to-read manner for programs and users, generally in text format. For example, the file */proc/mounts* contains the list of currently mounted filesystems:

```
$ cat /proc/mounts
/dev/root / ext2 rw 0 0
/proc /proc proc rw 0 0
/dev/hda9 /var ext2 rw 0 0
...
```

but if you examine the file listing:

```
$ ls -l /proc/mounts
-r--r--r--    1 root     root              0 Feb 23 17:07 /proc/mounts
```

you'll see several curious things. The file has zero size, yet it "contains" the mounted filesystem data, because it's a simulated file. Also its "last modified" timestamp is the current time. The permission bits are accurate: this file is world-readable but not writable.[a] The kernel enforces these access restrictions just as for ordinary files.

You can read */proc* files directly, but it's usually more convenient to use programs like ps, netstat, and lsof because:

- They combine data from a wide range of */proc* files into an informative report.
- They have options to control the output format or select specific information.
- Their output format is usually more portable than the format of the corresponding */proc* files, which are Linux-specific and can change between kernel versions (although considerable effort is expended to provide backward compatibility). For instance, the output of lsof -F is in a standardized format, and therefore easily parsed by other programs.

Nevertheless, */proc* files are sometimes ideal for scripts or interactive use. The most important files for networking are */proc/net/tcp* and */proc/net/udp*, both consulted by netstat. Kernel parameters related to networking can be found in the */proc/sys/net* directory.

Information for individual processes is located in */proc/<pid>* directories, where *<pid>* is the process ID. For example, the file */proc/12345/cmdline* contains the original command line that invoked the (currently running) process 12345. Programs like ps summarize the data in these files. Each process directory contains a */proc/<pid>/fd* subdirectory with links for open files: this is used by the lsof command.

For more details about the format of files in the */proc* filesystem, see the proc(5) manpage, and documentation in the Linux kernel source distribution, specifically:

/usr/src/linux*/Documentation/filesystems/proc.txt

[a] Imagine the havoc one could wreak by writing arbitrary text into a kernel data structure.

To answer these kinds of questions, you need tools for observing network use and for correlating activities with specific processes. Use these tools frequently so you will be familiar with normal network usage, and equipped to focus on suspicious behavior when you encounter it.

The netstat command prints a summary of the state of networking on your machine, and is a good way to start investigations. The --inet option prints active connections:

```
$ netstat --inet
Active Internet connections (w/o servers)
Proto   Recv-Q Send-Q Local Address          Foreign Address         State
tcp     0      240    myhost.example.com:ssh  client.example.com:3672 ESTABLISHED
tcp     0      0      myhost.example.com:4099 server.example.com:ssh  TIME_WAIT
```

This example shows inbound and outbound ssh connections; the latter is shutting down (as indicated by TIME_WAIT). If you see an unusually large number of connections in the SYN_RECV state, your system is probably being probed by a port scanner like nmap. [9.13]

Add the --listening option to instead see server sockets that are ready to accept new connections (or use --all to see both kinds of sockets):

```
$ netstat --inet --listening
Active Internet connections (only servers)
Proto Recv-Q Send-Q Local Address   Foreign Address   State
tcp     0      0     *:ssh           *:*               LISTEN
tcp     0      0     *:http          *:*               LISTEN
tcp     0      0     *:814           *:*               LISTEN
udp     0      0     *:ntp           *:*
udp     0      0     *:811           *:*
```

This example shows the ssh daemon, a web server (http), a network time server (which uses udp), and two numerical mystery ports, which might be considered suspicious. On a typical system, you would expect to see many more server sockets, and you should try to understand the purpose of each. Consider disabling services that you don't need, as a security precaution.

Port numbers for RPC services are assigned dynamically by the portmapper. The rpcinfo command shows these assignments:

```
$ rpcinfo -p | egrep -w "port|81[14]"
   program vers proto   port
   100007    2  udp     811  ypbind
   100007    1  udp     811  ypbind
   100007    2  tcp     814  ypbind
   100007    1  tcp     814  ypbind
```

This relieves our concerns about the mystery ports found by netstat.

You can even query the portmapper on a different machine, by specifying the hostname on the command line. This is one reason why your firewall should block access to your portmapper, and why you should run it only if you need RPC services.

The netstat -p option adds a process ID and command name for each socket, and the -e option adds a username.

 Only the superuser can examine detailed information for processes owned by others. If you need to observe a wide variety of processes, run these commands as root.

The lsof command lists open files for individual processes, including network connections. With no options, lsof reports on all open files for all processes, and you can hunt for information of interest using grep or your favorite text editor. This technique can be useful when you don't know precisely what you are looking for, because all of the information is available, which provides context. The voluminous output, however, can make specific information hard to notice.

lsof provides many options to select files or processes for more refined searches. By default, lsof prints information that matches *any* of the selections. Use the -a option to require matching *all* of them instead.

The -i option selects network connections: lsof -i is more detailed than but similar to netstat --inet --all -p. The -i option can be followed by an argument of the form [TCP|UDP][@*host*][:*port*] to select specific network connections—any or all of the components can be omitted. For example, to view all ssh connections (which use TCP), to or from any machine:

```
# lsof -iTCP:ssh
COMMAND PID  USER     FD TYPE DEVICE SIZE NODE NAME
sshd    678 root     3u IPv4   1279      TCP  *:ssh (LISTEN)
sshd   7122 root     4u IPv4 211494      TCP  myhost:ssh->client:367  (ESTABLISHED)
sshd   7125 katie    4u IPv4 211494      TCP  myhost:ssh->client:3672 (ESTABLISHED)
ssh    8145 marianne 3u IPv4 254706      TCP  myhost:3933->server:ssh (ESTABLISHED)
```

Note that a single network connection (or indeed, any open file) can be shared by several processes, as shown in this example. This detail is not revealed by netstat -p.

 Both netstat and lsof convert IP addresses to hostnames, and port numbers to service names (e.g., ssh), if possible. You can inhibit these conversions and force printing of numeric values, e.g., if you are have many network connections and some nameservers are responding slowly. Use the netstat --numeric-hosts or --numeric-ports options, or the lsof -n, -P, or -l options (for host addresses, port numbers, and user IDs, respectively) to obtain numeric values, as needed.

To examine processes that use RPC services, the +M option is handy for displaying portmapper registrations:

```
# lsof +M -iTCP:814 -iUDP:811
COMMAND PID  USER FD TYPE DEVICE SIZE NODE NAME
ypbind  633 root 6u IPv4   1202      UDP  *:811[ypbind]
ypbind  633 root 7u IPv4   1207      TCP  *:814[ypbind] (LISTEN)
```

```
ypbind   635  root  6u  IPv4  1202       UDP  *:811[ypbind]
ypbind   635  root  7u  IPv4  1207       TCP  *:814[ypbind] (LISTEN)
ypbind   636  root  6u  IPv4  1202       UDP  *:811[ypbind]
ypbind   636  root  7u  IPv4  1207       TCP  *:814[ypbind] (LISTEN)
ypbind   637  root  6u  IPv4  1202       UDP  *:811[ypbind]
ypbind   637  root  7u  IPv4  1207       TCP  *:814[ypbind] (LISTEN)
```

This corresponds to `rpcinfo -p` output from our earlier example. The RPC program names are enclosed in square brackets, after the port numbers.

You can also select processes by ID (-p), command name (-c), or username (-u):

```
# lsof -a -c myprog -u tony
COMMAND  PID  USER  FD  TYPE  DEVICE   SIZE  NODE   NAME
myprog   8387  tony  cwd  DIR   0,15     4096  42329  /var/tmp
myprog   8387  tony  rtd  DIR   8,1      4096     2   /
myprog   8387  tony  txt  REG   8,2     13798  31551  /usr/local/bin/myprog
myprog   8387  tony  mem  REG   8,1     87341  21296  /lib/ld-2.2.93.so
myprog   8387  tony  mem  REG   8,1     90444  21313  /lib/libnsl-2.2.93.so
myprog   8387  tony  mem  REG   8,1     11314  21309  /lib/libdl-2.2.93.so
myprog   8387  tony  mem  REG   8,1    170910  81925  /lib/i686/libm-2.2.93.so
myprog   8387  tony  mem  REG   8,1     10421  21347  /lib/libutil-2.2.93.so
myprog   8387  tony  mem  REG   8,1     42657  21329  /lib/libnss_files-2.2.93.so
myprog   8387  tony  mem  REG   8,1     15807  21326  /lib/libnss_dns-2.2.93.so
myprog   8387  tony  mem  REG   8,1     69434  21341  /lib/libresolv-2.2.93.so
myprog   8387  tony  mem  REG   8,1   1395734  81923  /lib/i686/libc-2.2.93.so
myprog   8387  tony   0u  CHR  136,3              2   /dev/pts/3
myprog   8387  tony   1u  CHR  136,3              2   /dev/pts/3
myprog   8387  tony   2u  CHR  136,3              2   /dev/pts/3
myprog   8387  tony   3r  REG   8,5        0  98315  /var/tmp/foo
myprog   8387  tony   4w  REG   8,5        0  98319  /var/tmp/bar
myprog   8387  tony   5u  IPv4 274331          TCP  myhost:2944->www:http (ESTABLISHED)
```

Note that the arrow does not indicate the direction of data transfer for network connections: the order displayed is always *local->remote*.

The letters following the file descriptor (FD) numbers show that myprog has opened the file *foo* for reading (r), the file *bar* for writing (w), and the network connection bidirectionally (u).

The complete set of information printed by lsof can be useful when investigating suspicious processes. For example, we can see that myprog's current working directory (cwd) is */var/tmp*, and the pathname for the program (txt) is */usr/local/bin/ myprog*. Be aware that rogue programs may try to disguise their identity: if you find sshd using the executable */tmp/sshd* instead of */usr/sbin/sshd*, that is cause for alarm. Similarly, it would be troubling to discover a program called "ls" with network connections to unfamiliar ports![*]

---

[*] Even ls can legitimately use the network, however, if your system uses NIS for user or group ID lookups. You need to know what to expect in each case.

See Also

netstat(8), rpcinfo(8), lsof(8).

9.15   Tracing Processes

Problem

You want to know what an unfamiliar process is doing.

Solution

To attach to a running process and trace system calls:

```
# strace -p pid
```

To trace network system calls:

```
# strace -e trace=network,read,write ...
```

Discussion

The strace command lets you observe a given process in detail, printing its system calls as they occur. It expands all arguments, return values, and errors (if any) for the system calls, showing all information passed between the process and the kernel. (It can also trace signals.) This provides a very complete picture of what the process is doing.

Use the strace -p option to attach to and trace a process, identified by its process ID, say, 12345:

```
# strace -p 12345
```

To detach and stop tracing, just kill strace. Other than a small performance penalty, strace has no effect on the traced process.

Tracing all system calls for a process can produce overwhelming output, so you can select sets of interesting system calls to print. For monitoring network activity, the -e trace=network option is appropriate. Network sockets often use the generic read and write system calls as well, so trace those too:

```
$ strace -e trace=network,read,write finger katie@server.example.com
...
socket(PF_INET, SOCK_STREAM, IPPROTO_TCP) = 4
connect(4, {sin_family=AF_INET,
            sin_port=htons(79),
            sin_addr=inet_addr("10.12.104.222")}, 16) = 0
write(4, "katie", 5)                    = 5
write(4, "\r\n", 2)                     = 2
read(4, "Login: katie       \t\t\tName: K"..., 4096) = 244
read(4, "", 4096)                       = 0
...
```

The trace shows the creation of a TCP socket, followed by a connection to port 79 for the finger service at the IP address for the server. The program then follows the finger protocol by writing the username and reading the response.

By default, strace prints only 32 characters of string arguments, which can lead to the truncated output shown. For a more complete trace, use the -s option to specify a larger maximum data size. Similarly, strace abbreviates some large structure arguments, such as the environment for new processes: supply the -v option to print this information in full.

You can trace most network activity effectively by following file descriptors: in the previous example, the value is 4 (returned by the socket-creation call, and used as the first argument for the subsequent system calls). Then match these values to the file descriptors displayed in the FD column by lsof. [9.14]

When you identify an interesting file descriptor, you can print the transferred data in both hexadecimal and ASCII using the options -e [read|write]=fd:

```
$ strace -e trace=read -e read=4 finger katie@server.example.com
...
read(4, "Login: katie          \t\t\tName: K"..., 4096) = 244
 | 00000   4c 6f 67 69 6e 3a 20 6b  61 74 69 65 20 20 20 20  Login: k atie     |
 | 00010   20 20 20 20 20 20 09 09  09 4e 61 6d 65 3a 20 4b           .. .Name: K |
...
```

strace watches data transfers much like network packet sniffers do, but it also can observe input/output involving local files and other system activities.

If you trace programs for long periods, ask strace to annotate its output with timestamps. The -t option records absolute times (repeat the option for more detail), the -r option records relative times between system calls, and -T records time spent in the kernel within system calls. Finally, add the strace -f option to follow child processes.[*]

Each line of the trace has the process ID added for children. Alternatively, you can untangle the system calls by directing the trace for each child process to a separate file, using the options:

```
$ strace -f -ff -o filename ...
```

See Also

strace(1), and the manpages for the system calls appearing in strace output.

---

[*] To follow child processes created by vfork, include the -F option as well, but this requires support from the kernel that is not widely available at press time. Also, strace does not currently work well with multithreaded processes: be sure you have the latest version, and a kernel Version 2.4 or later, before attempting thread tracing.

9.16   Observing Network Traffic

Problem

You want to watch network traffic flowing by (or through) your machine.

Solution

Use a packet sniffer such as `tcpdump`.[*]

To sniff packets and save them in a file:

```
# tcpdump -w filename [-c count] [-i interface] [-s snap-length] [expression]
```

To read and display the saved network trace data:

```
$ tcpdump -r filename [expression]
```

To select packets related to particular TCP services to or from a host:

```
# tcpdump tcp port service [or service] and host server.example.com
```

For a convenient and powerful GUI, use Ethereal. [9.17]

To enable an unconfigured interface, for a "stealth" packet sniffer:

```
# ifconfig interface-name 0.0.0.0 up
```

To print information about all of your network interfaces with loaded drivers: [3.1]

```
$ ifconfig -a
```

Discussion

Is your system under attack? Your firewall is logging unusual activities, you see lots of half-open connections, and the performance of your web server is degrading. How can you learn what is happening so you can take defensive action? Use a *packet sniffer* to watch traffic on the network!

In normal operation, network interfaces are programmed to receive only the following:

- *Unicast packets*, addressed to a specific machine
- *Multicast packets*, targeted to systems that choose to subscribe to services like streaming video or sound
- *Broadcast packets*, for when an appropriate destination is not known, or for important information that is probably of interest to all machines on the network

---

[*] In spite of its name, tcpdump is not restricted to TCP. It can capture entire packets, including the link-level (Ethernet) headers, IP, UDP, etc.

The term "unicast" is not an oxymoron: all packets on networks like Ethernet are in fact sent (conceptually) to all systems on the network. Each system simply ignores unicast packets addressed to other machines, or uninteresting multicast packets.

A packet sniffer puts a network interface into *promiscuous mode*, causing it to receive all packets on the network, like a wiretap. Almost all network adapters support this mode nowadays. Linux restricts the use of promiscuous mode to the superuser, so always run packet-sniffing programs as root. Whenever you switch an interface to promiscuous mode, the kernel logs the change, so we advise running the logger command [9.27] to announce your packet-sniffing activities.

If promiscuous mode doesn't seem to be working, and your kernel is sending complaints to the system logger (usually in */var/log/messages*) that say:

```
modprobe: can't locate module net-pf-17
```

then your kernel was built without support for the packet socket protocol, which is required for network sniffers.

Rebuild your kernel with the option CONFIG_PACKET=y (or CONFIG_PACKET=m to build a kernel module). Red Hat and SuSE distribute kernels with support for the packet socket protocol enabled, so network sniffers should work.

Network switches complicate this picture. Unlike less intelligent hubs, switches watch network traffic, attempt to learn which systems are connected to each network segment, and then send unicast packets only to ports known to be connected to the destination systems, which defeats packet sniffing. However, many network switches support packet sniffing with a configuration option to send all traffic to designated ports. If you are running a network sniffer on a switched network, consult the documentation for your switch.

The primary purpose of network switches is to improve performance, not to enhance security. Packet sniffing is more difficult on a switched network, but not impossible: dsniff [9.19] is distributed with a collection of tools to demonstrate such attacks. Do not be complacent about the need for secure protocols, just because your systems are connected to switches instead of hubs.

Similarly, routers and gateways pass traffic to different networks based on the destination address for each packet. If you want to watch traffic between machines on different networks, attach your packet sniffer somewhere along the route between the source and destination.

Packet sniffers tap into the network stack at a low level, and are therefore immune to restrictions imposed by firewalls. To verify the correct operation of your firewall, use a packet sniffer to watch the firewall accept or reject traffic.

Your network interface need not even be configured in order to watch traffic (it does need to be up, however). Use the ifconfig command to enable an unconfigured interface by setting the IP address to zero:

```
# ifconfig eth2 0.0.0.0 up
```

Unconfigured interfaces are useful for dedicated packet-sniffing machines, because they are hard to detect or attack. Such systems are often used on untrusted networks exposed to the outside (e.g., right next to your web servers). Use care when these "stealth" packet sniffers are also connected (by normally configured network interfaces) to trusted, internal networks: for example, disable IP forwarding. [2.3]

 Promiscuous mode can degrade network performance. Avoid running a packet sniffer for long periods on important, production machines: use a separate, dedicated machine instead.

Almost all Linux packet-sniffing programs use libpcap, a packet capture library distributed with tcpdump. As a fortunate consequence, network trace files share a common format, so you can use one tool to capture and save packets, and others to display and analyze the traffic. The file command recognizes and displays information about libpcap-format network trace files:

```
$ file trace.pcap
trace.pcap: tcpdump capture file (little-endian) - version 2.4 (Ethernet, capture
length 96)
```

 Kernels of Version 2.2 or higher can send warnings to the system logger like:

```
    tcpdump uses obsolete (PF_INET,SOCK_PACKET)
```

These are harmless, and can be safely ignored. To avoid the warnings, upgrade to a more recent version of libpcap.

To sniff packets and save them in a file, use the tcpdump -w option:

```
# tcpdump -w trace.pcap [-c count] [-i interface] [-s snap-length] [expression]
```

Just kill tcpdump when you are done, or use the -c option to request a maximum number of packets to record.

If your system is connected to multiple networks, use the -i option to listen on a specific interface (e.g., eth2). The ifconfig command prints information about all of your network interfaces with loaded drivers: [3.1]

```
$ ifconfig -a
```

The special interface name "any" denotes *all* of the interfaces by any program that uses libpcap, but these interfaces are not put into promiscuous mode automatically. Before using tcpdump -i any, use ifconfig to enable promiscuous mode for specific interfaces of interest:

```
# ifconfig interface promisc
```

Remember to disable promiscuous mode when you are done sniffing:

```
# ifconfig interface -promisc
```

Support for the "any" interface is available in kernel Versions 2.2 or later.

Normally, tcpdump saves only the first 68 bytes of each packet. This snapshot length is good for analysis of low-level protocols (e.g., TCP or UDP), but for higher-level ones (like HTTP) use the -s option to request a larger snapshot. To capture entire packets and track all transmitted data, specify a snapshot length of zero. Larger snapshots consume dramatically more disk space, and can impact network performance or even cause packet loss under heavy load.

By default, tcpdump records all packets seen on the network. Use a *capture filter expression* to select specific packets: the criteria can be based on any data in the protocol headers, using a simple syntax described in the tcpdump(8) manpage. For example, to record FTP transfers to or from a server:

```
# tcpdump -w trace.pcap tcp port ftp or ftp-data and host server.example.com
```

By restricting the kinds of packets you capture, you can reduce the performance implications and storage requirements of larger snapshots.

To read and display the saved network trace data, use the tcpdump -r option:

```
$ tcpdump -r trace.pcap [expression]
```

Root access is not required to analyze the collected data, since it is stored in ordinary files. You may want to protect those trace files, however, if they contain sensitive data.

Use a *display filter expression* to print information only about selected packets; display filters use the same syntax as capture filters.

The capture and display operations can be combined, without saving data to a file, if neither the -w nor -r options are used, but we recommend saving to a file, because:

- Protocol analysis often requires displaying the data multiple times, in different formats, and perhaps using different tools.

- You might want to analyze data captured at some earlier time.

- It is hard to predict selection criteria in advance. Use more inclusive filter expressions at capture time, then more discriminating ones at display time, when you understand more clearly which data is interesting.

- Display operations can be inefficient. Memory is consumed to track TCP sequence numbers, for example. Your packet sniffer should be lean and mean if you plan to run it for long periods.

- Display operations sometimes interfere with capture operations. Converting IP addresses to hostnames often involves DNS lookups, which can be confusing if you are watching traffic to and from your nameservers! Similarly, if you tunnel tcpdump output through an SSH connection, that generates additional SSH traffic.

Saving formatted output from tcpdump is an even worse idea. It consumes large amounts of space, is difficult for other programs to parse, and discards much of the information saved in the libpcap-format trace file. Use tcpdump -w to save network traces.

tcpdump prints information about packets in a terse, protocol-dependent format meticulously described in the manpage. Suppose a machine 10.6.6.6 is performing a port scan*of another machine, 10.9.9.9, by running nmap -r. [9.13] If you use tcpdump to observe this port scan activity, you'll see something like this:

```
# tcpdump -nn
...
23:08:14.980358 10.6.6.6.6180 > 10.9.9.9.20: S 5498218:5498218(0) win 4096 [tos 0x80]
23:08:14.980436 10.9.9.9.20 > 10.6.6.6.6180: R 0:0(0) ack 5498219 win 0 (DF) [tos 0x80]
23:08:14.980795 10.6.6.6.6180 > 10.9.9.9.21: S 5498218:5498218(0) win 4096 [tos 0x80]
23:08:14.980893 10.9.9.9.21 > 10.6.6.6.6180: R 0:0(0) ack 5498219 win 0 (DF) [tos 0x80]
23:08:14.983496 10.6.6.6.6180 > 10.9.9.9.22: S 5498218:5498218(0) win 4096
23:08:14.984488 10.9.9.9.22 > 10.6.6.6.6180: S 3458349:3458349(0) ack 5498219 win 5840
<mss 1460> (DF)
23:08:14.983907 10.6.6.6.6180 > 10.9.9.9.23: S 5498218:5498218(0) win 4096 [tos 0x80]
23:08:14.984577 10.9.9.9.23 > 10.6.6.6.6180: R 0:0(0) ack 5498219 win 0 (DF) [tos 0x80]
23:08:15.060218 10.6.6.6.6180 > 10.9.9.99.22: R 5498219:5498219(0) win 0 (DF)
23:08:15.067712 10.6.6.6.6180 > 10.9.9.99.24: S 5498218:5498218(0) win 4096
23:08:15.067797 10.9.9.9.24 > 10.6.6.6.6180: R 0:0(0) ack 5498219 win 0 (DF)
23:08:15.068201 10.6.6.6.6180 > 10.9.9.9.25: S 5498218:5498218(0) win 4096 [tos 0x80]
23:08:15.068282 10.9.9.9.25 > 10.6.6.6.6180: R 0:0(0) ack 5498219 win 0 (DF) [tos 0x80]
...
```

The nmap -r process scans the ports sequentially. For each closed port, we see an incoming TCP SYN packet, and a TCP RST reply from the target. An open SSH port (22) instead elicits a TCP SYN+ACK reply, indicating that a server is listening: the scanner responds a short time later with a TCP RST packet (sent out of order) to tear down the half-open SSH connection. Protocol analysis is especially enlightening when a victim is confronted by sneakier probes and denial of service attacks that don't adhere to the usual network protocol rules.

The previous example used -nn to print everything numerically. The -v option requests additional details; repeat it (-v -v ...) for increased verbosity. Timestamps are recorded by the kernel (and saved in libpcap-format trace files), and you can select a variety of formats by specifying the -t option one or more times. Use the -e option to print link-level (Ethernet) header information.

See Also

ifconfig(8), tcpdump(8), nmap(8). The `tcpdump` home page is *http://www.tcpdump.org*, and the `nmap` home page is *http://www.insecure.org/nmap*.

A good reference on Internet protocols is found at *http://www.protocols.com*. Also, the book *Internet Core Protocols: The Definitive Guide* (O'Reilly) covers similar material.

9.17   Observing Network Traffic (GUI)

Problem

You want to watch network traffic via a graphical interface.

Solution

Use Ethereal and `tethereal`.

Discussion

Prolonged perusing of `tcpdump` output [9.16] can lead to eyestrain. Fortunately, alternatives are available, and Ethereal is one of the best.

Ethereal is a GUI network sniffer that supports a number of enhancements beyond the capabilities of `tcpdump`. When Ethereal starts, it presents three windows:

Packet List
   A summary line for each packet, in a format similar to `tcpdump`.

Tree View
   An expandable protocol tree for the packet selected in the previous window. An observer can drill down to reveal individual fields at each protocol level. Ethereal understands and can display an astounding number of protocols in detail.

Data View
   Hexadecimal and ASCII dumps of all bytes captured in the selected packet. Bytes are highlighted according to selections in the protocol tree.

Ethereal uses the same syntax as `tcpdump` for capture filter expressions. However, it uses a different, more powerful syntax for display filter expressions. Our previous `tcpdump` example, to select packets related to FTP transfers to or from a server: [9.16]

```
tcp port ftp or ftp-data and host server.example.com
```

would be rewritten using Ethereal's display filter syntax as:

```
ftp or ftp-data and ip.addr == server.example.com
```

The display filter syntax is described in detail in the ethereal(1) manpage.

If you receive confusing and uninformative syntax error messages, make sure you are not using *display* filter syntax for *capture* filters, or vice-versa.

Ethereal provides a GUI to construct and update display filter expressions, and can use those expressions to find packets in a trace, or to colorize the display.

Ethereal also provides a tool to follow a TCP stream, reassembling (and reordering) packets to construct an ASCII or hexadecimal dump of an entire TCP session. You can use this to view many protocols that are transmitted as clear text.

Menus are provided as alternatives for command-line options (which are very similar to those of tcpdump). Ethereal does its own packet capture (using libpcap), or reads and writes network trace files in a variety of formats. On Red Hat systems, the program is installed with a wrapper that asks for the root password (required for packet sniffing), and allows running as an ordinary user (if only display features are used).

The easiest way to start using Ethereal is:

1. Launch the program.
2. Use the Capture Filters item in the Edit menu to select the traffic of interest, or just skip this step to capture all traffic.
3. Use the Start item in the Capture menu. Fill out the Capture Preferences dialog box, which allows specification of the interface for listening, the snapshot (or "capture length"), and whether you want to update the display in real time, as the packet capture happens. Click OK to begin sniffing packets.
4. Watch the dialog box (and the updated display, if you selected the real time update option) to see the packet capture in progress. Click the Stop button when you are done.
5. The display is now updated, if it was not already. Try selecting packets in the Packet List window, drill down to expand the Tree View, and select parts of the protocol tree to highlight the corresponding sections of the Data View. This is a *great* way to learn about internal details of network protocols!
6. Select a TCP packet, and use the Follow TCP Stream item in the Tools menu to see an entire session displayed in a separate window.

Ethereal is amazingly flexible, and this is just a small sample of its functionality. To learn more, browse the menus and see the Ethereal User's Guide for detailed explanations and screen shots.

tethereal is a text version of Ethereal, and is similar in function to tcpdump, except it uses Ethereal's enhanced display filter syntax. The -V option prints the protocol tree for each packet, instead of a one-line summary.

Use the tethereal -b option to run in "ring buffer" mode (Ethereal also supports this option, but the mode is designed for long-term operation, when the GUI is not as useful). In this mode, tethereal maintains a specified number of network trace files, switching to the next file when a maximum size (determined by the -a option) is reached, and discarding the oldest files, similar to logrotate. [9.30] For example, to keep a ring buffer with 10 files of 16 megabytes each:

```
# tethereal -w ring-buffer -b 10 -a filesize:16384
```

See Also

ethereal(1), tethereal(1). The Ethereal home page is *http://www.ethereal.com.*

9.18   Searching for Strings in Network Traffic

Problem

You want to watch network traffic, searching for strings in the transmitted data.

Solution

Use ngrep.

To search for packets containing data that matches a regular expression and protocols that match a filter expression:

```
# ngrep [grep-options] regular-expression [filter-expression]
```

To search instead for a sequence of binary data:

```
# ngrep -X hexadecimal-digits [filter-expression]
```

To sniff packets and save them in a file:

```
# ngrep -O filename [-n count] [-d interface] [-s snap-length] \
    regular-expression [filter-expression]
```

To read and display the saved network trace data:

```
$ ngrep -I filename regular-expression [filter-expression]
```

Discussion

ngrep is supplied with SuSE but not Red Hat; however, it is easy to obtain and install if you need it. Download it from *http://ngrep.sourceforge.net* and unpack it:

```
$ tar xvpzf ngrep-*.tar.gz
```

compile it:

```
$ cd ngrep
$ ./configure --prefix=/usr/local
$ make
```

and install it into *usr/local* as root:[*]

```
# mkdir -p /usr/local/bin /usr/local/man/man8
# make install
```

Sometimes we are interested in observing the data delivered by network packets, known as the *payload*. Tools like tcpdump [9.16] and especially Ethereal [9.17] can display the payload, but they are primarily designed for protocol analysis, so their ability to select packets based on arbitrary data is limited.[†]

The ngrep command searches network traffic for data that matches extended regular expressions, in the same way that the egrep command (or grep -E) searches files. In fact, ngrep supports many of the same command-line options as egrep, such as -i (case-insensitive), -w (whole words), or -v (nonmatching). In addition, ngrep can select packets using the same filter expressions as tcpdump. To use ngrep as an ordinary packet sniffer, use the regular expression ".", which matches any nonempty payload.

ngrep is handy for detecting the use of insecure protocols. For example, we can observe FTP transfers to or from a server, searching for FTP request command strings to reveal usernames, passwords, and filenames that are transmitted as clear text:

```
$ ngrep -t -x 'USER|PASS|RETR|STOR' tcp port ftp and host server.example.com
interface: eth0 (10.44.44.0/255.255.255.0)
filter: ip and ( tcp port ftp )
match: USER|PASS|RETR|STOR
#############
T 2003/02/27 23:31:20.303636 10.33.33.33:1057 -> 10.88.88.88:21 [AP]
  55 53 45 52 20 6b 61 74    69 65 0d 0a                  USER katie..
#####
T 2003/02/27 23:31:25.315858 10.33.33.33:1057 -> 10.88.88.88:21 [AP]
  50 41 53 53 20 44 75 6d    62 6f 21 0d 0a               PASS Dumbo!..
#############
T 2003/02/27 23:32:15.637343 10.33.33.33:1057 -> 10.88.88.88:21 [AP]
  52 45 54 52 20 70 6f 6f    68 62 65 61 72 0d 0a         RETR poohbear..
########
T 2003/02/27 23:32:19.742193 10.33.33.33:1057 -> 10.88.88.88:21 [AP]
  53 54 4f 52 20 68 6f 6e    65 79 70 6f 74 0d 0a         STOR honeypot..
################exit
58 received, 0 dropped
```

---

[*] We explicitly install in */usr/local*, because otherwise the configure script would install into */usr*, based on the location of gcc. We recommend */usr/local* to avoid clashes with vendor-supplied software in */usr*; this recommendation is codified in the Filesystem Hierarchy Standard (FHS), *http://www.pathname.com/fhs*. The configure script used for ngrep is unusual—such scripts typically install into */usr/local* by default, and therefore do not need an explicit --prefix option. We also create the installation directories if they don't already exist, to overcome deficiencies in the make install command.

† The concept of a packet's payload is subjective. Each lower-level protocol regards the higher-level protocols as its payload. The highest-level protocol delivers the user data; for example, the files transferred by FTP.

The -t option adds timestamps; use -T instead for relative times between packets. The -x option prints hexadecimal values in addition to the ASCII strings.

ngrep prints a hash character (#) for each packet that matches the filter expression: only those packets that match the regular expression are printed in detail. Use the -q option to suppress the hashes.

To search for binary data, use the -X option with a sequence of hexadecimal digits (of any length) instead of a regular expression. This can detect some kinds of buffer overflow attacks, characterized by known signatures of fixed binary data.

 ngrep matches data only within individual packets. If strings are split between packets due to fragmentation, they will not be found. Try to match shorter strings to reduce (but not entirely eliminate) the probability of these misses. Shorter strings can also lead to false matches, however—a bit of experimentation is sometimes required. dsniff does not have this limitation. [9.19]

Like other packet sniffers, ngrep can write and read libpcap-format network trace files, using the -O and -I options. [9.16] This is especially convenient when running ngrep repeatedly to refine your search, using data captured previously, perhaps by another program. Usually ngrep captures packets until killed, or it will exit after recording a maximum number of packets requested by the -n option. The -d option selects a specific interface, if your machine has several. By default, ngrep captures entire packets (in contrast to tcpdump and ethereal), since ngrep is interested in the payloads. If your data of interest is at the beginning of the packets, use the -s option to reduce the snapshot and gain efficiency.

When ngrep finds an interesting packet, the adjacent packets might be of interest too, as context. The ngrep -A option prints a specified number of extra (not necessarily matching) packets for trailing context. This is similar in spirit to the grep -A option, but ngrep does not support a corresponding -B option for leading context.

 A recommended practice: Save a generous amount of network trace data with tcpdump, then run ngrep to locate interesting data. Finally, browse the complete trace using Ethereal, relying on the timestamps to identify the packets matched by ngrep.

See Also

ngrep(8), egrep(1), grep(1), tcpdump(8). The home page for ngrep is *http://ngrep. sourceforge.net*, and the tcpdump home page is *http://www.tcpdump.org*.

Learn more about extended regular expressions in the O'Reilly book *Mastering Regular Expressions*.

9.19　Detecting Insecure Network Protocols

Problem

You want to determine if insecure protocols are being used on the network.

Solution

Use dsniff.

To monitor the network for insecure protocols:

```
# dsniff -m [-i interface] [-s snap-length] [filter-expression]
```

To save results in a database, instead of printing them:

```
# dsniff -w gotcha.db [other options...]
```

To read and print the results from the database:

```
$ dsniff -r gotcha.db
```

To capture mail messages from SMTP or POP traffic:

```
# mailsnarf [-i interface] [-v] [regular-expression [filter-expression]]
```

To capture file contents from NFS traffic:

```
# filesnarf [-i interface] [-v] [regular-expression [filter-expression]]
```

To capture URLs from HTTP traffic:

```
# urlsnarf  [-i interface] [-v] [regular-expression [filter-expression]]
```

ngrep is also useful for detecting insecure network protocols. [9.18]

Discussion

dsniff is not supplied with Red Hat or SuSE, but installation is straightforward. A few extra steps are required for two prerequisite libraries, libnet and libnids, not distributed by Red Hat. SuSE provides these libraries, so you can skip ahead to the installation of dsniff itself on such systems.

If you need the libraries, first download libnet, a toolkit for network packet manipulation, from *http://www.packetfactory.net/projects/libnet*, and unpack it:

```
$ tar xvzpf libnet-1.0.*.tar.gz
```

Then compile it:*

```
$ cd Libnet-1.0.*
$ ./configure --prefix=/usr/local
$ make
```

---

* At press time, dsniff 2.3 (the latest stable version) cannot be built with the most recent version of libnet. Be sure to use the older libnet 1.0.2a with dsniff 2.3.

and install it as root:

```
# make install
```

We explicitly configure to install in */usr/local* (instead of */usr*), to match the default location for our later configuration steps. Next, download `libnids`, which is used for TCP stream reassembly, from *http://www.packetfactory.net/projects/libnids*, and unpack it:

```
$ tar xvzpf libnids-*.tar.gz
```

Then compile it:

```
$ cd `ls -d libnids-* | head -1`
$ ./configure
$ make
```

and install it as root:

```
# make install
```

 dsniff also requires the Berkeley database library, which is provided by both Red Hat and SuSE. Unfortunately, some systems such as Red Hat 7.0 are missing */usr/include/db_185.h* (either a plain file or a symbolic link) that dsniff needs. This is easy to fix:

```
# cd /usr/include
# test -L db.h -a ! -e db_185.h \
    && ln -sv `readlink db.h | sed -e 's,/db,&_185,'` .
```

Your link should look like this:

```
$ ls -l db_185.h
lrwxrwxrwx    1 root root 12 Feb 14 14:56 db_185.h -> db4/db_185.h
```

It's OK if the link points to a different version (e.g., db3 instead of db4).

Finally, download `dsniff` from *http://naughty.monkey.org/~dugsong/dsniff*, and unpack it:

```
$ tar xvzpf dsniff-*.tar.gz
```

Then compile it:

```
$ cd `ls -d dsniff-* | head -1`
$ ./configure
$ make
```

and install it as root:

```
# make install
```

Whew! With all of the software in place, we can start using `dsniff` to audit the use of insecure network protocols:

```
# dsniff -m
dsniff: listening on eth0
-----------------
03/01/03 20:11:07 tcp client.example.com.2056 -> server.example.com.21 (ftp)
```

```
USER katie
PASS Dumbo!
-----------------
03/01/03 20:11:23 tcp client.example.com.1112 -> server.example.com.23 (telnet)
marianne
aspirin?
ls -l
logout
-----------------
03/01/03 20:14:56 tcp client.example.com.1023 -> server.example.com.514 (rlogin)
[1022:tony]
rm junque
-----------------
03/01/03 20:16:33 tcp server.example.com.1225 -> client.example.com.6000 (x11)
MIT-MAGIC-COOKIE-1 c166a754fdf243c0f93e9fecb54abbd8
-----------------
03/01/03 20:08:20 udp client.example.com.688 -> server.example.com.777 (mountd)
/home [07 04 00 00 01 00 00 00 0c 00 00 00 02 00 00 00 3b 11 a1 36 00 00 00 00 00 00
00 00 00 00 00 00 ]
```

dsniff understands a wide range of protocols, and recognizes sensitive data that is transmitted without encryption. Our example shows passwords captured from FTP and Telnet sessions, with telnet commands and other input. (See why typing the root password over a Telnet connection is a very bad idea?) The rlogin session used no password, because the source host was trusted, but the command was captured. Finally, we see authorization information used by an X server, and filehandle information returned for an NFS mount operation.

dsniff uses libnids to reassemble TCP streams, because individual characters for interactively-typed passwords are often transmitted in separate packets. This reassembly relies on observation of the initial three-way handshake that starts all TCP sessions, so dsniff does not trace sessions already in progress when it was invoked.

The dsniff -m option enables automatic pattern-matching of protocols used on nonstandard ports (e.g., HTTP on a port other than 80). Use the -i option to listen on a specific interface, if your system is connected to multiple networks. Append a filter-expression to restrict the network traffic that is monitored, using the same syntax as tcpdump. [9.16] dsniff uses libpcap to examine the first kilobyte of each packet: use the -s option to adjust the size of the snapshot if necessary.

dsniff can save the results in a database file specified by the -w option; the -r option reads and prints the results. If you use a database, be sure to protect this sensitive data from unwanted viewers. Unfortunately, dsniff cannot read or write libpcap-format network trace files—it performs live network-monitoring only.

A variety of more specialized sniffing tools are also provided with dsniff. The mailsnarf command captures mail messages from SMTP or POP traffic, and writes them in the standard mailbox format:

```
# mailsnarf
mailsnarf: listening on eth0
```

```
From engh@example.com Sat Mar  1 21:00:02 2003
Received: (from engh@example.com)
        by mail.example.com (8.11.6/8.11.6) id h1DJAPe10352
        for liberace@example.com; Sat, 1 Mar 2003 21:00:02 -0500
Date: Sat, 1 Mar 2003 21:00:02 -0500
From: Engelbert Humperdinck <engh@example.com>
Message-Id: <200303020200.AED1D74A1@example.com>
To: liberace@example.com
Subject: Elvis lives!

I ran into Elvis on the subway yesterday.
He said he was on his way to Graceland.
```

Suppose you want to encourage users who are sending email as clear text to encrypt their messages with GnuPG (see Chapter 8). You could theoretically inspect every email message, but of course this would be a gross violation of their privacy. You just want to detect whether encryption was used in each message, and to identify the correspondents if it was not. One approach is:

```
# mailsnarf -v "-----BEGIN PGP MESSAGE-----" | \
  perl -ne 'print if /^From / .. /^$/;' | \
  tee insecure-mail-headers
```

Our regular expression identifies encrypted messages, and the mailsnarf -v option (similar to grep -v) captures only those messages that were *not* encrypted. A short Perl script then discards the message bodies and records only the mail headers. The tee command prints the headers to the standard output so we can watch, and also writes them to a file, which can be used later to send mass mailings to the offenders. This strategy never saves your users' sensitive email data in a file.

dsniff comes with similar programs for other protocols, but they are useful mostly as convincing demonstrations of the importance of secure protocols. We hope you are already convinced by now!

The filesnarf command captures files from NFS traffic, and saves them in the current directory:

```
# filesnarf
filesnarf: listening on eth0
filesnarf: 10.220.80.1.2049 > 10.220.80.4.800: known_hosts (1303@0)
filesnarf: 10.220.80.1.2049 > 10.220.80.4.800: love-letter.doc (8192@0)
filesnarf: 10.220.80.1.2049 > 10.220.80.4.800: love-letter.doc (4096@8192)
filesnarf: 10.220.80.1.2049 > 10.220.80.4.800: .Xauthority (204@0)
filesnarf: 10.220.80.1.2049 > 10.220.80.4.800: myprog (8192@0)
filesnarf: 10.220.80.1.2049 > 10.220.80.4.800: myprog (8192@8192)
filesnarf: 10.220.80.1.2049 > 10.220.80.4.800: myprog (8192@16384)
filesnarf: 10.220.80.1.2049 > 10.220.80.4.800: myprog (8192@40960)
```

The last values on each line are the number of bytes transferred, and the file offsets. Of course, you can capture only those parts of the file transmitted on the network, so the saved files can have "holes" (which read as null bytes) where the missing data would be. No directory information is recorded. You can select specific filenames using a regular expression (and optionally with the -v option, to invert the sense of the match, as for `mailsnarf` or `grep`).

The `urlsnarf` command captures URLs from HTTP traffic, and records them in the Common Log Format (CLF). This format is used by most web servers, such as Apache, and is parsed by many web log analysis programs.

```
# urlsnarf
urlsnarf: listening on eth1 [tcp port 80 or port 8080 or port 3128]
client.example.com - - [ 1/Mar/2003:21:06:36 -0500] "GET http://naughty.monkey.org/
cgi-bin/counter?ft=0|dd=E|trgb=ffffff|df=dugsong-dsniff.dat HTTP/1.1" - - "http://
naughty.monkey.org/~dugsong/dsniff/" "Mozilla/5.0 (X11; U; Linux i686; en-US; rv:0.9.
9) Gecko/20020513"
client.example.com - - [ 1/Mar/2003:21:06:46 -0500] "GET http://naughty.monkey.org/
~dugsong/dsniff/faq.html HTTP/1.1" - - "http://naughty.monkey.org/~dugsong/dsniff/"
"Mozilla/5.0 (X11; U; Linux i686; en-US; rv:0.9.9) Gecko/20020513"
```

By default, `urlsnarf` watches three ports that commonly carry HTTP traffic: 80, 3128, and 8080. To monitor a different port, use a capture filter expression:

```
# urlsnarf tcp port 8888
urlsnarf: listening on eth1 [tcp port 8888]
...
```

To monitor all TCP ports, use a more general expression:

```
# urlsnarf -i eth1 tcp
urlsnarf: listening on eth1 [tcp]
...
```

A regular expression can be supplied to select URLs of interest, optionally with -v as for `mailsnarf` or `filesnarf`.

A few other programs are provided with `dsniff` as a proof of concept for attacks on switched networks, man-in-the-middle attacks, and slowing or killing TCP connections. Some of these programs can be quite disruptive, especially if used incorrectly, so we don't recommend trying them unless you have an experimental network to conduct penetration testing.

See Also

dsniff(8), mailsnarf(8), filesnarf(8), urlsnarf(8). The `dsniff` home page is *http://naughty.monkey.org/~dugsong/dsniff*.

9.20 Getting Started with Snort

Problem

You want to set up Snort, a network-intrusion detection system.

Solution

Snort is included with SuSE but not Red Hat. If you need it (or you want to upgrade), download the source distribution from *http://www.snort.org* and unpack it:

```
$ tar xvpzf snort-*.tar.gz
```

Then compile it:

```
$ cd `ls -d snort-* | head -1`
$ ./configure
$ make
```

and install the binary and manpage as root:

```
# make install
```

Next, create a logging directory. It should not be publicly readable, since it will contain potentially sensitive data:

```
# mkdir -p -m go-rwx /var/log/snort
```

Finally, install the configuration files and rules database:

```
# mkdir -p /usr/local/share/rules
# cp etc/* rules/*.rules  /usr/local/share/rules
```

Discussion

Snort is a *network intrusion detection system* (NIDS), sort of an early-warning radar system for break-ins. It sniffs packets from the network and analyzes them according to a collection of well-known signatures characteristic of suspicious or hostile activities. This may remind you of an anti-virus tool, which looks for patterns in files to identify viruses.

By examining the protocol information and payload of each packet (or a sequence of packets) and applying its pattern-matching rules, Snort can identify the telltale fingerprints of attempted buffer overflows, denial of service attacks, port scans, and many other kinds of probes. When Snort detects a disturbing event, it can log network trace information for further investigation, and issue alerts so you can respond rapidly.

See Also

snort(8). The Snort home page is *http://www.snort.org*.

9.21 Packet Sniffing with Snort

Problem

You want to use Snort as a simple packet sniffer.

Solution

To format and print network trace information:

```
# snort -v [-d|-X] [-C] [-e] [filter-expression]
```

To sniff packets from the network:

```
# snort [-i interface] [-P snap-length] [filter-expression]
```

To read network trace data you have saved previously:

```
$ snort -r filename [filter-expression]
```

Discussion

Snort can act as a simple packet sniffer, providing a level of detail between the terseness of tcpdump [9.16] and the verbosity of tethereal. [9.17] The -v option prints a summary of the protocol information for each packet. To dump the payload data in hexadecimal and ASCII, add the -d option (with the -C option if you care only about the characters). For more information about lower-level protocols, add -e to print a summary of the link-level (Ethernet) headers, or use -X instead of -d to dump the protocol headers along with the payload data:

```
# snort -veX
02/27-23:32:15.641528 52:54:4C:A:6B:CD -> 0:50:4:D5:8E:5A type:0x800 len:0x9A
192.168.33.1:20 -> 192.168.33.3:1058 TCP TTL:60 TOS:0x8 ID:28465 IpLen:20 DgmLen
:140
***AP*** Seq: 0xDCE2E01  Ack: 0xA3B50859  Win: 0x1C84  TcpLen: 20
0x0000: 00 50 04 D5 8E 5A 52 54 4C 0A 6B CD 08 00 45 08  .P...ZRTL.k...E.
0x0010: 00 8C 6F 31 00 00 3C 06 4B DE C0 A8 21 01 C0 A8  ..o1..<.K...!...
0x0020: 21 03 00 14 04 22 0D CE 2E 01 A3 B5 08 59 50 18  !...."...... YP.
0x0030: 1C 84 34 BB 00 00 54 6F 75 72 69 73 74 73 20 2D  ..4...Tourists -
0x0040: 2D 20 68 61 76 65 20 73 6F 6D 65 20 66 75 6E 20  - have some fun
0x0050: 77 69 74 68 20 4E 65 77 20 59 6F 72 6B 27 73 20  with New York's
...
```

Addresses and ports are always printed numerically.

If your system is connected to multiple networks, use the -i option to select an interface for sniffing. Alternately, you can read libpcap-format trace files [9.16] saved by Snort or some other compatible network sniffer, by using the -r option.

Append a filter expression to the command line to limit the data collected, using the same syntax as for tcpdump. [9.16] Filter expressions can focus attention on specific machines (such as your production web server), or efficiently ignore uninteresting traffic, especially if it is causing false alarms. When Snort is displaying data from network trace files, the filter expression selects packets to be printed, a handy feature when playing back previously logged data.

By default, Snort captures entire packets to examine their payloads. If you are looking at only a few specific protocols, and you know that the data of interest is at the start of the packets, use the -P option to specify smaller snapshots and achieve an efficiency gain.

See Also

snort(8), tcpdump(1), tethereal(1). The Snort home page is *http://www.snort.org*.

9.22   Detecting Intrusions with Snort

Problem

You want to notice if your system is under attack from the network.

Solution

To run as a network intrusion detection system, with binary logging, and alerts sent to the system logger:

```
# snort -c /usr/local/share/rules/snort.conf -b -s
```

To run Snort in the background, as a daemon:

```
# snort -D [-u user] [-g group] [-m umask] -c ...
```

Discussion

Snort is most valuable when run as a full-fledged NIDS:

```
# snort -c /etc/snort/snort.conf ...              SuSE installation
# snort -c /usr/local/share/rules/snort.conf ...  Manual installation
```

The configuration file includes a large number of pattern matching rules that control logging and alerts.

In this mode of operation, packets are recorded (logged) when they match known *signatures* indicating a possible intrusion. Use the -b option for efficient logging to binary libpcap-format files. [9.24] The -N option disables logging if you want alerts only, but we don't recommend this: the logs provide valuable context about the events that triggered the alerts.

Alerts can be directed to a wide range of destinations. We recommend the system logger [9.27] because:

- It's efficient.
- It's convenient (and enlightening) to correlate Snort's messages with those of other daemons, your firewall, and the kernel—these are all recorded in the system log.

- Tools like logwatch [9.36] can scan the log files effectively and provide notification by email, which works well with high-priority alerts.

Use the -s option to direct alerts to the system logger. By default, alerts are sent using the auth facility and info priority. This can be changed by uncommenting and changing a line in *snort.conf*, e.g.:

```
output alert_syslog: LOG_LOCAL3 LOG_WARNING
```

At press time, the latest version of Snort (1.9.1) has an unfortunate bug: it incorrectly requires an extra argument after the -s option. If you are experiencing confusing command-line syntax errors, try providing this extra argument (which will be ignored).

The Snort documentation also erroneously claims that the default facility and priority are authpriv and alert, respectively. If you are not seeing alert messages in */var/log/secure* (typically used for authpriv), check */var/log/messages* (which is used for auth) instead.

To disable alerts entirely (e.g., for rules-based logging only), use the -A none option. We don't recommend this for routine operation, unless you have some other special mechanism for producing alerts by examining the logs.

To run Snort in the background, as a daemon, use the -D option. This is the recommended way to launch Snort for continuous, long-term operation. Also, Snort is best run on a dedicated monitoring system, ideally sniffing traffic on an unconfigured, "stealth" interface. [9.16]

On SuSE systems, you can enable Snort to start automatically at boot time with the chkconfig command:

```
# chkconfig snort on
```

Edit */var/adm/fillup-templates/sysconfig.snort* to specify the desired snort command-line options.

On Red Hat systems, the simplest way to start Snort at boot time is to add a command to */etc/rc.d/rc.local*. Alternately, you can copy one of the other scripts in */etc/init.d* to create your own snort script, and then use chkconfig.

Snort must be run as root initially to set the network interfaces to promiscuous mode for sniffing, but it can run subsequently as a less privileged user—this is always a good idea for added security. Use the -u and -g options to designate this lesser user and group ID, respectively. The permissions of the logging directory need to allow only write access for this user or group. If you want to allow a set of other authorized users to analyze the logging data (without root access), add the users to Snort's group, make the logging directory group readable, and use -m 007 to set Snort's umask so that all of the files created by Snort will be group readable as well. [5.10]

You can ask Snort to dump statistics to the system logger (the same report that is produced before Snort exits) by sending it a SIGUSR1 signal:

```
# kill -USR1 `pidof snort`
```

Snort writes its process ID to the file */var/run/snort_<interface>.pid*. If you are running multiple copies of snort, with each listening on a separate interface, these files can be handy for signaling specific invocations, e.g.:

```
# kill -USR1 `cat /var/run/snort_eth2.pid`
```

See Also

snort(8). The Snort home page is *http://www.snort.org*.

9.23   Decoding Snort Alert Messages

Problem

You want to understand a Snort alert message.

Solution

Consult the Snort signature database at *http://www.snort.org/snort-db*, using the signature ID as an index, or searching based on the text message. Most alerts are described in detail, and many include links to other NIDS databases with even more information, such as the arachNIDS database at *http://www.whitehats.com*.

Discussion

Let's decode an alert message produced when Snort detects a port scan by nmap [9.13]:

```
Mar 18 19:40:52 whimsy snort[3115]: [1:469:1] ICMP PING NMAP [Classification:
Attempted Information Leak] [Priority: 2]: <eth1> {ICMP} 10.120.66.1 -> 10.22.33.106
```

Breaking apart this single line, we first have the usual syslog information:

```
Mar 18 19:40:52 whimsy snort[3115]:
```

which includes a timestamp, the hostname where Snort was running, and the Snort identifier with its process ID. Next we have:

```
[1:469:1] ICMP PING NMAP
```

In this portion of the alert, the first number, 1, is a generator ID, and identifies the Snort subsystem that produced the alert. The value 1 means Snort itself. The next number, 469, is a signature ID that identifies the alert, and corresponds to the subsequent text message (ICMP PING NMAP). The final number, 1, is a version for the alert.

If the alert were produced by a Snort preprocessor, it would have a higher value for the generator ID, and the name of the preprocessor would be listed in parentheses before the text message. For example:

```
[111:10:1] (spp_stream4) STEALTH ACTIVITY (XMAS scan) detection
```

Signature IDs are assigned by each preprocessor: to learn more about these alerts, see the *snort.conf* file, and the *Snort User's Manual*. Continuing our example, we see the classification of the alert:

```
[Classification: Attempted Information Leak] [Priority: 2]:
```

Each alert is classified into one of a set of broad categories: see the file *classification. config* in the rules directory. Alerts are also assigned priority levels, with lower values meaning more severe events. Finally, the alert identifies the receiving network interface and lists the IP protocol, source address, and destination address:

```
<eth1> {ICMP} 10.120.66.1 -> 10.22.33.106
```

It's optional to identify the receiving network interface: use the -I option to enable this feature, say, if your system is connected to multiple networks. Finally, even though the source address is listed, you cannot trust it in general: attackers often use spoofed addresses to implicate innocent third parties.

If you are replaying a network trace using snort -r, you probably don't want to send alerts to the system logger: use the -A fast or -A full options to write the alerts to a file called *alert* in the logging directory. The fast alert format is very similar to syslog's. Full alerts provide more protocol details, as well as cross-references like:

```
[Xref => arachnids 162]
```

These usually correspond to links in the Snort signature database. See the file *reference.config* in the rules directory to convert the ID numbers to URLs to obtain more information for each alert.

Use the -A console option to write alerts (in the fast alert format) to the standard output instead of the *alert* file.

See Also

snort(8). The Snort home page is *http://www.snort.org*.

9.24 Logging with Snort

Problem

You want to manage Snort's output and log files in an efficient, effective manner.

Solution

To log network trace data for later analysis:

```
# snort -b [-l logging-directory] [-L basename]
```

To examine the network trace data:

```
$ snort -r logfile
```

or use any other program that reads libpcap-format files, like Ethereal. [9.17]

To manage the logs, don't use logrotate. [9.30] Instead, periodically tell Snort to close all of its files and restart, by sending it a SIGHUP signal:

```
# kill -HUP `pidof snort`
```

Then, use find to remove all files that are older than (say) a week:

```
# find /var/log/snort -type f -mtime +7 -print0 | xargs -0 -r rm
```

Finally, use find again to remove empty subdirectories:

```
# find /var/log/snort -mindepth 1 -depth -type d -print0 | \
    xargs -0 -r rmdir -v --ignore-fail-on-non-empty
```

To run these commands (for example) every night at 3:30 a.m., create a cleanup script (say, */usr/local/sbin/clean-up-snort*) and add a *crontab* entry for root:

```
30 3 * * * /usr/local/sbin/clean-up-snort
```

Discussion

To log network trace data for later analysis, use the -b option. This creates a libpcap-format binary file in the logging directory (by default, */var/log/snort*) with a name like *snort.log.1047160213*: the digits record the start time of the trace, expressed as seconds since the epoch.* To convert this value to a more readable format, use either Perl or the date command:

```
$ perl -e 'print scalar localtime 1047160213, "\n";'
Sat Mar  8 16:50:13 2003

$ date -d "1970-01-01 utc + 1047160213 sec"
Sat Mar  8 16:50:13 EST 2003
```

To learn the ending time of the trace, see the modification time of the file:

```
# ls --full-time -o snort.log.1047160213
-rw-------    1 root        97818 Sat Mar 08 19:05:47 2003 snort.log.1047160213
```

or use snort -r to examine the network trace data.

---

* The Unix "epoch" occurred on January 1, 1970, at midnight UTC.

You can specify a different logging directory with the -l option, or an alternate base-name (instead of *snort.log*) with the -L option: the start timestamp is still added to the filename.

Since Snort filenames contain timestamps, and the formatted logging files might be split into separate directories, logrotate [9.30] is not an ideal mechanism for managing your log files. Use the method we suggest, or something similar.

See Also

snort(8), logrotate(8). The Snort home page is *http://www.snort.org*.

9.25 Partitioning Snort Logs Into Separate Files

Problem

You want to split Snort's log output into separate files, based on the IP addresses and protocols detected.

Solution

```
# snort -l /var/log/snort -h network -r snort.log.timestamp
```

Discussion

Snort can split its formatted output into separate files, with names based on the remote IP address and protocols used: these files contain the same information printed by snort -v. Select this mode of operation by using the -l option without -b, plus the -h option to specify the "home network" for identification of the remote packets:

```
# cd /var/log/snort
# snort -l /var/log/snort -h 10.22.33.0/24 -r snort.log.1047160213
...
# find [0-9A-Z]* -type f -print | sort
10.30.188.28/TCP:1027-22
192.168.33.1/IP_FRAG
192.168.33.1/UDP:2049-800
192.168.33.2/TCP:6000-1050
192.168.33.2/TCP:6000-1051
192.168.33.2/TCP:6000-1084
ARP
```

The digits following the filenames for TCP and UDP traffic refer to the remote and local port numbers, respectively. Information about fragmented IP packets that could not otherwise be classified is stored in files named IP_FRAG. Details for ARP packets are stored in a file named ARP in the top-level logging directory.

Don't use split formatted output for logging while sniffing packets from the network —it's inefficient and discards information. For logging, we recommend binary libpcap-format files (produced by the -b option) for speed and flexibility. [9.16] You can always split and format the output later, using the technique in this recipe.

See Also

snort(8). The Snort home page is *http://www.snort.org*.

9.26 Upgrading and Tuning Snort's Ruleset

Problem

You want Snort to use the latest intrusion signatures.

Solution

Download the latest rules from *http://www.snort.org* and install them in */usr/local/ share* to be consistent with our other Snort recipes:

```
# tar xvpzf snortrules-stable.tar.gz -C /usr/local/share
```

To test configuration changes, or to verify the correct usage of command-line options:

```
# snort -T ...
```

To omit the verbose initialization and summary messages:

```
# snort -q ...
```

Discussion

The field of NIDS is an area of active research, and Snort is undergoing rapid development. Furthermore, the arms race between attackers and defenders of systems continues to escalate. You should upgrade your Snort installation frequently to cope with the latest threats.

If you have locally modified your rules, then before upgrading them, preserve your changes and merge them into the new versions. If you confine your site-specific additions to the file *local.rules*, merging will be a lot easier.

Although the *snort.conf* file can be used without modification, it is worthwhile to edit the file to customize Snort's operation for your site. Comments in the file provide a guided tour of Snort's features, and can be used as a step-by-step configuration guide, along with the *Snort User's Manual*.

The most important parameters are the network variables at the beginning of the configuration file. These define the boundaries of your networks, and the usage patterns within those networks. For quick testing, you can override variables on the command line with the -S option, e.g.:

```
# snort -S HOME_NET=10.22.33.0/24 ...
```

Depending on your interests and needs, you may also wish to enable or tune some of the Snort preprocessors that are designed to respond to various threats. IP defragmentation and TCP stream reassembly are enabled by default, to detect denial of service attacks and to support the other preprocessors. If you are being subjected to anti-NIDS attacks such as noise generators that attempt to overwhelm Snort with a flood of alert-inducing traffic, use:

```
# snort -z est ...
```

to limit alerts to known, established connections only. Several preprocessors are available to defeat attempts to escape detection during attacks on specific protocols. These often take the form of path name or instruction sequence mutations, and the preprocessors work to convert the input streams into a canonical form that can be more readily recognized by the pattern matching rules. Port scans are noticed by preprocessors that watch a range of protocols over time.

Finally, a variety of output plugins can direct alerts to databases, XML files, SNMP traps, a local Unix socket, or even WinPopup messages on Windows workstations, using Samba. Many of these features are experimental, or require special configuration options when Snort is installed; consult the documentation in the source distribution for details.

 Whenever you modify the Snort configuration or add or customize rules, use the -T option to verify that your changes are correct. This will prevent Snort from dying unexpectedly when it next restarts, e.g., at boot time.

See Also

snort(8). The Snort home page is *http://www.snort.org*. The Honeynet project's web site, *http://www.honeynet.org*, contains a wealth of information about network monitoring, including Snort. See *http://www.honeynet.org/papers/honeynet/tools/snort.conf* for a sample Snort configuration file.

9.27 Directing System Messages to Log Files (syslog)

Problem

You want to configure the system logger to use an organized collection of log files.

Solution

Set up */etc/syslog.conf* for local logging:

```
/etc/syslog.conf:
# Messages of priority info or higher, that are not logged elsewhere
*.info;\
mail,authpriv,cron.none;\
local0,local1,local2,local3,local4,local5,local6,local7.none \
                                /var/log/messages

# Messages of priority debug, that are not logged elsewhere
*.=debug;\
mail,authpriv,cron.none;\
local0,local1,local2,local3,local4,local5,local6,local7.none \
                                -/var/log/debug

# Facilities with log files that require restricted access permissions
mail.*                  /var/log/maillog
authpriv.*              /var/log/secure
cron.*                  /var/log/cron

# Separate log files for local use
local0.*                /var/log/local0
local1.*                /var/log/local1
local2.*                /var/log/local2
local3.*                /var/log/local3
local4.*                /var/log/local4
local5.*                /var/log/local5
local6.*                /var/log/local6

# Red Hat usurps the local7 facility for boot messages from init scripts
local7.*                /var/log/boot.log
```

After you modify */etc/syslog.conf*, you must send a signal to force `syslogd` to reread it and apply your changes. Any of these will do:

```
# kill -HUP `pidof syslogd`
```

or:

```
# kill -HUP `cat /var/run/syslogd.pid`
```

or:

```
# /etc/init.d/syslog reload
```

or:

```
# service syslog reload        Red Hat
```

Discussion

When your kernel needs to tell you something important, will you notice? If you are investigating a potential break-in last night, will you have all of the information you need? Staying informed requires careful configuration and use of the system logger.

The system logger collects messages from programs and even from the kernel. These messages are tagged with a *facility* that identifies the broad category of the source, e.g., mail, kern (for kernel messages), or authpriv (for security and authorization messages). In addition, a *priority* specifies the importance (or severity) of each message. The lowest priorities are (in ascending order) debug, info, and notice; the highest priority is emerg, which is used when your disk drive is on fire. The complete set of facilities and priorities are described in syslog.conf(5) and syslog(3).

Messages can be directed to different log files, based on their facility and priority; this is controlled by the configuration file */etc/syslog.conf*. The system logger conveniently records a timestamp and the machine name for each message.

It is tempting, but ill-advised, to try selecting the most important or interesting messages into separate files, and then to ignore the rest. The problem with this approach is that you can't possibly know in advance which information will be crucial in unforeseen circumstances.

Furthermore, the facilities and priorities are insufficient as message selection criteria, because they are general, subjective, and unevenly applied by various programs. Consider the authpriv facility: it is intended for security issues, but many security-related messages are tagged with other facilities. For example, the message that your network interface is in "promiscuous mode" is tagged as a kernel message, even though it means someone could be using your machine as a packet sniffer. Likewise, if a system daemon emits a complaint about a ridiculously long name, perhaps filled with control characters, someone might be trying to exploit a buffer overflow vulnerability.

Vigilance requires the examination of a wide range of messages. Even messages that are not directly associated with security can provide a valuable context for security events. It can be reassuring to see that the kernel's "promiscuous mode" message was preceded by a note from a system administrator about using Ethereal to debug a network problem. [9.17] Similarly, it is nice to know that the nightly tape backups finished before a break-in occurred in the wee hours of the morning.

There is only one way to guarantee you have all of the information available when you need it: log everything. It is relatively easy to ignore messages after they have been saved in log files, but it is impossible to recover messages once they have been discarded by the system logger: the fate of messages that do not match any entries in */etc/syslog.conf*.

Auxiliary programs, like logwatch [9.36], can scan log files and effectively select messages of interest using criteria beyond the facility and priority: the name of the program that produced the message, the timestamp, the machine name, and so forth. This is a good strategy in order to avoid being overwhelmed by large amounts of logging data: you can use reports from logwatch to launch investigations of suspicious activities, and be confident that more detailed information will always be available in your log files for further sleuthing.

Even very busy systems using the most verbose logging typically produce only a few megabytes of logging data per day. The modest amount of disk space required to store the log files can be reduced further by logrotate. [9.30] There are, nevertheless, some good reasons to direct messages to different log files:

- Some of the messages might contain sensitive information, and hence deserve more restrictive file permissions.

- Messages collected at a higher rate can be stored in log files that are rotated more frequently.

Our recipe shows one possible configuration for local logging. Higher priority messages from a range of sources are collected in the traditional location */var/log/ messages*. Lower priority (debug) messages are directed to a separate file, which we rotate more frequently because they may arrive at a higher rate. By default, the system logger synchronizes log files to the disk after every message, to avoid data loss if a system crash occurs. The dash ("-") character before the */var/log/debug* filename disables this behavior to achieve a performance boost: use this with other files that accumulate a lot of data. Exclusions are used to prevent messages from being sent to multiple files. This is not strictly necessary, but is a nice property if you later combine log files [9.35], as there will be no duplicate messages.

Priority names in the configuration file normally mean the specified priority *and* all higher priorities. Therefore, info means all priorities except debug. To specify only a single priority (but not all higher priorities), add "=" before the priority name. The special priority none excludes facilities, as we show for */var/log/messages* and */var/log/ debug*. The "*" character is used as a wildcard to select all facilities or priorities. See the syslog.conf(5) manpage for more details about this syntax.

Messages tagged with the authpriv, mail, and cron facilities are sent to separate files that are usually not readable by everyone, because they could contain sensitive information.

Finally, the local[0-7] facilities, reserved for arbitrary local uses, are sent to separate files. This provides a convenient mechanism for categorizing your own logging messages. Note that some system daemons use these facilities, even though they really are not supposed to do so. For example, the local7 facility is used by Red Hat for boot messages.

 The facility local7 is used by Red Hat Linux for boot messages. Use care when redirecting or ignoring messages with this facility.

The system logger notices changes in */etc/syslog.conf* only when it receives a signal, so send one as shown. The same commands also cause the system logger to close and reopen all its log files; this feature is leveraged by logrotate. [9.30]

When adding new log files, it is best to create new (empty) files manually so that the correct permissions can be set. Otherwise, the log files created by the system logger will be publicly readable, which isn't always appropriate.

See Also

syslogd(8), syslog.conf(5).

9.28 Testing a syslog Configuration

Problem

You want to find out where all your syslog messages go.

Solution

```
#!/bin/sh
PROG=`basename "$0"`
FACILITIES='auth authpriv cron daemon ftp kern lpr mail news syslog user uucp
    local0 local1 local2 local3 local4 local5 local6 local7'
PRIORITIES='emerg alert crit err warning notice info debug'
for f in $FACILITIES
do
    for p in $PRIORITIES
    do
        logger -p $f.$p "$PROG[$$]: testing $f.$p"
    done
done
```

Discussion

This script simply iterates through all syslog facilities and priorities, sending a message to each combination. After running it, examine your log files to see which messages ended up where.

If you don't want to hard-code the facilities and priorities (in case they change), write an analogous program in C and reference the names directly in /usr/include/sys/syslog.h.

See Also

logger(1), syslogd(8), syslog.conf(5).

syslog-ng ("new generation") is a more powerful replacement for the standard system logger. If you crave more features or are frustrated by limitations of facilities and priorities, check out *http://www.balabit.com/products/syslog_ng*.

9.29 Logging Remotely

Problem

You want system logger messages saved on a remote machine rather than locally.

Solution

Configure */etc/syslog.conf* for remote logging, using the "@" syntax:

```
/etc/syslog.conf:
# Send all messages to remote system "loghost"
*.*             @loghost
```

On *loghost*, tell syslogd to accept messages from the network by adding the -r option:

```
# syslogd -r ...
```

or within */etc/sysconfig/syslog*:

```
SYSLOGD_OPTIONS="... -r ..."         Red Hat
SYSLOGD_PARAMS="... -r ..."          SuSE
```

Remember to send a signal to syslogd to pick up any changes to */etc/syslog.conf* [9.27], or to restart the daemon on *loghost* if you have changed command-line options.

Discussion

The system logger can redirect messages to another machine: this is indicated in */etc/syslog.conf* by an "@" character followed by a machine name as the destination. Our recipe shows a simple remote logging configuration that sends all messages to a remote machine, conventionally named *loghost*.

The remote configuration can be convenient for collecting messages from several machines in log files on a single centralized machine, where they can be monitored and examined. You might also want to use this configuration on a machine like a web server, so that log files cannot be read, tampered with, or removed by an intruder if a break-in occurs.

Local and remote rules can be combined in the same *syslog.conf* configuration, and some categories of messages can be sent to both local and remote destinations.

The system logger will not accept messages from another machine by default. To allow this, add the syslogd -r command-line option on *loghost*. Your *loghost* can even collect messages from other types of systems, e.g., routers and switches. Protect your *loghost* with your firewall, however, to prevent others from bombarding your server with messages as a denial of service attack.

To allow the *loghost* to be changed easily, set up a "loghost" CNAME record on your nameserver that points to a specific machine:

```
loghost IN CNAME watchdog.example.com.
```

(Don't forget the final period.) You can then redirect messages by simply modifying the CNAME record, rather than a potentially large number of *etc/syslog.conf* files. Add the syslogd -h option on your old *loghost* to forward your messages to the new *loghost*, until you have a chance to reconfigure those routers and switches unaware of the change.

See Also

syslogd(8), syslog.conf(5).

9.30 Rotating Log Files

Problem

You want to control and organize your ever-growing log files.

Solution

Use logrotate, a program to compress and/or delete log files automatically when they are sufficiently old, perhaps after they have been stashed away on tape backups.

Add entries to */etc/logrotate.d/syslog*, e.g.:

```
/etc/logrotate.d/syslog:
/var/log/local0 /var/log/local1 ...others... {
    sharedscripts
    postrotate
        /bin/kill -HUP `cat /var/run/syslogd.pid`
    endscript
}
```

Discussion

Log files should be rotated so they won't grow indefinitely. Our recipe shows a simple configuration that can be used with logrotate to do this automatically. After the files are shuffled around, the postrotate script sends a signal to the system logger to reopen the log files, and the sharedscripts directive ensures that this is done only once, for all of the log files.

You can add a separate configuration file (with any name) in the */etc/logrotate.d* directory, as an alternative to editing the */etc/logrotate.d/syslog* file. Separate entries can be used to tune the default behavior of logrotate, which is described by */etc/ logrotate.conf*, e.g., to rotate some log files more frequently.

See Also

logrotate(8), syslogd(8).

9.31   Sending Messages to the System Logger

Problem

You want to add information about interesting events to the system log.

Solution

Use the logger program. A simple example:

```
$ logger "using Ethereal to debug a network problem"
```

Suppose "food" is the name of a program, short for "Foo Daemon." Log a simple message:

```
$ logger -t "food[$$]" -p local3.warning "$count connections from $host"
```

Direct stdout and stderr output to syslog:

```
$ food 2>&1 | logger -t "food[$$]" -p local3.notice &
```

Send stdout and stderr to syslog, using different priorities (bash only):

```
$ food 1> >(logger -t "food[$$]" -p local3.info) \
       2> >(logger -t "food[$$]" -p local3.err)  &
```

You can also write to the system log from shell scripts [9.32], Perl programs [9.33], or C programs [9.34].

Discussion

The system logger isn't just for system programs: you can use it with your own programs and scripts, or even interactively. This is a great way to record information for processes that run in the background (e.g., as cron jobs), when stdout and stderr aren't necessarily connected to anything useful. Don't bother to create, open, and maintain your own log files: let the system logger do the work.

Interactively, logger can be used almost like echo to record a message with the default user facility and notice priority. Your username will be prepended to each message as an identifier.

Our recipe shows a sample "Foo Daemon" (food) that uses the local3 facility and various priority levels, depending on the importance of each message. By convention, the script uses its name "food" as an identifier that is prepended to each message.

It is a good idea to add a process ID to each message, so that a series of messages can be untangled when several copies of the script are running simultaneously. For example, consider the log file entries from a computer named *cafeteria*:

```
Feb 21 12:05:41 cafeteria food[1234]: customer arrived: Alison
Feb 21 12:06:15 cafeteria food[5678]: customer arrived: Bob
Feb 21 12:10:22 cafeteria food[1234]: devoured tofu
Feb 21 12:11:09 cafeteria food[5678]: consumed beef
Feb 21 12:15:34 cafeteria food[5678]: ingested pork
Feb 21 12:18:23 cafeteria food[1234]: gobbled up broccoli
Feb 21 12:22:52 cafeteria food[5678]: paid $7.89
Feb 21 12:24:35 cafeteria food[1234]: paid $4.59
```

In this case, the process IDs allow us to distinguish carnivores and herbivores, and to determine how much each paid. We use the process ID of the invoking shell by appending "[$$]" to the program name.* Other identifiers are possible, like the customer name in our example, but the process ID is guaranteed to be unique: consider the possibility of two customers named Bob! The system logger can record the process ID with each message automatically.

> It is a good practice to run logger before engaging in activities that might otherwise be regarded as suspicious, such as running a packet sniffing program like Ethereal. [9.17]

Programs that don't use the system logger are unfortunately common. Our recipe shows two techniques for capturing stdout and stderr from such programs, either combined or separately (with different priorities), using logger. The latter uses process substitution, which is available only if the script is run by bash (not the standard Bourne shell, sh).

See Also

logger(1), bash(1).

9.32 Writing Log Entries via Shell Scripts

Problem

You want to add information to the system log using a shell script.

---

* logger's own option to log a process ID, -i, is unfortunately useless. It prints the process ID of logger itself, which changes on each invocation.

Solution

Use logger and this handy API, which emulates that of Perl and C:

syslog-api.sh:
```
#!/bin/sh
ident="$USER"
facility="user"
openlog() {
    if [ $# -ne 3 ]
    then
        echo "usage: openlog ident option[,option,...] facility" 1>&2
        return 1
    fi
    ident="$1"
    local option="$2"
    facility="$3"
    case ",$option," in
        *,pid,*)    ident="$ident[$$]";;
    esac
}

syslog() {
    if [ $# -lt 2 ]
    then
        echo "usage: syslog [facility.]priority format ..." 1>&2
        return 1
    fi
    local priority="$1"
    local format="$2"
    shift 2
    case "$priority" in
        *.*)    ;;
        *)      priority="$facility.$priority";;
    esac
    printf "$format" "$@" | logger -t "$ident" -p "$priority"
}

closelog() {
    ident="$USER"
    facility="user"
}
```

To use the functions in a shell script:

```
#!/bin/sh
source syslog-api.sh
openlog `basename "$0"` pid local3
syslog warning "%d connections from %s" $count $host
syslog authpriv.err "intruder alert!"
closelog
```

The syslog API

The standard API for the system logger provides the following three functions for Perl scripts and C programs, and we provide an implementation for Bash shell scripts as well. [9.32]

openlog
> Specify the identifier prepended to each message, conventionally the basename of the program or script. An option is provided to add the process ID as well; other options are less commonly used. Finally, a default facility is established for subsequent messages: local0 through local6 are good choices.

syslog
> Send messages. It is used like printf, with an added message priority. Specify a facility to override the default established by openlog: this should be done sparingly, e.g., to send security messages to authpriv. Each message should be a single line—omit newlines at the end of the messages too. Don't use data from untrusted sources in the format string, to avoid security holes that result when the data is maliciously crafted to contain unexpected "%" characters (this advice applies to any function using printf-style formatting): use "%s" as the format string instead, with the insecure data as a separate argument.

closelog
> Close the socket used to communicate with the system logger. This function can be employed to clean up file descriptors before forking, but in most cases is optional.

Discussion

Our recipe shows how to use shell functions to implement the syslog API (see the sidebar "The syslog API") within shell scripts. The openlog function can be readily extended to recognize other, comma-separated options. The syslog function uses the same syntax as logger for the optional facility. The closelog function just restores the defaults for the identifier and facility, which are stored in global variables. These functions can be stored in a separate file and sourced by other shell scripts, as a convenient alternative to the direct use of logger.

See Also

logger(1), syslog(3).

9.33   Writing Log Entries via Perl

Problem

You want to add information to the system log from a Perl program.

Solution

Use the Perl module Sys::Syslog, which implements the API described in the side-bar, "The syslog API."

```
syslog-demo.pl
#!/usr/bin/perl
use Sys::Syslog qw(:DEFAULT setlogsock);
use File::Basename;
my $count = 0;
my $host = "some-machine";
setlogsock("unix");
openlog(basename($0), "pid", "local3");
syslog("warning", "%d connections from %s", $count, $host);
syslog("authpriv|err", "intruder alert!");
syslog("err", "can't open configuration file: %m");
closelog();
```

Discussion

The system logger by default refuses to accept network connections (assuming you have not used the syslogd -r option). Unfortunately, the Perl module uses network connections by default, so our recipe calls setlogsock to force the use of a local socket instead. If your syslog messages seem to be disappearing into thin air, be sure to use setlogsock. Recent versions of Sys::Syslog resort to a local socket if the network connection fails, but use of setlogsock for reliable operation is a good idea, since the local socket should always work. Note that setlogsock must be explicitly imported.

Perl scripts can pass the %m format specifier to syslog to include system error messages, as an alternative to interpolating the $! variable. Be sure to use %m (or $!) only when a system error has occurred, to avoid misleading messages.

See Also

Sys::Syslog(3pm), syslog(3).

9.34 Writing Log Entries via C

Problem

You want to add information to the system log from a C program.

Solution

Use the system library functions openlog, syslog, and closelog (see sidebar "The syslog API"):

```
syslog-demo.c:
#define _GNU_SOURCE      /* for basename( ) in <string.h> */
#include <syslog.h>
#include <string.h>
int count = 0;
char *host = "some-machine";
int main(int argc, char *argv[]) {
    openlog(basename(argv[0]), LOG_PID, LOG_LOCAL3);
    syslog(LOG_WARNING, "%d connection attempts from %s", count, host);
    syslog(LOG_AUTHPRIV|LOG_ERR, "intruder alert!");
    syslog(LOG_ERR, "can't open configuration file: %m");
    closelog( );
    return(0);
}
```

Discussion

Like Perl scripts [9.33], C programs can pass the %m format specifier to syslog to include system error messages, corresponding to strerror(errno). Be sure to use %m only when a system error has occurred, to avoid misleading messages.

See Also

syslog(3).

9.35   Combining Log Files

Problem

You want to merge a collection of log files into a single, chronological log file.

Solution

```
#!/bin/sh
perl -ne \
    'print $last, /last message repeated \d+ times$/ ? "\0" : "\n" if $last;
    chomp($last = $_);
    if (eof) {
        print;
        undef $last;
    }' "$@" | sort -s -k 1,1M -k 2,2n -k 3,3 | tr '\0' '\n'
```

Discussion

The system logger automatically prepends a timestamp to each message, like this:

```
Feb 21 12:34:56 buster kernel: device eth0 entered promiscuous mode
```

To merge log files, sort each one by its timestamp entries, using the first three fields (month, date, and time) as keys.

A complication arises because the system logger inserts "repetition messages" to conserve log file space:

```
Feb 21 12:48:16 buster last message repeated 7923 times
```

The timestamp for the repetition message is often later than the last message. It would be terribly misleading if possibly unrelated messages from other log files were merged between the last message and its associated repetition message.

To avoid this, our Perl script glues together the last message with a subsequent repetition message (if present), inserting a null character between them: this is reliable because the system logger never writes null characters to log files. The script writes out the final line before the end of each file and then forgets the last line, to avoid any possibility of confusion if the next file happens to start with an unrelated repetition message.

The sort command sees these null-glued combinations as single lines, and keeps them together as the files are merged. The null characters are translated back to newlines after the files are sorted, to split the combinations back into separate lines.

We use sort -s to avoid sorting entire lines if all of the keys are equal: this preserves the original order of messages with the same timestamp, at least within each original log file.

If you have configured the system logger to write messages to multiple log files, then you may wish to remove duplicates as you merge. This can be done by using sort -u instead of -s, and adding an extra sort key -k 4 to compare the message contents. There is a drawback, however: messages could be rearranged if they have the same timestamp. All of the issues related to sort -s and -u are consequences of the one-second resolution of the timestamps used by the system logger.

We'll note a few other pitfalls related to timestamps. The system logger does not record the year, so if your log files cross a year boundary, then you will need to merge the log files for each year separately, and concatenate the results. Similarly, the system logger writes timestamps using the local time zone, so you should avoid merging log files that cross a daylight saving time boundary, when the timestamps can go backward. Again, split the log files on either side of the discontinuity, merge separately, and then concatenate.

If your system logger is configured to receive messages from other machines, note that the timestamps are generated on the machine where the log files are stored. This allows consistent sorting of messages even from machines in different time zones.

See Also

sort(1).

9.36   Summarizing Your Logs with logwatch

Problem

You want to scan your system log files for reports of problems.

Solution

Use logwatch, from *http://www.logwatch.org*. For example:

```
# logwatch --range all --archives --detail High --print | less
```

to see all the useful data logwatch can display, or:

```
# logwatch --print | less
```

to see only yesterday's entries.

Discussion

logwatch is a handy utility to scan system log files and display unexpected entries. Red Hat includes it but SuSE does not. If you need it, download the binary RPM from *http://www.logwatch.org*,[*] and install it, as root:

```
# rpm -Uhv logwatch-*.noarch.rpm
```

The easiest way to see what logwatch does is to run it:

```
$ logwatch --range all --print | less
################### LogWatch 4.2.1 (10/27/02) ###################
    Processing Initiated: Sun Nov 10 20:53:49 2002
    Date Range Processed: all
    Detail Level of Output: 0
    Logfiles for Host: myhost
###############################################################
 -------------------- Connections (secure-log) Begin -----------------------
Unauthorized sudo commands attempted (1):
smith:
```

---

[*] Actually, there are no binaries: logwatch is a collection of Perl scripts. Therefore, you don't need to worry about which RPM is right for your system's architecture.

```
    /usr/bin/tail -30 /var/log/maillog
--------------------- Connections (secure-log) End ------------------------

-------------------- SSHD Begin -----------------------
SSHD Killed: 2 Time(s)
SSHD Started: 1 Time(s)
Users logging in through sshd:
    smith logged in from foo.example.com (128.91.0.3) using publickey: 1 Time(s)
Refused incoming connections:
    200.23.18.56: 1 Time(s)
-------------------- SSHD End -----------------------
...
```

Once installed, logwatch is often run daily by cron, emailing its results to root. This is not necessarily the most secure way to do things: if your system is compromised, then you cannot trust email or logwatch itself. Like tripwire (Chapter 1), logwatch is best run on a remote machine, or from a secure medium like CD-ROM or write-protected floppy disk.

logwatch processes most but not all common log files. For the rest, you can define your own logwatch *filters* to parse and summarize them. [9.37]

If logwatch seems to do nothing when you run it, be aware of the --print option. By default, logwatch does not write its results on standard output: it sends them by email. Specify --print to see the results on screen. Also be aware that the default range is "yesterday," which might not be what you want.

See Also

See logwatch(8) for full usage information or run:

```
$ logwatch --help
```

9.37   Defining a logwatch Filter

Problem

You want logwatch to print reports for a service it does not support.

Solution

Create your own logwatch filter for that service or log file. Suppose you have a service called foobar that writes to the log file */var/log/foobar.log*.

1. Create */etc/log.d/conf/logfiles/foobar.conf* containing:
   ```
   LogFile = /var/log/foobar.log
   Archive = foobar.log.*
   ...
   ```

---

2. Create */etc/log.d/conf/services/foobar.conf* containing:

```
LogFile = foobar
```

3. Create */etc/log.d/scripts/services/foobar*.

This is a script (Perl, shell, etc.) that matches the desired lines in *foobar.log* and produces your desired output. logwatch automatically strips the datestamps from syslog-format output, so your script needn't do this.

Discussion

logwatch is more a framework than a log parser. In fact, all parsing is done by auxiliary scripts in */etc/log.d/scripts/services*, so for unsupported services, you must write your own scripts. You might think, "Hey, if I have to write these scripts myself, what's the value of logwatch?" The answer is convenience, as well as consistency of organization. It's helpful to have all your log groveling scripts together under one roof. Plus logwatch supplies tons of scripts; use them as examples for writing your own.

To integrate a given service into logwatch, you must define three files:

A logfile group configuration file
Found in */etc/log.d/conf/logfiles*, it defines where the service's logs are stored.

A service filter executable
Found in */etc/log.d/scripts/services*, it must read log entries from standard input and write whatever you like on standard output.

A service filter configuration file
Found in */etc/log.d/conf/services*, it defines the association between the above two files. It specifies that the above-mentioned logs will be fed to the above-mentioned filter.

Our recipe uses minimal configuration files. Plenty of other options are possible.

See Also

/usr/share/doc/logwatch*/HOWTO-Make-Filter documents the full syntax of logwatch filters.

9.38 Monitoring All Executed Commands

Problem

You want to record information about executed commands, a.k.a., process accounting.

Solution

Prepare to enable process accounting:

```
# umask 077                          Be sure that the accounting data isn't publicly readable
# touch /var/account/pacct           Create the log file if necessary
```

Enable it:

```
# accton /var/account/pacct
```

or:

```
# /etc/init.d/psacct start           Red Hat
# /etc/init.d/acct start             SuSE
```

or:

```
# service psacct start               Red Hat
```

To disable it:

```
# accton                             Note: no filename
```

or:

```
# /etc/init.d/psacct stop            Red Hat
# /etc/init.d/acct stop              SuSE
```

or:

```
# service psacct stop                Red Hat
```

To enable process accounting automatically at boot time:

```
# chkconfig psacct on                Red Hat
# chkconfig acct on                  SuSE
```

By default, the process accounting RPM is not installed for Red Hat 8.0 or SuSE 8.0, but both distributions include it. The package name is psacct for Red Hat, and acct for SuSE.

Discussion

Sometimes, investigating suspicious activity requires time travel—you need detailed information about what happened during some interval in the past. *Process accounting* can help.

The Linux kernel can record a wealth of information about processes as they exit. This feature originally was designed to support charging for resources such as CPU time (hence the name "process accounting"), but today it is used mostly as an audit trail for detective work.

The accton command enables process accounting, and specifies the file used for the audit trail, conventionally */var/account/pacct*. This file must already exist, so manually create an empty file first if necessary, carefully restricting access to prevent public viewing of the sensitive accounting data. If the filename is omitted, then the accton command disables process accounting.

Usually process accounting is enabled automatically at boot time. On SuSE and Red Hat 8.0 or later systems, the chkconfig command installs the necessary links to run the scripts acct and psacct (respectively) in the */etc/init.d* directory. The behavior of earlier Red Hat versions is slightly different, and less flexible: the boot script */etc/init.d/rc.sysinit* always enables process accounting if the psacct RPM is installed, and the accounting files are stored in */var/log* instead of */var/account*.

Accounting data will accumulate fairly rapidly on a busy system, so the log files must be aggressively rotated [9.30]: the daily rotation specified by */etc/logrotate.d/psacct* on Red Hat systems is typical. SuSE does not provide a logrotate script, but you can install one in */etc/logrotate.d/acct*:

```
/var/account/pacct {
    prerotate
        /usr/sbin/accton
    endscript
    compress
    notifempty
    daily
    rotate 31
    create 0600 root root
    postrotate
        /usr/sbin/accton /var/account/pacct
    endscript
}
```

The prerotate and postrotate scripts use the accton command to disable accounting temporarily while the log files are being rotated. Compressed log files are retained for a month.

An alternative is to use the sa command with the -s option to truncate the current log file and write a summary of totals by command name or user ID in the files *savacct* and *usracct*, respectively (in the same directory as *pacct*). The logrotate method is more suitable for sleuthing, since it preserves more information.

See Also

accton(8), sa(8).

9.39 Displaying All Executed Commands

Problem

You want to display information about executed commands, as recorded by process accounting.

Solution

To view the latest accounting information:

```
$ lastcomm [command-name] [user-name] [terminal-name]
```

To view the complete record using `lastcomm`:

```
# umask 077                          Avoid publicly-readable accounting data in /var/tmp
# zcat `ls -tr /var/account/pacct.*.gz` > /var/tmp/pacct
# cat /var/account/pacct >> /var/tmp/pacct
# lastcomm -f /var/tmp/pacct
# rm /var/tmp/pacct
```

For more detailed information:

```
# dump-acct [--reverse] /var/account/pacct
```

Discussion

The GNU accounting utilities are a collection of programs for viewing the audit trail. The most important is `lastcomm`, which prints the following information for each process:

- The *command name*, truncated to sixteen characters.
- A set of *flags* indicating if the command used superuser privileges, was killed by a signal, dumped core, or ran after a `fork` without a subsequent `exec` (many daemons do this).
- The *user* who ran the command.
- The controlling *terminal* for the command (if any).
- The *CPU time* used by the command.
- The *start time* of the command.

 The latest version of `lastcomm` available at press time suffers from some unfortunate bugs. Terminals are printed incorrectly, usually as either "stdin" or "stdout", and are not recognized when specified on the command line. The reported CPU times are slightly more than five times the actual values for Red Hat 8.0 kernels; they are correct for earlier versions and for SuSE.

Some documentation errors should also be noted. The "X" flag means that the command was killed by any signal, not just SIGTERM. The last column is the start time, not the exit time for the command.

If you encounter these problems with `lastcomm`, upgrade to a more recent version if available.

Information about commands is listed in reverse chronological order, as determined by the time when each process exited (which is when the kernel writes the accounting records). Commands can be selected by combinations of the command name, user, or terminal; see lastcomm(1) for details.

`lastcomm` can read an alternative log file with the `-f` option, but it cannot read from a pipe, because it needs to seek within the accounting file, so the following will not work:

Fails:
```
$ zcat pacct.gz | lastcomm -f /dev/stdin
```

The kernel records much more information than is displayed by `lastcomm`. The undocumented `dump-acct` command prints more detailed information for each process:

- The *command name* (same as `lastcomm`).

- The *CPU time*, split into user and system (kernel) times, expressed as a number of ticks. The sum of these two times corresponds to the value printed by `lastcomm`.

- The *elapsed (wall clock) time*, also in ticks. This can be combined with the start time to determine the exit time.

- The *numerical user and group IDs*. These are real, not effective IDs. The user ID corresponds to the username printed by `lastcomm`.

- The *average memory usage*, in kilobytes.

- A measure of the *amount of I/O* (always zero for Version 2.4 or earlier kernels).

- The *start time*, with one second precision (`lastcomm` prints the time truncated to only one minute precision).

 A *tick* is the most basic unit of time used by the kernel, and represents the granularity of the clock. It is defined as 1/HZ, where HZ is the system timer interrupt frequency. The traditional value of HZ is 100, which leads to a ten millisecond tick.* Red Hat 8.0 kernels increased HZ to 512 for better time resolution, with a correspondingly shorter tick. The `tickadj` command prints the current value of the tick, in microseconds:

```
$ tickadj
tick = 10000
```

By default, `dump-acct` lists commands in chronological order; use the `-r` or `--reverse` options for behavior similar to `lastcomm`. One or more accounting files must be explicitly specified on the command line for `dump-acct`.

See Also

lastcomm(1).

---

* Known in Linux lore as a *jiffy*.

9.40 Parsing the Process Accounting Log

Problem

You want to extract detailed information such as exit codes from the process accounting log.

Solution

Read and unpack the accounting records with this Perl script:

```perl
#!/usr/bin/perl
use POSIX qw(:sys_wait_h);
use constant ACORE => 0x08; # for $flag, below
$/ = \64;                   # size of each accounting record
while (my $acct = <>) {
    my ( $flag,
         $uid,
         $gid,
         $tty,
         $btime,
         $utime,
         $stime,
         $etime,
         $mem,
         $io,
         $rw,
         $minflt,
         $majflt,
         $swaps,
         $exitcode,
         $comm) =
             unpack("CxS3LS9x2LA17", $acct);
    printf("%s %-16s", scalar(localtime($btime)), $comm);
    printf(" exited with status %d", WEXITSTATUS($exitcode))
        if WIFEXITED($exitcode);
    printf(" was killed by signal %d", WTERMSIG($exitcode))
        if WIFSIGNALED($exitcode);
    printf(" (core dumped)")
        if $flag & ACORE;
    printf("\n"); }
exit(0);
```

Discussion

Even the dump-acct command [9.39] misses some information recorded by the kernel, such as the exit code. This is really the status that would have been returned by wait(2), and includes the specific signal for commands that were killed. To recover this information, attack the accounting records directly with a short Perl script.

Our recipe shows how to read and unpack the records, according to the description in */usr/include/sys/acct.h*. When we run the script, it produces a chronological report that describes how each process expired, e.g:

```
Sun Feb 16 21:23:56 2003 ls        exited with status 0
Sun Feb 16 21:24:05 2003 sleep     was killed by signal 2
Sun Feb 16 21:24:14 2003 grep      exited with status 1
Sun Feb 16 21:25:05 2003 myprogram was killed by signal 7 (core dumped)
```

See Also

acct(5). The C language file */usr/include/sys/acct.h* describes the accounting records written by the kernel.

9.41   Recovering from a Hack

Problem

Your system has been hacked via the network.

Solution

1. Think. Don't panic.
2. Disconnect the network cable.
3. Analyze your running system. Document everything (and continue documenting as you go). Use the techniques described in this chapter.
4. Make a full backup of the system, ideally by removing and saving the affected hard drives. (You don't know if your backup software has been compromised.)
5. Report the break-in to relevant computer security incident response teams. [9.42]
6. Starting with a blank hard drive, reinstall the operating system from trusted media.
7. Apply all security patches from your vendor.
8. Install all other needed programs from trusted sources.
9. Restore user files from a backup taken before the break-in occurred.
10. Do a post-mortem analysis on the original copy of your compromised system. The Coroner's Toolkit (TCT) can help determine what happened and sometimes recover deleted files.
11. Reconnect to the network only after you've diagnosed the break-in and closed the relevant security hole(s).

Discussion

Once your system has been compromised, trust nothing on the system. Anything may have been modified, including applications, shared runtime libraries, and the kernel. Even innocuous utilities like */bin/ls* may have been changed to prevent the attacker's tracks from being viewed. Your only hope is a complete reinstall from trusted media, meaning your original operating system CD-ROMs or ISOs.

The Coroner's Toolkit (TCT) is a collection of scripts and programs for analyzing compromised systems. It collects forensic data and can sometimes recover (or at least help to identify) pieces of deleted files from free space on filesystems. It also displays access patterns of files, including deleted ones. Become familiar with TCT before any break-in occurs, and have the software compiled and ready on a CD-ROM in advance.

The post-mortem analysis is the most time-consuming and open-ended task after a break-in. To obtain usable results may require a lot of time and effort.

See Also

CERT's advice on recovery is at *http://www.cert.org/tech_tips/win-UNIX-system_ compromise.html*. The Coroner's Toolkit is available from *http://www.porcupine.org/ forensics/tct.html* or *http://www.fish.com/tct*.

9.42   Filing an Incident Report

Problem

You want to report a security incident to appropriate authorities, such as a computer security incident response team (CSIRT).

Solution

In advance of any security incident, develop and document a security policy that includes reporting guidelines. Store CSIRT contact information offline, in advance.

When an incident occurs:

1. Decide if the incident merits an incident report. Consider the impact of the incident.

2. Gather detailed information about the incident. Organize it, so you can communicate effectively.

3. Contact system administrators at other sites that were involved in the incident, either as attackers or victims.

4. Submit incident reports to appropriate CSIRTs. Be sure to respond to any requests for additional information.

Discussion

If your system has been hacked [9.41], or you have detected suspicious activity that might indicate an impending break-in, report the incident. A wide range of computer security incident response teams (CSIRTs) are available to help.

CSIRTs act as clearinghouses for security information. They collect and distribute news about ongoing security threats, analyze statistics gathered from incident reports, and coordinate defensive efforts. Collaboration with CSIRTs is an important part of being a responsible network citizen: any contribution, however small, to improving the security of the Internet will help you, too.

Develop a security policy, including procedures and contact information for applicable CSIRTs, *before* a break-in occurs. Most CSIRTs accept incident reports in a variety of formats, including Web forms, encrypted email, phone, FAX, etc. Since your network access might be disrupted by break-ins or denial of service attacks, store some or all of this information offline.

The Computer Emergency Response Team (CERT) serves the entire Internet, and is one of the most important CSIRTs: this is a good starting point. The Forum of Incident Response and Security Teams (FIRST) is a consortium of CSIRTs (including CERT) that serve more specialized constituencies. See their list of members to determine if any apply to your organization.

Government agencies are increasingly acting as CSIRTs, with an emphasis on law enforcement and prevention. Contact them to report activities that fall within their jurisdiction. An example in the United States is the National Infrastructure Protection Center (NIPC).

What activities qualify as bona fide security incidents? Clearly, malicious activities that destroy data or disrupt operations are included, but every Snort alert [9.20] does not merit an incident report. Consider the impact and potential effect of the activities, but if you are in doubt, report what you have noticed. Even reports of well-known security threats are useful to CSIRTs, as they attempt to correlate activities to detect widespread patterns and determine longer-term trends.

Before filing a report, gather the relevant information, including:

- A detailed description of activities that you noticed
- Monitoring techniques: *how* you noticed
- Hosts and networks involved: yours, apparent attackers, and other victims
- Supporting data such as log files and network traces

Start by contacting system administrators at other sites. If you are (or were) under attack, note the source, but be aware that IP addresses might have been spoofed. If your system has been compromised and used to attack other sites, notify them as well. ISPs might be interested in activities that involve large amounts of network traffic.

The whois command can obtain technical and administrative contact information based on domain names:

```
$ whois example.com
```

Save all of your correspondence—you might need it later. CSIRTs will want copies, and the communication might have legal implications if you are reporting potentially criminal activity.

Next, contact the appropriate CSIRTs according to your security policy. Follow each CSIRT's reporting guidelines, and note the incident tracking numbers assigned to your case, for future reference.

Provide good contact information, and try your best to respond in a timely manner to requests for more details. Don't be disappointed or surprised if you don't receive a reply, though. CSIRTs receive many reports, and if yours is a well-known threat, they might use it primarily for statistical analysis, with no need for a thorough, individual investigation.

In many cases, however, you will at least receive the latest available information about recognized activities. If you have discovered a new threat, you may even receive important technical assistance. CSIRTs often possess information that has not been publicly released.

See Also

The Computer Emergency Response Team (CERT) home page is *http://www.cert. org*. For incident reporting guidelines, see *http://www.cert.org/tech_tips/incident_ reporting.html*.

The CERT Coordination Center (CERT/CC) incident reporting form is available at the secure web site *https://irf.cc.cert.org*.

The Forum of Incident Response and Security Teams (FIRST) home page is *http:// www.first.org*. Their member list, with applicable constituencies, is available at *http:// www.first.org/team-info*.

The National Infrastructure Protection Center (NIPC) home page is *http://www. nipc.gov*.

Index

Symbols

@ character, redirecting log messages to another machine, 262

: (colons), current directory in empty search path element, 212

$! variable (Perl), for system error messages, 268

! (exclamation point)
  escaping for shells, 30
  excluding commands in sudoers file, 115
  preventing file inclusion in Tripwire database, 17

%m format specifier to syslog to include system error messages, 268, 269

. (period), in search path, 212

"" (quotes), empty, 116

/ (slash), beginning absolute directory names, 212

A

absolute directory names, 212

access control lists (ACLs), creating with PAM, 76

access_times attribute (xinetd), 62

accounting (see process accounting)

acct RPM, 274

accton command (for process accounting), 274

addpol command (Kerberos), 91

administrative privileges, Kerberos user, 92

administrative system, Kerberos (see kadmin utility)

agents, SSH
  forwarding, disabling for authorized keys, 141
  terminating on logout, 141
  using with Pine, 195
  (see also ssh-agent)

Aide (integrity checker), 3

alerts, intrusion detection (see Snort)

aliases
  for hostnames, 142
    changing SSH client defaults, 143
  for users and commands (with sudo), 114

ALL keyword (sudo), 106, 109

AllowUsers keyword (sshd), 65

Andrew Filesystem kaserver, 96

ank command (adding new Kerberos principal), 91

"any" interface, 236

apache (/etc/init.d startup file), 114

append-only directories, 149

apply keyword (PAM, listfile module), 78

asymmetric encryption, 147
  (see also public-key encryption)

attacks
  anti-NIDS attacks, 257
  buffer overflow
    detection with ngrep, 242
    indications from system daemon messages, 259
  dictionary attacks on terminals, 71
  dsniff, using to simulate, 247
  inactive accounts still enabled, using, 208

We'd like to hear your suggestions for improving our indexes. Send email to *index@oreilly.com*.

attacks (*continued*)
    man-in-the-middle (MITM)
        risk with self-signed certificates, 83
        services deployed with dummy
            keys, 187
    operating system vulnerability to forged
        connections, 225
    setuid root program hidden in
        filesystems, 216
    on specific protocols, 257
    system hacked via the network, 279
    vulnerability to, factors in, 221
attributes (file), preserving in remote file
    copying, 128
authconfig utility, 76
    imapd, use of general system
        authentication, 187
    Kerberos option, turning on, 100
AUTHENTICATE command (IMAP), 98
authentication
    cryptographic, for hosts, 51
    for email sessions (see email; IMAP)
    interactive, without password (see
        ssh-agent)
    Internet Protocol Security (IPSec), 73
    Kerberos (see Kerberos authentication)
    OpenSSH (see SSH)
    PAM (Pluggable Authentication Modules)
        (see PAM)
    SMTP (see SMTP)
    specifying alternate username for remote
        file copying, 128
    SSH (Secure Shell) (see SSH)
    SSL (Secure Sockets Layer) (see SSL)
    by trusted host (see trusted-host
        authentication)
authentication keys for Kerberos users and
    hosts, 89
authorization, 102–123
    root user
        ksu (Kerberized su) command, 104
        multiple root accounts, 103
        privileges, dispensing, 102
        running root login shell, 104
        running X programs as, 105
        SSH, use of, 103, 120
        sudo command, 103
    sharing files using groups, 111
    sharing root privileges
        via Kerberos, 121–123
        via SSH, 118

sudo command
    allowing user authorization privileges
        per host, 108
    bypassing password
        authentication, 106
    forcing password authentication, 108
    granting privileges to a group, 110
    killing processes with, 115
    logging remotely, 118
    password changes, 113
    read-only access to shared file, 112
    restricting root privileges, 115
    running any program in a
        directory, 110
    running commands as another
        user, 106
    starting/stopping daemons, 114
    unauthorized attempts to invoke,
        listing, 117
    weak controls in trusted-host
        authentication, 137
authorized_keys file (~/.ssh/ directory), 131
    forced commands, adding to, 120
authpriv facility (system messages), 260

B

backups, encrypting, 171
bash shell, xiv
    process substitution, 265
benefits of computer security, tradeoffs with
    risks and costs, xiii
Berkeley database library, use by dsniff, 244
binary data
    encrypted files, 151
    libpcap-format files, 250
    searching for with ngrep -X option, 242
binary format (DER), certificates, 79
    converting to PEM, 87
binary-format detached signature
    (GnuPG), 160
bootable CD-ROM, creating securely, 12
broadcast packets, 233
btmp file, processing with Sys::Utmp
    module, 210
buffer overflow attacks
    detection with ngrep, 242
    indicated by system daemon messages
        about names, 259

C

C programs
    functions provided by system logger
        API, 267
    writing to system log from, 264, 268
CA (Certifying Authority), 80
    setting up your own for self-signed
        certificates, 84
    SSL Certificate Signing Request (CSR),
        sending to, 81
    Verisign, Thawte, and Equifax, 82
CA.pl (Perl script), 84–87
cage, chroot (restricting a service to a
        particular directory), 65
canonical hostname for SSH client, 136
    finding with Perl script, 137
    inconsistencies in, 137
capture filter expressions, 236
    Ethereal, use of, 238
CERT Coordination Center (CERT/CC),
        incident reporting form, 282
certificates
    generating self-signed X.509
        certificate, 192
    revocation certificates for keys, 153
        distributing, 169
    SSL
        converting from DER to PEM, 87
        creating self-signed certificate, 83
        decoding, 79
        dummy certificates for imapd and
            pop3d, 186
        generating Certificate Signing Request
            (CSR), 81–83
        installing new, 80
        mutt mail client, use of, 191
        setting up CA and issuing
            certificates, 84–87
        validating, 78
        verifying, 184, 186
    testing of pre-installed trusted certificates
        by Evolution, 191
Certifying Authority (see CA)
cert.pem file
    adding new SSL certificate to, 80
    validating SSL certificates in, 79
certutil, 191
challenge password for certificates, 82
checksums (MD5), verifying for
        RPM-installed files, 18

chkconfig command
    enabling load commands for firewall, 44
    KDC and kadmin servers, starting at
        boot, 92
    process accounting packages, running at
        boot, 275
    Snort, starting at boot, 251
chkrootkit program, 219
    commands invoked by, 220
chmod (change mode) command, 147, 149
    preventing directory listings, 150
    removing setuid or setgid bits, 217
    setting sticky bit on world-writable
        directory, 149
    world-writable files access, disabling, 218
chroot program, restricting services to
        particular directories, 65
CIAC (Computer Incident Advisory
        Capability), Network Monitoring
        Tools page, 202
Classless InterDomain Routing (CIDR) mask
        format, 33
client authentication (see Kerberos
        authentication; PAM; SSH; SSL;
        trusted-host authentication)
client programs, OpenSSH, 124
closelog function, 267
    using in C program, 269
colons (:), referring to current working
        directory, 212
command-line arguments
    avoiding long, 214
    prohibiting for command run via
        sudo, 111
Common Log Format (CLF) for URLs, 247
Common Name, 82
    self-signed certificates, 84
compromised systems, analyzing, 280
Computer Emergency Response Team
        (CERT), 281
Computer Incident Advisory Capability
        (CIAC) Network Monitoring Tools
        page, 202
computer security incident response team
        (CSIRT), 280
copying files
    remotely, 127
        name-of-source and
            name-of-destination, 128
        rsync program, using, 19
        scp program, 125
            remote copying of multiple files, 127

Coroner's Toolkit (TCT), 280
cps keyword (xinetd), 67
cracking passwords
    Crack utility (Alec Muffet), 205
    CrackLib program, using, 75, 205
    John the Ripper software, using, 203–205
CRAM-MD5 authentication (SMTP), 199
credentials, Kerberos, 73
    forwardable, 98
    listing with klist command, 94
    obtaining and listing for users, 88
cron utility
    authenticating in jobs, 140
    cron facility in system messages, 260
    integrity checking at specific times or
        intervals, 13
    restricting service access by time of day
        (with inetd), 63
    secure integrity checks, running, 12
crypt++ (Emacs package), 169
cryptographic authentication
    for hosts, 51
    Kerberos (see Kerberos authentication)
    plaintext keys, 139
        using with forced command, 140–141
    public-key authentication, 129–131
        between OpenSSH client and SSH2
            server, using OpenSSH
            key, 131–133
        between OpenSSH client and SSH2
            server, using SSH2 key, 133
        between SSH2 client/OpenSSH
            server, 134
        with ssh-agent, 138
    SSH (see SSH)
    SSL (see SSL)
    by trusted hosts (see trusted-host
        authentication)
cryptographic hardware, 85
csh shell, terminating SSH agent on
        logout, 142
CSR (Certificate Signing Request), 81
    passphrase for private key, 82
current directory
    colons (:) referring to, 212
    Linux shell scripts in, xiv
CyberTrust SafeKeyper (cryptographic
        hardware), 85

D

daemons
    IMAP, within xinetd, 185
    imapd (see imapd)
    inetd (see inetd)
    Kerberized Telnet daemon, enabling, 97
    mail, receiving mail without running, 197
    POP, enabling within xinetd or inetd, 185
    sendmail, security risks with visibility
        of, 198
    Snort, running as, 251
    sshd (see sshd)
    starting/stopping via sudo, 114
    tcpd
        using with inetd, 62
        using with xinetd, 60
    Telnet, disabling standard, 97
    xinetd (see xinetd)
dangling network connections, avoiding, 126
date command, 254
DATE environment variable, 14
datestamps, handling by logwatch, 273
Debian Linux, debsums tool, 18
debugging
    debug facility, system messages, 260
    Kerberized authentication on Telnet, 98
    Kerberos authentication on POP, 100
    Kerberos for SSH, 96
    PAM modules, 78
    SSL connection problems from
        server-side, 190
dedicated server, protecting with firewall, 38
denial-of-service (DOS) attacks
    preventing, 67
    Snort detection of, 257
    vulnerability to using REJECT, 27
DENY
    absorbing incoming packets (ipchains)
        with no response, 28
    pings, preventing, 39
    REJECT vs. (firewalls), 27
DER (binary format for certificates), 79
    converting to PEM, 87
DES-based crypt( ) hashes in passwd
        file, 204
destination name for remote file
        copying, 128
detached digital signature (GnuPG), 160
/dev directory, 218
devfs, 71

device special files
  inability to verify with manual integrity
      check, 20
  securing, 217
/dev/null, redirecting standard input
      from, 126
DHCP, initialization scripts, 53
dictionary attacks against terminals, 71
diff command, using for integrity checks, 20
DIGEST-MD5 authentication (SMTP), 199
digital signatures, 148
  ASCII-format detached signature, creating
      in GnuPG, 160
  binary-format detached signature
      (GnuPG), creating, 160
  email messages, verifying with mc-verify
      function, 176
  encrypted email messages, checking with
      mc-verify, 177
  GnuPG-signed file, checking for
      alteration, 161
  signing a text file with GnuPG, 159
  signing and encrypting files, 159
  signing email messages with mc-sign
      function, 176
  uploading new to keyserver, 165
  verifying for keys imported from
      keyserver, 166
  verifying on downloaded software, 167
  for X.509 certificates, 72
directories
  encrypting entire directory tree, 164
  fully-qualified name, 110
  inability to verify with manual integrity
      check, 20
  marking files for inclusion or exclusion
      from Tripwire database, 17
  recurse=n attribute (Tripwire), 16
  recursive remote copying with scp, 128
  restricting a service to a particular
      directory, 65
  setgid bit, 112
  shared, securing, 149
  skipping with find -prune command, 214
  specifying another directory for remote
      file copying, 127
  sticky bit set on, 219
disallowed connections (see hosts.deny file)
DISPLAY environment variable (X
      windows), 105, 127

display filter expressions
  using with Ethereal, 238
  using with tcpdump, 236
display-filters for email (PinePGP), 179
Distinguished Encoding Rules (see DER)
DNS
  Common Name for certificate
      subjects, 82
  using domain name in Kerberos realm
      name, 89
dormant accounts, 207
  monitoring login activity, 211
DOS (see denial-of-service attacks)
DROP
  pings, preventing, 39
  REJECT and, refusing packets
      (iptables), 27
  specifying targets for iptables, 28
dsniff program, 234
  Berkeley database library, requirement
      of, 244
  downloading and installing, 244
  filesnarf command, 246
  insecure network protocols
      auditing use of, 244
      detecting, 243
  libnet, downloading and compiling, 243
  libnids
      downloading and installing, 244
      reassembling TCP streams with, 245
  libpcap snapshot, adjusting size of, 245
  -m option (matching protocols used on
      nonstandard ports), 245
  mailsnarf command, 245
  urlsnarf command, 247
dual-ported disk array, 13
dump-acct command, 277

E

editing encrypted files, 170
elapsed time (displayed in ticks), 277
elm mailer, 182
ELMME+, 182
Emacs
  encrypted email with, 175–177
      Mailcrypt package, using with
          GnuPG, 176
  encrypted files, maintaining with, 169
email, 175–201
  encryption
      with elm, 182
      with Emacs, 175–177

email, encryption (*continued*)
    with Evolution, 180
    with MH, 183
    with mutt, 181
    with vim, 177
    Mailcrypt package (see Mailcrypt)
    POP/IMAP security
        with SSH, 193
        with SSH and Pine, 195–197
        with SSL, 183–187
        with SSL and Evolution, 191
        with SSL and mutt, 190
        with SSL and Pine, 188
        with stunnel and SSL, 192
    protecting
        encouraging use of encryption, 246
        encrypted mail with Mozilla, 179
        at the mail server, 175
        between mail client and mail
            server, 175
        receiving Internet email without visible
            server, 197
        from sender to recipient, 175
        sending/receiving encrypted email with
            Pine, 178
        testing SSL mail connection, 188
    sending Tripwire reports by, 15
    SMTP server, using from arbitrary
        clients, 198–201
empty passphrase in plaintext key, 139
empty quotes (""), 116
encryption, 146
    asymmetric (see public-key encryption)
    of backups, 171
    decrypting file encrypted with
        GnuPG, 152
    email (see email, encryption)
    files
        entire directory tree, 164
        with password, 151
        (see also files, protecting)
    public-key (see public-key encryption)
    symmetric (see symmetric encryption)
encryption software, 147
Enigmail (Mozilla), 180
env program
    changes after running su, 104
    X windows DISPLAY and
        XAUTHORITY, setting, 105
environment variables, 105
Equifax (Certifying Authority), 82

error messages (system), including in
    syslog, 268, 269
errors
    onerr keyword, PAM listfile module, 77
    PAM modules, debugging, 78
Ethereal (network sniffing GUI)
    observing network traffic, 238–240
        capture and display filter
            expressions, 238
        data view window, 238
        packet list window, 238
        tree view window, 238
    payload display, 241
    tethereal (text version), 239
    tool to follow TCP stream, 239
    verifying secure mail traffic, 190
Evolution mailer, 180
    certificate storage, 81
    POP/IMAP security with SSL, 191
exclamation point (see !, under Symbols)
executables
    ignoring setuid or setgid attributes
        for, 216
    linked to compromised libraries, 22
    prohibiting entirely, 216
execute permission, controlling directory
    access, 150
executed commands (see process accounting)
expiration for GnuPG keys, 153
exporting PGP key into file, 173
extended regular expressions, matching with
    ngrep, 241

F

facilities, system messages, 259
    sensitive information in messages, 260
FascistCheck function (CrackLib), 205
fetchmail, 197
    mail delivery with, 198
fgrep command, 11
file attributes, preserving in remote file
    copying, 128
file command, 235
file permissions (see permissions)
files, protecting, 147–174
    encrypted, maintaining with Emacs, 169
    encrypting directories, 164
    encrypting with password, 151
    encryption, using, 147
    maintaining encrypted files with vim, 170

permissions (see permissions)
PGP keys, using with GnuPG, 173
prohibiting directory listings, 150
revoking a public key, 168
shared directory, 149
sharing public keys, 156
uploading new signatures to
    keyserver, 165
world-writable, finding, 218
(see also Gnu Privacy Guard)
files, searching effectively (see find
    command)
filesnarf command, 246
filesystems
    Andrew Filesystem kaserver, 96
    device special files, potential security
        risks, 217
    mounted, listing in /proc/mounts, 227
    /proc, 227
    searching for security risks, 212–215
        filenames, handling carefully, 214
        information about your
            filesystems, 213
        local vs. remote filesystems, 213
        permissions, examining, 214
        preventing crossing filesystem
            boundaries (find -xdev), 214
        rootkits, 202
        skipping directories (find -prune), 214
    Windows VFAT, checking integrity of, 17
filtered email messages (PineGPG), 179
filters
    capture expressions
        Ethereal, using with, 238
        selecting specific packets, 236
    display expressions
        Ethereal, using with, 238
        tcpdump, using with, 236
    logwatch, designing for, 272
    protocols matching filter expression,
        searching network traffic for, 240
    Snort, use by, 249
find command
    device special files, searching for, 217
    manual integrity checks, running with, 20
    searching filesystems effectively, 212
        -exec option (one file at a time), 215
        -perm (permissions) option, 214
        -print0 option, 214
        -prune option, 214
        running locally on its server, 213

setuid and setgid bits, 217
-xdev option, preventing crossing
    filesystem boundaries, 214
world-writable files, finding and
    fixing, 219
finger connections, 50
    redirecting to another machine, 69
    redirecting to another service, 69
fingerprints
    checking for keys imported from
        keyserver, 167
    operating system, 221, 222
        nmap -O command, 225
    public key, verifying for, 157
firewalls
    blocking access from a remote host, 31
    blocking access to a remote host, 32
    blocking all network traffic, 28
    blocking incoming network traffic, 28
    blocking incoming service requests, 30
    blocking incoming TCP port for
        service, 57
    blocking outgoing access to all web
        servers on a network, 33
    blocking outgoing network traffic, 30
    blocking outgoing Telnet connections, 37
    blocking remote access while permitting
        local, 34
    blocking spoofed addresses, 26
    controlling remote access by MAC
        address, 35
    decisions based on source addresses,
        testing with nmap, 225
    designing for Linux host, philosophies
        for, 25
    limiting number of incoming
        connections, 68
    Linux machine acting as, 26
    loading configuration, 43
    logging, 47
    network access control, 49
    open ports not protected by, finding with
        nmap, 222
    permitting SSH access only, 36
    pings, blocking, 39, 223
    portmapper access, reason to block, 228
    protecting dedicated server, 38
    remote logging host, protecting, 263
    rules
        building complex rule trees, 46
        deleting, 41

firewalls, rules (*continued*)
    hostnames instead of IP addresses,
        using in rules, 34
    inserting, 42
    listing, 39
    loading at boot time, 43
  saving configuration, 42
  source address verification,
      enabling, 24–26
  TCP ports blocked by, 223
  TCP RST packets for blocked ports,
      returning, 224
  testing configuration, 45
  vulnerability to attacks and, 221
flushing a chain, 41
forced commands
  limiting programs user can run as
      root, 120
  plaintext key, using with, 140–141
  security considerations with, 121
  server-side restrictions on public keys in
      authorized keys, 141
Forum of Incident Response and Security
    Teams (FIRST), 281
  home page, 282
forwardable credentials (Kerberized
    Telnet), 98
FreeS/WAN (IPSec implementation), 73
fstab file
  grpid, setting, 112
  nodev option to prohibit device special
      files, 217
  prohibiting executables, 216
  setuid or setgid attributes for
      executables, 216
FTP
  open server, testing for exploitation as a
      proxy, 225
  passwords captured from sessions with
      dsniff, 245
  sftp, 128
fully-qualified directory name, 110

G

gateways, packet sniffers and, 234
generator ID (Snort alerts), 252
Generic Security Services Application
    Programming Interface
    (GSSAPI), 95
  Kerberos authentication on IMAP, 98
  Kerberos authentication on POP, 100
gethostbyname function, 137

GNU Emacs (see Emacs)
Gnu Privacy Guard (GnuPG), 146, 147, 175
  adding keys to keyring, 157
  backing up private key, 162–164
  decrypting files, 152
  default secret key, designating, 155
  ELMME+ mailer, 182
  encrypting backups, 171
  encrypting files for others, 158
  Enigmail (Mozilla), using for encryption
      support, 180
  Evolution mailer, using with, 180
  files encrypted with, editing with
      vim, 170
  key, adding to keyserver, 165
  keyring, using, 154
  keys, adding to keyring, 157
  Mailcrypt, using with, 176
  MH, integrating with, 183
  mutt mailer, using with, 181
  obtaining keys from keyserver, 166–168
  PGP keys, using, 173
  PinePGP, sending/receiving encrypted
      email, 178
  piping email through gpg command, 182
  piping show command through gpg
      command, 183
  printing your public key in ASCII, 162
  producing single encrypted files from all
      files in directory, 164
  public-key encryption, 151
  revoking a key, 168
  setting up for public-key encryption, 152
  sharing public keys, 156
  signed file, checking for alteration, 161
  signing and encrypting files (to be not
      human-readable), 159
  signing text file, 159
  symmetric encryption, 151
  viewing keys on keyring, 154
  vim mail editor, composing encrypted
      email with, 177
government agencies acting as CSIRTs, 281
GPG (see Gnu Privacy Guard)
.gpg suffix (binary encrypted files), 151
grep command
  extracting passwords by patterns, 146
  -z (reading/writing data) and -Z (writing
      filenames), 214, 215
group permissions
  changes since last Tripwire check, 16
  read/write for files, 113

groups
    granting privileges to with sudo
        command, 110
    logfile group configuration file, 273
    sharing files in, 111
        setgid bit on directory, 112
        setting umasks as group writable, 112
grpid option (mount), 112
GSSAPI (see Generic Security Services
        Application Programming Interface)
GUI (graphical user interface), observing
        network traffic via, 238–240

H

hard links for encrypted files, 172
hardware, cryptographic, 85
Heimdal Kerberos, 73
highly secure integrity checks, 11
    dual-ported disk array, using, 13
history of all logins and logouts, 208
Honeynet project web site (network
        monitoring information), 257
host aliases (see aliases)
host discovery (with nmap), 222
    disabling port scanning with -sP
        options, 225
    for IP address range only, 221
    TCP and ICMP pings, 223
Host keyword, 142
host principal for KDC host, 88
host program, problems with canonical
        hostname, 137
hostbased authentication (see trusted-host
        authentication)
HostbasedAuthentication
    in ssh_config, 136
    in sshd_config, 135
HostbasedUsesNameFromPacketOnly
        keyword (sshd_config), 138
HOSTNAME environment variable, 14
hostnames
    conversion to IP addresses by netstat and
        lsof commands, 229
    in remote file copying, 128
    using instead of IP addresses in firewall
        rules, 34
hosts
    controlling access by (instead of IP source
        address), 51
    firewall design, philosophies for, 25
    IMAP server, adding Kerberos principals
        for mail service, 99

Kerberos
    adding new principal, 91
    adding to existing realm, 93
    modifying KDC database for, 90
    Kerberos KDC principal database of, 89
    Kerberos on SSH, localhost and, 96
    tailoring SSH per host, 142
    trusted, authenticating by (see
        trusted-host authentication)
hosts.allow file, 60
    access control for remote hosts
        inetd with tcpd, 62
    restricting access by remote hosts, 60
        sshd, 64
        xinetd with tcpd, 60
hosts.deny file, 51, 60
    access control for remote hosts
        inetd with tcpd, 62
    restricting access by remote hosts, 60
        sshd, 64
        xinetd with tcpd, 60
HTTP
    blocking all incoming service requests, 31
    capturing and recording URLs from traffic
        with urlsnarf, 247
httpd (/etc/init.d startup file), 114
HTTPS, checking certificate for secure web
        site, 79

I

ICMP
    blocking messages, 29
    blocking some messages, 39
    closed ports, detecting with
        messages, 224
    pings for host discovery, use by
        nmap, 223
    rate-limiting functions of Linux kernel, 27
IDENT
    checking with TCP-wrappers, 51
    DROP, problems with, 27
    testing server with nmap -I for
        security, 225
identification file (SSH2 key files), 132, 135
identity, 72
idfile script (manual integrity checker), 20
IDs for cryptographic keys (GnuPG default
        secret key), 156
ifconfig program
    -a option (information about all network
        interfaces and loaded drivers), 235
    controlling network interfaces, 50

ifconfig program (*continued*)
   enabling promiscuous mode for specific
      interfaces, 236
   enabling unconfigured interface, 235
   listing network interfaces, 52
   observing network traffic, 233
   stopping network device, 28
ifdown script, 53
ifup script, 53
IgnoreRhosts option, 137
IMAP
   access control list (ACL) for server,
      creating with PAM, 77
   enabling IMAP daemon within xinetd or
      inetd, 185
   in /etc/pam.d startup file, 187
   Kerberos authentication, using with, 98
   mail session security
      with SSH, 193
      with SSH and Pine, 195–197
      with SSL, 183–187
      with SSL and Evolution, 191
      with SSL and mutt, 190
      with SSL and Pine, 188
      with SSL and stunnel, 192
      with stunnel and SSL, 192
   remote polling of server by fetchmail, 198
   SSL certificate, validating server with, 79
   STARTTLS command, 184
   testing SSL connection to server, 188
   unsecured connections, permitting, 187
imapd
   enabling within xinetd or inetd, 186
   Kerberos support, 99
   SSL, using with, 183
   validation of passwords, controlling with
      PAM, 187
IMAP/SSL certificate on Red Hat server, 82
importing keys
   from a keyserver, 166
   PGP, importing into GnuPG, 173
incident report (security), filing, 280–282
   gathering information for, 281
includedir (xinetd.conf), 56
incoming network traffic, controlling (see
      firewalls; networks, access control)
incorrect net address (sshd), 96
inetd, 51
   adding new network service, 56
   enabling/disabling TCP service invocation
      by, 54

IMAP daemon, enabling, 185
POP daemon, enabling, 185
-R option, preventing denial-of-service
      attacks, 68
restricting access by remote hosts, 61
inetd.conf file
   adding new network service, 56
   restricting service access by time of
      day, 63
inode numbers
   changes since last Tripwire check, 16
   rsync tool, inability to check with, 20
   Windows VFAT filesystems, instructing
      Tripwire not to compare, 17
input/output
   capturing stdout/stderr from programs
      not using system logger, 265
   Snort alerts, 257
   stunnel messages, 193
Insecure.org's top 50 security tools, 203
instances keyword (xinetd), 67
instruction sequence mutations (attacks
      against protocols), 257
integrity checkers, 1
   Aide, 3
   runtime, for the kernel, 3
   Samhain, 3
   (see also Tripwire)
integrity checks
   automated, 13
   checking for file alteration since last
      snapshot, 7
   highly secure, 11
      dual-ported disk array, using, 13
   manual, 20–22
   printing latest tripwire report, 14
   read-only, 8
   remote, 9
   reports, 2
   rsync, using for, 19
interactive programs, invoking on remote
      machine, 126
interfaces, network
   bringing up, 52
   enabling/disabling, levels of control, 53
   listing, 51, 52
Internet email, acceptance by SMTP
      server, 200
Internet Protocol Security (IPSec), 73
Internet protocols, references for, 238
Internet services daemon (see inetd)

intrusion detection for networks, 202
  anti-NIDS attacks, 257
  Snort system, 247
    decoding alert messages, 252
    detecting intrusions, 250
    logging, 253
    ruleset, upgrading and tuning, 256
  testing with nmap stealth operations, 226
IP addresses
  conversion to hostnames by netstat and
    lsof commands, 229
  in firewall rules, using hostnames instead
    of, 34
  host discovery for (without port
    scanning), 221
  for SSH client host, 137
IP forwarding flag, 25
ipchains, 23
  blocking access for particular remote host
    for a particular service, 32
  blocking access for some remote hosts but
    not others, 32
  blocking all access by particular remote
    host, 31
  blocking all incoming HTTP traffic, 31
  blocking incoming HTTP traffic while
    permitting local HTTP traffic, 31
  blocking incoming network traffic, 29
  blocking outgoing access to all web
    servers on a network, 33
  blocking outgoing Telnet connections, 37
  blocking outgoing traffic, 30
  blocking outgoing traffic to particular
    remote host, 32
  blocking remote access, while permitting
    local, 34
  blocking spoofed addresses, 26
  building chain structures, 47
  default policies, 24
  deleting firewall rules, 41
  DENY and REJECT. DROP, refusing
    packets with, 27
  disabling TCP service invocation by
    remote request, 55
  inserting firewall rules in particular
    position, 42
  listing firewall rules, 40
  logging and dropping certain packets, 48
  permitting incoming SSH access only, 37
  preventing pings, 39
  protecting dedicated server, 38

  restricting telnet service access by source
    address, 54
  simulating packet traversal through to
    verify firewall operation, 221
  testing firewall configuration, 45
ipchains-restore, 43
  loading firewall configuration, 43
ipchains-save
  checking IP addresses, 34
  saving firewall configuration, 42
  viewing rules with, 40
IPSec, 51
iptables, 23
  blocking access for particular remote host
    for a particular service, 31
  blocking access for some remote hosts but
    not others, 32
  blocking all access by particular remote
    host, 31
  blocking all incoming HTTP traffic, 31
  blocking incoming HTTP traffic while
    permitting local HTTP traffic, 31
  blocking incoming network traffic, 29
  blocking outgoing access to all web
    servers on a network, 33
  blocking outgoing Telnet connections, 37
  blocking outgoing traffic, 30
  blocking outgoing traffic to particular
    remote host, 32
  blocking remote access, while permitting
    local, 34
  blocking spoofed addresses, 26
  building chain structures, 46
  controlling access by MAC address, 35
  default policies, 24
  deleting firewall rules, 41
  disabling reverse DNS lookups (-n
    option), 40
  disabling TCP service invocation by
    remote request, 55
  DROP and REJECT, refusing packets
    with, 27
  error packets, tailoring, 28
  inserting firewall rules in particular
    position, 42
  listing firewall rules, 40
  permitting incoming SSH access only, 37
  preventing pings, 39
  protecting dedicated server, 38
  restricting telnet service access by source
    address, 54

iptables (*continued*)
  rule chain for logging and dropping
      certain packets, 47
  --syn flag to process TCP packets, 29
  testing firewall configuration, 45
  web site, 24
iptables-restore, 43
  loading firewall configuration, 43
iptables-save
  checking IP addresses, 34
  saving firewall configuration, 42
  viewing rules with, 40
IPv4-in-IPv6 addresses, problems with, 96
ISP mail servers, acceptance of relay
      mail, 200
issuer (certificates), 72
  self-signed, 83

J

John the Ripper (password-cracking
      software), 203–205
  dictionaries for, 204
  download site, 203
  wordlist directive, 204

K

kadmin utility, 88
  adding Kerberos principals to IMAP mail
      server, 99
  adding users to existing realm, 92
  modifying KDC database for host, 90
  running on new host, 93
  setting server to start at boot, 92
kadmind command (Kerberos), 88
kaserver (Andrew Filesystem), 96
kdb5_util command (Kerberos), 89
KDC (see Key Distribution Center)
KDE applications, certificate storage, 81
Kerberos authentication, 73
  in /etc/pam.d startup file, 100
  hosts, adding to existing realm, 93
  IMAP, using with, 98
  Key Distribution Centers (KDCs), 73
  ksu, 104
  ksu command, 122
  PAM, using with, 100
  without passwords, 137
  POP, using with, 100
  setting up MIT Kerberos-5 KDC, 88–92
  sharing root privileges via, 121–123

SSH, using with, 94–96
  debugging, 96
  SSH-1 protocol, 95
Telnet, using with, 96
users, adding to existing realm, 92
web site (MIT), 73
KerberosTgtPassing (in sshd_config), 96
kernel
  collection of messages from by system
      logger, 259
  enabling source address verification, 27
  IP forwarding flag, 25
  ipchains (Versions 2.2 and up), 23
  iptables (Versions 2.4 and up), 23
  /proc files and, 227
  process information recorded on exit, 274
  runtime integrity checkers, 3
  source address verification, enabling, 24
Key Distribution Center (KDC)
  setting up for MIT Kerberos-5, 88–92
      protecting your KDC server, 90
keyring files (GnuPG), 156
  adding keys to, 157
  viewing keys on, 154
      information listed for keys, 155
keys, cryptographic
  adding to GnuPG keyring, 157
  backing up GnuPG private key, 162–164
  dummy keypairs for imapd and
      pop3d, 186
  encrypting files for others with
      GnuPG, 158
  generating key pair for GnuPG, 152
  GnuPG, viewing on your keyring, 154
  key pairs in public-key encryption, 147
  keyring files for GnuPG keys, 156
  obtaining from keyserver and
      verifying, 166–168
  OpenSSH programs for
      creating/using, 124
  PGP keys, using in GnuPG, 173
  revoking a public key, 168
  sharing public keys securely, 156
  Tripwire, 3
  viewing on GnuPG keyring, 155
  (see also cryptographic authentication)
keyserver
  adding key to, 165
  informing that a public keys is no longer
      valid, 168
  obtaining keys from, 166–168
  uploading new signatures to, 165

killing processes
   authorizing users to kill via sudo
      command, 115
   pidof command, using, 116
   terminating SSH agent on logout, 142
kinit command (Kerberos), 88, 91, 94
   -f option (forwardable credentials), 98
klist command (Kerberos), 88, 94
known hosts database (OpenSSH
      server), 136
kpasswd command (Kerberos), 92
krb5.conf file, copying to new Kerberos
      host, 93
krb5kdc, 89
krb5.keytab file, 91
kstat (integrity checker), 3
ksu (Kerberized su)
   authentication via Kerberos, 122
   sharing root privileges via, 121–123

L

last command, 207, 210
lastb command, 210
lastcomm utility, 276
   bugs in latest version, 276
lastdb command, 207
lastlog command, 207
   databases from several systems,
      merging, 209
   multiple systems, monitoring problems
      with, 210
ldd command, 67
libnet (toolkit for network packet
      manipulation), 243
libnids (for TCP stream reassembly), 244
libpcap (packet capture library), 235, 245
   binary files, Snort logging directory,
      creating in, 254
   logging Snort data to libpcap-format
      files, 250
   network trace files, ngrep, 242
   Snort, use by, 249
libwrap, using with xinetd, 59
Linux
   differing locations for binaries and
      configuration files in
      distributions, xv
   encryption software included with, 147
   operating system vulnerabilities, 225
   /proc filesystem, 227
   Red Hat (see Red Hat Linux)

supported distributions for security
      recipes, xiv
   SuSE (see SuSE Linux)
ListenAddress statements, adding to
      sshd_config, 96
listfile module (PAM), 76
   ACL file entries, 77
local acces, permitting while blocking remote
      access, 34
local facilities (system messages), 260
local filesystems, searching, 213
local key (Tripwire), 3
   creating with twinstall.sh script, 4
   fingerprints, creating in secure integrity
      checks, 12
   read-only integrity checking, 8
local mail (acceptance by SMTP server), 200
local password authentication, using
      Kerberos with PAM, 101
localhost
   problems with Kerberos on SSH, 96
   SSH port forwarding, use in, 193
   unsecured mail sessions from, 187
logfile group configuration file
      (logwatch), 273
logger program, 264
   writing system log entries via shell scripts
      and syslog API, 266
logging
   access to services, 70
   combining log files, 269
   firewalls, configuring for, 47
   nmap -o options, formats of, 225
   PAM modules, error messages, 78
   process accounting logs, parsing, 278
   rotating log files, 263
   service access via xinetd, 70
   shutdowns, reboots, and runlevel changes
      in /var/log/wtmp, 208
   Snort, 248, 253
      to binary files, 250
      partitioning into separate files, 255
      permissions for directory, 251
   stunnel messages, 193
   sudo command, 103
      remotely, 118
   system (see system logger)
   testing with nmap stealth operations, 226
loghost
   changing, 263
   remote logging of system messages, 262
login shells, root, 104

logins
  adding another Kerberos principal to your
    ~/.k5login file, 96
  Kerberos, using with PAM, 101
  monitoring suspicious activity, 202
  printing information about for each
    user, 207
  recent logins to system accounts,
    checking, 207
  testing passwords for strength, 203–206
    CrackLib, using, 205
    John the Ripper, using, 203–205
logouts, history of all on system, 208
logrotate program, 260, 263, 275
logwatch
  filter, defining, 272
  integrating services into, 273
  listing all sudo invocation attempts, 117
  scanning log files for messages of
    interest, 259
  scanning Snort logs and sending out
    alerts, 251
  scanning system log files for problem
    reports, 271
lsh (SSH implementation), 197
lsof command, 229
  -c option (command name for
    processes), 230
  -i option (for network connections), 229
  IP addresses, conversion to
    hostnames, 229
  +M option (for processes using RPC
    services), 229
  network connections for processes,
    listing, 226
  -p option (selecting processes by ID), 230
  /proc files, reading, 227
  -u option (username for processes), 230

M

m4 macro processor, 63
MAC addresses
  controlling access by, 35
  spoofed, 36
mail (see email; IMAP; POP)
Mail application (Mozilla), 179
mail clients
  connecting to mail server over SSL, 186
  support for secure POP and IMAP using
    SSL, 184
mail facility (system messages), 260

mail servers
  receiving Internet email without visible
    server, 197
  support for SSL, 184
  testing SSL connection locally, 185
Mailcrypt
  mc-deactivate-passwd to force passphrase
    erasure, 177
  official web site, 177
  using with GnuPG, 176
mailpgp (script for encrypting/sending
    email), 182
mailsnarf command, 245
  -v option, capturing only unencrypted
    messages, 246
malicious program, /tmp/ls, 211
man-in-the-middle (MITM) attacks
  dsniff, proof of concept with, 247
  self-signed certificates, risk of, 83
  services deployed with dummy keys, 187
manual integrity checks, 20–22
mask format, CIDR, 33
Massachusetts Institute of Technology (MIT)
    Kerberos, 73
matching anything (ALL keyword), 106, 109
max_load keyword (xinetd), 67, 68
mc-encrypt function, 176
MD5 checksum, verifying for RPM-installed
    files, 18
merging system log files, 269
MH (mail handler), 183
mirroring a set of files securely between
    machines, 129
MIT Kerberos, 73
MITM (see man-in-the-middle attacks)
modules
  PAM, 74
    CrackLib, 75
    listfile, 76, 77
    pam_stack, 76
  Perl
    Sys::Lastlog and Sys::Utmp, 210
    Sys::Syslog, 268
    XML::Simple, 225
monitoring systems for suspicious
    activity, 202–282
  account use, 207
    checking on multiple
      systems, 209–211
  device special files, 217
  directing system messages to log
    files, 257–261

displaying executed commands, 275

executed command, monitoring, 273

filesystems, 202
    searching effectively, 212–215

finding accounts with no password, 206

finding superuser accounts, 207

finding writable files, 218

insecure network protocols,
    detecting, 243–247

local network activities, 226–231

log files, combining, 269

logging, 202

login passwords, 203–206

logins and passwords, 202

logwatch filter for services not
    supported, 272

lsof command, investigating processes
    with, 230

networking, 202

network-intrusion detection with
    Snort, 247, 250
    decoding alert messages, 252
    logging output, 253
    partitioning logs into files, 255
    ruleset, upgrading and tuning, 256

observing network traffic, 233–238
    with Ethereal GUI, 238–240

open network ports, testing for, 220–226

packet sniffing with Snort, 248

parsing process accounting logs, 278

recovering from a hack, 279

rootkits, 219

rotating log files, 263

scanning log files for problem
    reports, 271

search path, testing, 211

searching for strings in network
    traffic, 240–242

security incident report, filing, 280–282

sending messages to system logger, 264

setuid and setgid programs,
    insecure, 215–217

syslog configuration, testing, 261

syslog messages, logging remotely, 262

tracing processes, 231

writing system log entries
    shell scripts, 265–267
    with C, 268
    with Perl scripts, 267

monitoring tools for networks
    NIH page, 203
    web page information on, 202

morepgp (script for decrypting/reading
    email), 182

mount command, 213
    grpid option, 112
    noexec option, 216
    nosuid option, 216
    -o nodev (prohibiting device special
        files), 217
    setuid and setgid programs, protecting
        against misuse, 217

mounts file, 227

Mozilla
    certificate storage, 81
    encrypted mail with Mail &
        Newsgroups, 179

Muffet, Alec (Crack utility), 205

multicast packets, 233

multi-homed hosts
    firewall for, 25
    SSH client, problems with canonical
        hostname, 137

multi-homed server machines, socket mail
    server is listening on, 194

multithreaded services (in inetd.conf), 56

mutt mailer, 181
    home web page, 182
    securing POP/IMAP with SSL, 190

N

NAMEINARGS flag for xinetd, 61

NAT gateway, canonical client hostname
    and, 137

National Infrastructure Protection Center
    (NIPC) (U.S.), 281
    home page, 282

National Institutes of Health, "Network and
    Network Monitoring Software"
    page, 203

nc command
    probing ports with, 223
    -u option (for UDP ports), 224

netgroups
    customizing shosts.equiv file to restrict
        hostbased authentication, 138
    defining, 109

Netscape, certificate storage, 81

netstat command
    --all option, 228
    conversion of IP addresses to
        hostnames, 229
    -e option (adding username), 229

netstat command (*continued*)
    examining network state on your
        machines, 221
    --inet option (printing active
        connections), 228
    --listening option, 228
    -p option (process ID and command name
        for each socket), 229
    printing summary of network use, 226
    /proc files, reading, 227
    summary for networking on a
        machine, 228
network configuration of your systems,
        attack vulnerability and, 221
network (/etc/init.d startup file), 53
network filesystems
    remote integrity checks, 11
    searching, 213
    snooping with filesnarf, 246
network interfaces, 49
    bringing up, 52
network intrusion detection systems
        (NIDS), 248
    attacks against, 257
    rapid development in, 256
    Snort (see Snort)
network monitoring tools
    NIH page, 203
    web page information on, 202
network protocols, detecting
        insecure, 243–247
network script, 53
network services, access control facilities, 49
network switches, packet sniffers and, 234
networking
    disabling for secure integrity checks, 12
    monitoring and intrusion detection (see
        intrusion detection for networks;
        monitoring systems for suspicious
        activity)
    /proc/net/tcp and /proc/net/upd
        files, 227
    summary for, printing with netstat, 228
networks
    access control
        adding a new service (xinetd), 55
        adding a new service (inetd), 56
        denial-of-service attacks,
            preventing, 67
        enabling/disabling a service, 53
        levels of control, 49
        listing network interfaces, 51

logging access to services, 70
prohibiting root logins on terminal
        devices, 71
redirecting connections to another
        socket, 69
restricting access by remote hosts
        (inetd), 61
restricting access by remote hosts
        (xinetd), 58
restricting access by remote hosts
        (xinetd with libwrap), 59
restricting access by remote hosts
        (xinetd with tcpd), 60
restricting access by remote users, 57
restricting access to service by time of
        day, 62
restricting access to SSH server by
        account, 64
restricting access to SSH server by
        host, 64
restricting services to specific
        directories, 65
starting/stopping network
        interface, 52
(see also firewalls)
hacks, system recovery from, 279
intrusion detection (see intrusion
        detection for networks; Snort)
local activities, examining, 226–231
    lsof command, examining
        processes, 230
    printing summary of use with
        netstat, 226
    /proc filesystem, 227
monitoring traffic on, 233–238
    observing via GUI, 238–240
    searching for strings in, 240–242
protecting outgoing traffic, 124–146
    authenticating between SSH2 client
        and OpenSSH server, 134
    authenticating between SSH2 server
        and OpenSSH client with OpenSSH
        key, 131–133
    authenticating between SSH2 server
        and OpenSSH client with SSH2
        key, 133
    authenticating by public key in
        OpenSSH, 129–131
    authenticating by trusted host, 135
    authenticating in cron jobs, 140
    authenticating interactively without
        password, 138

copying files remotely, 127
invoking remote programs, 126
keeping track of passwords, 146
logging into remote host, 125
SSH client defaults, changing, 143
SSH, using, 124
tailoring SSH per host, 142
terminating SSH agent on logout, 141
tunneling TCP connection through
    SSH, 144
refusal of connections by system
    logger, 268
tracing system calls, 226, 231
Newsgroups application (Mozilla), 179
ngrep program, 240–242
    -A option, printing extra packets for
        trailing context, 242
    detecting use of insecure protocols, 241
    download site, 240
    home page for, 242
    libcap-format network trace files, 242
    searching network traffic for data
        matching extended regular
        expressions, 241
    -T option (relative times between
        packets), 242
    -t option (timestamps), 242
    -X option (searching for binary data), 242
NIDS (see network intrusion detection
    systems; Snort)
nmap command, 221–226
    host discovery, use of TCP and ICMP
        pings, 223
    information gathered in network security
        testing, 222
    probing a single target, 222
    -r option, sequential port scan, 237
    running as root, 224
    scanning range of addresses, 222
    stealth options, using to test logging and
        intrusion detection, 226
    testing for open ports, 221
        customizing number and ranges of
            ports scanned, 224
        -O option for operating system
            fingerprints, 225
        port scans, 223
        -sU options (for UDP ports), 224
    testing for vulnerabilities of specific
        network services, 225
nmapfe program, 221, 223
nmh (mail handler), 183

NNTP, tunneling with SSH, 57, 144
no_access keyword, xinetd.conf, 58
noninteractive commands, invoking securely
    on remote machine, 126
non-local mail (acceptance by SMTP
    server), 200
NOPASSWD tag (sudo command), 107
notice priority, system messages, 264
null-terminated filenames, 214

O

onerr keyword (PAM, listfile module), 77
only_from and no_access keywords,
    xinetd.conf, 58
open relay mail servers, 200
open servers, testing FTP server for possible
    exploitation as a proxy, 225
openlog function, 267
    using in C program, 269
open-source integrity checkers (see Tripwire)
OpenSSH (see SSH)
OpenSSL, 73
    CA.pl, Perl script creating Certifying
        Authority, 84–87
    PEM encoding, converting DER certificate
        to, 87
    testing SSL connection to POP/IMAP
        server, 188
    web site, 73
Openwall Project, John the Ripper, 203
operating system fingerprints, 221
    nmap command, using for, 222, 225
@otherhost syntax, syslog.conf, 118
outgoing network connections (see networks,
    protecting outgoing traffic)
ownership, file
    inability to track with manual integrity
        check, 20
    verifying for RPM-installed files, 18

P

packet filtering
    Linux, web site for, 24
    stateful, 23
    stateless, 23
packet sniffers
    dsniff, for switched networks, 234
    enabling unconfigured network interfaces
        with ifconfig, 235
    network intrusion detection system
        (NIDS), 248

packet sniffers (*continued*)
  ngrep, using for, 240
  observing network traffic with, 233–238
    promiscuous mode on network
      interfaces, 234
    unconfigured interface for stealth
      sniffer, 233
  Snort, using as, 248
packets, refusing with DROP or REJECT, 27
PAM (Pluggable Authentication
      Modules), 72
  access control lists (ACLs), creating, 76
  controlling imapd password
      validation, 187
  creating PAM-aware application, 74
  enforcing password strength, 75
  imapd validation of passwords,
      controlling, 187
  Kerberos, using with, 100
  Linux Developers Guide, 75
  Linux-PAM, web site, 73
  modules, 74
pam_stack module, 76
passphrases
  backing up for GnuPG private keys, 163
  caching SSH private keys to avoid
      typing, 124
  forcing erasure by Mailcrypt with
      mc-deactivate-passwd, 177
  secret, for GnuPG public keys, 154
  SSH, 130
passwd file, DES-based crypt( ) hashes
      in, 204
passwd program, 75
passwords
  authorizing changes via sudo, 113
  dsniff program
    captured from FTP and Telnet
      sessions, 245
    using libnids to reassemble, 245
  encrypting files with, 151
  enforcing strength with PAM, 75
  interactive authentication without
      (ssh-agent), 138
  keeping track of, 146
  Kerberos (kpasswd command), 92
  local, authentication via (Kerberos with
      PAM), 101
  login, testing for strength, 203–206
    CrackLib, using, 205
    John the Ripper, using, 203–205

mail servers (IMAP/POP), protection by
      SSL, 186
master password for KDC database, 88
  storage of, 89
  protection with SSH, 125
  root, 102
  sudo command
    bypassing password
      authentication, 106
    forcing authentication with, 108
  testing and monitoring on system, 202
PATH environment variable, splitting with
      Perl script, 212
pathnames
  mutation in attacks against
      protocols, 257
  in remote file copying, 128
paths
  search path, testing, 211
  to server executable (inetd.conf), 56
pattern matching (see regular expressions)
payload, observing, 241
PEM format (certificates), 80
  converting DER format to, 87
performance, effects of promiscuous
      mode, 235
period (.), in search path, 212
Perl scripts
  canonical hostname for SSH client,
      finding, 137
  CA.pl, 84–87
  CrackLib, using with module, 206
  functions provided by system logger
      API, 267
  merging lastlog databases from several
      systems, 209
  merging log files, 269
  process accounting records, reading and
      unpacking, 278
  writing system log entries, 264, 267
permissions, 147, 148
  changes since last Tripwire check, 16
  examining carefully for security, 214
  inability to track with manual integrity
      check, 20
  log files, 261
  preventing directory listings, 150
  Snort logging directory, 251
  world-writable files and directories,
      finding, 218
PermitRootLogin (sshd_config), 119
per_source keyword (xinetd), 67

PGP (Pretty Good Privacy), 147
    Evolution mailer, using with, 180
    integrating with MH, 183
    keys, using in GnuPG operations, 173
    setting in mutt mailer headers, 181
PID (process ID)
    adding to system log messages, 265
    looking up, 115
pidof command, killing all processes with
    given name, 116
Pine
    securing POP/IMAP with SSH and
      Pine, 195–197
    securing POP/IMAP with SSL and, 188
    sending/receiving encrypted email, 178
PinePGP, 178
pings
    nmap, use of TCP and ICMP pings for
      host discovery, 223
    preventing responses to, 39
plaintext keys, 139
    including in system backups, security risks
      of, 141
    using with forced command, 140–141
Pluggable Authentication Modules (see PAM)
policies
    default, for ipchains and iptables, 24
    Tripwire, 1
      displaying, 5
      generating in human-readable format
        and adding file to, 16
      modifying, 6
      signing with site key, 4
POP
    capturing messages from with dsniff
      mailsnarf command, 245
    enabling POP daemon within xinetd or
      inetd, 185
    Kerberos authentication, using with, 100
    mail server, running with SSL, 183–187
    running mail server with SSL, 183
    securing email session with SSL and
      mutt, 190
    securing mail server with SSH, 193
    securing mail server with SSH and
      Pine, 195–197
    securing mail server with stunnel and
      SSL, 192
    securing with SSL and pine, 188
    STLS command, 184
    testing SSL connection to server, 188

port forwarding
    disabling for authorized keys, 141
    SSH, 193
    tunneling TCP session through SSH, 144
port numbers, conversion to service names by
    netstat and lsof, 229
port scanners, presence evidenced by
    SYN_RECV state, 228
portmappers
    displaying registrations with lsof +M, 229
    querying from a different machine, 228
ports
    assigned to RPC services, 228
    default, IMAP and POP over SSL, 191
    nonstandard, used by network
      protocols, 245
    SSL-port on mail servers, 184
    testing for open, 220–226
      nc command, using, 223
      nmap command, port scanning
        capabilities, 222
      port scans with nmap, 223
      TCP port, testing with telnet
        connection, 223
      TCP RST packets returned by firewalls
        blocking ports, 224
      UDP ports, problems with, 224
preprocessors, Snort
    alert messages produced by, 253
    enabling or tuning, 257
prerotate and postrotate scripts, 275
Pretty Good Privacy (see PGP)
principals, Kerberos, 73
    adding another principal to your
      ~/.k5login file, 96
    adding new with ank command, 91
    adding to IMAP service on server host, 99
    database, creating for KDC, 88
    database for, records for users and
      hosts, 89
    host principal, testing for new host, 94
    ksu authentication, 122
    new host, adding to KDC database, 93
    POP, adding to, 100
    setting up with admin privileges and host
      principal for KDC host, 88
priority
    levels for Snort alerts, 253
    for system messages, 259

private keys, 147
    GnuPG, backing up, 162–164
    PGP, exporting and using in GnuPG, 173
    (see also cryptographic authentication)
/proc files
    filesystems, 213
    networking, important files for
            (/proc/net/tcp and
            /proc/net/udp), 227
process accounting, 273
    displaying all executed commands, 275
        lastcomm utility, using, 276
    dump-acct command, 277
    enabling with accton command, 274
    parsing logs, 278
process IDs
    adding to system log messages, 265
    looking up, 115
process substitution, 265
processes
    killing
        with pidof command, 116
        with sudo command, 115
    listing
        all open files (and network
            connections) for all processes, 226
        all open files for specific, 226
        command name (lsof -c), 230
        by ID (lsof -p), 230
        network connections for all, 226
        by username (lsof -u), 230
    owned by others, examination by
            superuser, 229
    /proc/ directories, 227
    that use RPC services, examining with losf
            +M, 229
    tracing, 231
        strace command, using, 231
promiscuous mode (for network
            interfaces), 234
    enabling for specific interfaces with
            ifconfig, 236
    performance and, 235
    setting for Snort, 251
prosum (integrity checker), 3
protocol tree for selected packet
            (Ethereal), 238
protocols
    attacks on, detection by Snort
            preprocessors, 257
    insecure, detecting use of with ngrep, 241

matching a filter expression, searching
            network traffic for, 240
    network, detecting insecure, 243–247
ps command, reading /proc files, 227
psacct RPM, 274, 275
pseudo-ttys, 71
    disabling allocation of for authorized
            keys, 141
    forcing ssh to allocate, 126
PubkeyAuthentication (sshd_config), 131
public keys
    adding to GnuPG keyring, 157
    inserting into current mail buffer with
            mc-insert-public-key, 176
    keyserver, storing and retrieving
            with, 165
    listing for GnuPG, 154
    PGP, exporting and using in GnuPG, 173
public-key authentication (see cryptographic
            authentication)
public-key encryption, 147
    decrypting files encrypted with
            GNUPG, 152
    expiration for keys, 153
    find method, use by, 164
    GnuPG, 151, 152
        bit length of keys, 153
        generating key pair, 152
        secret passphrase for keys, 154
    sharing public keys, 156
    unique identifier for keys, 154

Q

queueing your mail on another ISP, 197
quotation marks, empty double-quotes
            (""), 116

R

race conditions during snapshot
            generation, 21
rc files, storing load commands for
            firewall, 44
read permission, preventing directory
            listing, 150
read-only access to shared file via sudo, 112
read-only integrity checks, 8
realms, Kerberos, 73
    adding hosts to existing realm, 93
    adding users to existing realm, 92
    choosing name for, 88, 89
reboots, records of, 208

recent logins to system accounts, checking
    for, 207
recipes in this book, trying, xiv
recurse=n attribute (Tripwire), 16
recursion in PAM modules, 76
recursive copying of remote directory, 128
Red Hat Linux
    authconfig utility, 76
    default dummy keypairs and certificates
        for imapd and pop3d, 186
    Evolution, testing of pre-installed trusted
        SSL certificates, 191
    facility local7, use for boot messages, 260
    firewall rules, saving and restoring, 43
    Guide to Password Security, 205
    imapd with Kerberos support, 99
    IMAP/SSL certificate on server, 82
    Kerberos packages, installing, 88
    loading firewall rules at boot time, 43
        rc files "iptables" and "ipchains", 44
    MD5-hashed passwords stored in shadow
        file (v. 8.0), 204
    MIT Kerberos-5, 73
    PAM, enforcing password strength
        requirements, 75
    preconfiguration to run tripwire nightly
        via cron, 14
    process accounting RPM, 274
    script allowing users to start/stop
        daemons, 114
    Snort, starting at boot, 251
    SSL certificates, 79
        adding new certificate, 80
    TCP-wrappers, 51, 64
redirect keyword (xinetd), 69
redirecting
    blocking redirects, 39
    connections to another socket, 69
    standard input from /dev/null, 126
regular expressions (and pattern matching)
    extracting passwords with grep
        patterns, 146
    fgrep command and, 11
    identifying encrypted mail messages, 246
    ngrep, finding strings in network
        traffic, 240
    urlsnarf, use with, 247
REJECT
    blocking incoming packet and sending
        error message, 28
    DROP and, refusing packets
        (iptables), 27

pings and, 39
preventing only SSH connections from
    nonapproved hosts, 37
relative pathnames
    directories in search path, 211
    in remote file copying, 128
relay server for non-local mail, 200
remote filesystems, searching, 213
remote hosts
    blocking access for some but not
        others, 32
    blocking access from particular remote
        host, 31
    blocking access to particular host, 32
    preventing from pretending to be local to
        network, 26
    restricting access by (xinetd with
        libwrap), 60
    restricting access to TCP service
        via inetd, 61
        via xinetd, 58
remote integrity checking, 9
remote programs, invoking securely
    interactive programs, 126
    noninteractive commands, 126
remote users, restricting access to network
    services, 57
renamed file, copying remotely with scp, 127
reports, Tripwire
    ignoring discrepancies by updating
        database, 15
    printing latest, 14
revocation certificate, 153
revoking a public key, 168
    revocation certificate, distributing, 169
rhost item (PAM), 78
RhostsRSAAuthentication keyword
    (OpenSSH), 136
"ring buffer" mode (for tethereal), 239
rlogin session that used no password,
    detection with dsniff, 245
root
    logins, preventing on terminal devices, 71
    multiple root accounts, 103
    packet-sniffing programs, running as, 234
    PermitRootLogin (sshd_config), 119
    privileges, dispensing, 102
    root login shell, running, 104
    running nmap as, 224
    running root commands via SSH, 120
    running X programs as root (while logged
        in as normal user), 105

root (*continued*)
    setuid root for ssh-keysign program, 136
    setuid root program hidden in
        filesystems, 216
    sharing privileges
        via Kerberos, 121–123
        via multiple superuser accounts, 207
        via SSH (without revealing
            password), 118
    sharing root password, 102
    sudo command, 103
        invoking programs with, 107
        restricting privileges via, 115
        running commands as another
            user, 106
rootkits
    looking for, 219
    searching system for, 202
    subversion of exec call to tripwire, 14
rotating log files, 263
    process accounting, 275
routers
    firewalls for hosts configured as, 25
    packet sniffers and, 234
RPC services
    displaying information about with nmap
        -sR, 225
    port numbers assigned to, 228
    printing dynamically assigned ports
        for, 226
    processes that use, examining with lsof
        +M, 229
rpcinfo command, 226, 228
RPM-installed files, verifying, 18
rsync utility, 10
    integrity checking with, 19
    -n option (not copying files), 11
    --progress option, 11
    remote integrity checking, 10
    with ssh, mirroring set of files securely
        between machines, 129
runlevel changes, records of, 208
runlevels (networking), loading firewall rules
    for, 44
runtime kernel integrity checkers, 3

S

sa -s command (truncating process
    accounting the log file), 275
Samhain (integrity checker), 3
/sbin/ifconfig, 53
/sbin/ifdown, 53

/sbin/ifup, 53
scp command
    mirroring set of files securely between
        computers, 129
    options for remote file copying, 127
    securely copying files between
        computers, 125
    syntax, 128
scripts, enabling/disabling network
    interfaces, 53
search path, testing, 211
    . (period) in, 212
    relative directories in, dangers of, 212
SEC_BIN global variable (Tripwire), 16
secret keys
    adding to GnuPG keyring, 157
    default key for GnuPG operations, 155
    listing for GnuPG, 154
secret-key encryption, 147
secure integrity checks, 11
    creating bootable CD-ROM securely, 12
    dual-ported disk array, using, 13
Secure Sockets Layer (see SSL)
securetty file, editing to prevent root logins
    via terminal devices, 71
security policies (see policies)
security tests (see monitoring systems for
    suspicious activity)
security tools (Insecure.org), 203
self-signed certificates, 72
    creating, 83
    generating X.509 certificate, 192
    man-in-the-middle attacks, risk of, 83
    setting up your own CA to issue
        certificates, 84
sending-filters for email (PinePGP), 179
sendmail
    accepting mail from other hosts, 200
    authentication mechanisms accepted as
        trusted, 200
    daemons (visible), security risks with, 198
    restriction on accepting connections from
        only same host, changing, 199
    SSL, using to protect entire SMTP
        session, 201
sense keyword (PAM, listfile module), 77
server arguments (inetd.conf file), 56
server authentication
    (see Kerberos authentication; PAM; SSH;
        SSL; trusted-host authentication)
server keyword (xinetd), 69
server program, OpenSSH, 124

service filter configuration file
    (logwatch), 273
service filter executable (logwatch), 273
service names
    conversion of port numbers to by netstat
        and lsof, 229
    executable, 61
    modifying to invoke tcpd in /etc/xinetd.d
        startup file, 61
    PAM, 76, 78
services file, adding service names to
        inetd.conf, 56
session protection for mail, 185
setgid bit on directories, 112
setgid/setuid programs, security checks
    finding and interactively fixing, 216
    listing all files, 215
    listing scripts only, 216
    removing setgid/setuid bits from a
        file, 216
    setuid programs for hostbased
        authentication, 138
setlogsock (Sys::Syslog), 268
setuid root, ssh-keysign program, 136
sftp, 128
shadow directive
    (/etc/pam.d/system-auth), 204
shadow password file, 204, 206
sharing files
    prohibiting directory listings, 150
    protecting shared directory, 149
shell command substitution, exceeding
        command line maximum, 214
shell item (PAM), 78
shell prompts, standards used, xvi
shell scripts
    in your current directory, xiv
    writing system log entries, 264, 265–267
shells
    bash, xiv
    invoking MH commands from
        prompt, 183
    invoking with root privileges by sudo,
        security risks, 107
    process substitution, 265
    root login shell, running, 104
    root shell vs. root login shell, 105
    terminating SSH agent on logout, 142
    umask command, 149
shell-style wildcard expansion, 114
.shosts file, 136
shosts.equiv file, 138

show command, decrypting email displayed
    with, 183
shutdowns (system), records of, 208
shutting down network interfaces, 52
signature ID (Snort alerts), 252
signed cryptographic keys, 148
signing files (see digital signatures)
single-threaded services (inetd.conf file), 56
site key (Tripwire), 3
    creating with twinstall.sh script, 4
    fingerprints, creating in secure integrity
        checks, 12
    read-only integrity checking, 8
size, file
    /bin/login, changes since last Tripwire
        check, 16
    verifying for RPM-installed files, 18
SLAC (Stanford Linear Accelerator), Network
        Monitoring Tools page, 202
S/MIME
    native support by Mozilla, 180
    support by Evolution mailer, 181
SMTP
    blocking requests for mail service from a
        remote host, 31
    capturing messages from with dsniff
        program mailsnarf, 245
    protecting dedicated server for smtp
        services, 38
    requiring authentication by server before
        relaying mail, 200
    using server from arbitrary
        clients, 198–201
snapshots (see Tripwire)
Snort, 247
    decoding alert messages, 252
        nmap port scan detected, 252
        priority levels, 253
        writing alerts for file instead of
            syslog, 253
    detecting intrusions with, 250
        dumping statistics to the system
            logger, 252
        promiscuous mode, setting, 251
        running in background as
            daemon, 251
    packet sniffing with, 248
    partitioning logs into separate files, 255
    upgrading and tuning ruleset, 256
socket type (inetd.conf file), 56
software packages, risk of Trojan horses
        in, 167

sort command, 270
   -z option for null filename separators, 214
source address verification
   enabling in firewall, 24–26
   enabling in kernel, 27
   web site information on, 26
source addresses
   controlling access by, 51
   limiting server sessions by, 68
source name for remote file copying, 128
source quench, blocking, 39
sources for system messages, 259
spoofed addresses
   blocking access from, 26
   MAC, 36
   source addresses, 51
SquirrelMail, 187
ssh command
   -t option (for pseudo-tty), 126
   using with rsync to mirror set of files
      between computers, 129
   -X option (for X forwarding), 127
~/.ssh directory, creating and setting
      mode, 131
ssh file, 124
SSH (Secure Shell), 124
   agents (see ssh-agent)
   authenticating between client/server by
      trusted host, 135
   authenticating between SSH2
      client/OpenSSH server, 134
   authenticating by public key, 129–131
   changing client defaults, 143
   client configurations in
      ~/.ssh/config, 142
   connecting via ssh with Kerberos
      authentication, 94
   cryptographic authentication, 73
   download site for OpenSSH, 64
   fetchmail, use of, 198
   important programs and files, 124
      scp (client program), 125
      ssh (client program), 125
   Kerberos, using with, 94–96
      debugging, 96
      Kerberos-5 support, 94
   permitting only incoming access via SSH
      with firewall, 36
   protecting dedicated server for ssh
      services, 38
   public-key and ssh-agent, using with
      Pine, 195

public-key authentication between SSH2
      client/OpenSSH server, 134
public/private authentication keys, 130
remote user access by public key
      authentication, 57
restricting access to server by account, 64
restricting access to server by host, 64
running root commands via, 120
securing POP/IMAP, 193
   with Pine, 195–197
sharing root privileges via, 118
SSH-2 connections, trusted-host
      authentication, 136
SSH2 server and OpenSSH client,
      authenticating between with
      OpenSSH key, 131–133
SSH2 server and OpenSSH client,
      authenticating between with SSH2
      key, 133
superusers, authentication of, 103
tailoring per host, 142
tunneling
   NNTP with, 57
   TCP connection through, 144
   transferring email from another
      ISP, 197
web site, 73
ssh-add, 138
ssh-agent, 131
   automatic authentication (without
      password), 137
   invoking between backticks (` `), 138
   public-key authentication without
      passphrase, 138
   terminating on logout, 141
~/.ssh/config file, 124
ssh_config file, 124
   client configuration keywords, 143
   HostbasedAuthentication, enabling, 136
   ~/.ssh file, using instead of, 138
sshd, 65
   AllowUsers keyword, 65
   authorizing users to restart, 116
   restricting access from specific remote
      hosts, 64
   TCP-wrappers support, 64
sshd_config file
   AllowUsers keyword, 65
   HostbasedAuthentication, enabling, 135
   HostbasedUsesNameFromPacketOnly,
      138
   KerberosTgtPassing, enabling, 96

ListenAddress statements, adding, 96
PermitRootLogin, setting, 119
PublicAuthentication, permitting, 131
X11Forwarding setting, 127
ssh-keygen, 130
conversion of SSH2 private key into
OpenSSH private key with -i
(import) option, 134
ssh-keysign, 138
setuid root on client, 136
ssh_known_hosts file, 136
OpenSSH client, using ~/.ssh file instead
of, 138
SSL (Secure Sockets Layer), 72
connection problems, server-side
debugging, 190
converting certificates from DER to
PEM, 87
creating self-signed certificate, 83
decoding SSL certificates, 79
generating Certificate Signing Request
(CSR), 81–83
installing new certificate, 80
OpenSSL, 73
web site, 73
POP/IMAP security, 184
mail server, running with, 183–187
mail sessions for Evolution, 191
mutt mail client, using with, 190
stunnel, using, 192
with pine mail client, 188
setting up CA and issuing
certificates, 84–87
STARTTLS command (IMAP),
negotiating protection for
mail, 183
STLS command (POP), negotiating
protection for email, 183
validating a certificate, 78
verifying connection to secure POP or
IMAP server, 188
SSL-port
on mail servers, 184
POP or IMAP connections for mutt
client, 190
testing use in pine mail client, 189
standard input, redirecting from
/dev/null, 126
Stanford Linear Accelerator (SLAC) Network
Monitoring Tools page, 202
starting network interfaces, 52

STARTTLS command (IMAP), 183
mail server support for SSL, 184
mutt client connection over IMAP,
testing, 190
testing use in pine mail client, 189
startup scripts (bootable CD-ROM),
disabling networking, 12
stateful, 23
stateless, 23
sticky bit
set on world-writable directories, 219
setting on world-writable directory, 149
STLS command (POP), 183, 184
strace command, 226, 231
strings
matching with fgrep command, 11
searching network traffic for, 240–242
strings command, 67
strong authentication for email sessions, 184
strong session protection for mail (by
SSL), 184
stunnel, securing POP/IMAP with SSL, 192
su command, 102
invoking with root privileges by sudo,
security risks, 107
ksu (Kerberized su), 104
authentication via Kerberos, 122
sharing root privileges via, 121–123
su -, running root login shell, 104
su configuration (PAM), 74
subject (certificates), 72
components of certificate subject name, 82
self-signed, 83
sudo command, 103
bypassing password authentication, 106
careful practices for using, 107
forcing password authentication, 108
killing processes via, 115
listing invocations, 117
logging remotely, 118
password changes, authorizing via, 113
prohibiting command-line arguments for
command run via, 111
read-only access to shared file, 112
running any program in a directory, 110
running commands as another user, 106
starting/stopping daemons, 114
user authorization privileges, allowing per
host, 108

sudoers file, 103
    argument lists for each command,
        specifying meticulously, 107
    editing with visudo program, 107
    listing permissible commands for root
        privileges, 115
    running commands as another user, 106
    timestamp_timeout variable, 108
    user authorization to kill certain
        processes, 115
superdaemons, 49
    inetd (see inetd)
    xinetd (see xinetd)
superuser, 102
    assigning privileges via ssh without
        disclosing root password, 119
    finding all accounts on system, 207
    ksu (Kerberized su), 104
    processes owned by others,
        examining, 229
    (see also root)
SuSE Linux
    firewall rules, building, 43
    Heimdal Kerberos, 73
    inetd superdaemon, 51
    loading firewall rules at boot time, 44
    process accounting RPM, 274
    script allowing users to start/stop
        daemons, 114
    Snort, starting automatically at boot, 251
    SSL certificates, 79, 81
    TCP-wrappers, 51, 64
switched networks
    packet sniffers and, 234
    simulated attacks with dsniff, 247
symbolic links
    for encrypted files on separate
        system, 172
    inability to verify with manual integrity
        check, 20
    permission bits, ignoring, 219
    scp command and, 129
symmetric encryption, 147
    files encrypted with GnuPG,
        decrypting, 152
    problems with, 151
    single encrypted file containing all files in
        directory, 164
synchronizing files on two machines
    (rsync), 10
    integrity checking with, 19

SYN_RECV state, large numbers of network
    connections in, 228
Sys::Lastlog and Sys::Utmp modules
    (Perl), 210
syslog function, 267
    using in C program, 269
syslog.conf file
    directing messages to different log files by
        facility and priority, 259
    remote logging, configuring, 118, 262
    setting up for local logging, 258
    signaling system logger about changes
        in, 260
    tracing configuration errors in, 71
syslogd
    -r flag to receive remote messages, 118
    signaling to pick up changes in
        syslog.conf, 262
syslog-ng ("new generation"), 262
Sys::Syslog module, 268
system accounts, login activity on, 210, 211
system calls, tracing on network, 231
system logger
    combining log files, 269
    debugging SSL connections, 190
    directing system messages to log
        files, 257–261
        testing syslog configuration, 261
    log files created by, permissions and, 261
    logging messages remotely, 262
    programs not using, 265
    scanning log files for problem
        reports, 271
    sending messages to, 264
    signaling changes in syslog.conf, 260
    standard API, functions provided by, 267
    testing and monitoring, 202
    writing system log entries
        in C, 264, 268
        in Perl, 267
        in shell scripts, 265–267
    xinetd, logging to, 70
system_auth (/etc/pam.d startup file)
    forbidding local password validation, 101
    Kerberos in, 100
systems
    authentication methods and policies
        (authconfig), 76
    security tests on (see monitoring systems
        for suspicious activity)
system-wide authentication (Kerberos with
    PAM), 100

T

tar utility
  bundling files into single file and encrypting the tarball, 151
  encrypted backups, creating with gpg, 172
  encrypting all files in directory, 164
TCP
  enabling/disabling service invocation by inetd, 54
  IPID Sequence tests and, measuring vulnerability to forged connections, 225
  pings for host discovery, use by nmap, 223
  preventing service invocation by xinetd, 53
  reassembling streams with libnids, 245
  redirection of connections with SSH tunneling, 57
  restricting access by remote hosts (inetd), 61
  restricting access by remote hosts (xinetd), 58
  restricting access by remote users, 57
  RST packets for blocked ports, returned by firewall, 224
  slowing or killing connections, simulation with dsniff, 247
  stream reassembly with libnids, 244
  testing for open port, 221
  testing port by trying to connect with Telnet, 223
  tunneling session through SSH, 144
tcpd
  restricting access by remote hosts using with xinetd, 60
  using with inetd to restrict remote host access, 62
tcpdump (packet sniffer), 233–238
  -i option (to listen on a specific interface), 235
  libcap (packet capture library), 235
  payload display, 241
  printing information about nmap port scan, 237
  -r option, reading/displaying network trace data, 236
  selecting specific packets with capture filter expression, 236
  snapshot length, 236

verifying secure mail traffic, 190
-w option (saving packets to file), 235
TCP/IP connections
  DROP vs. REJECT, 27
  rejecting TCP packets that initiate connections, 29
TCP-wrappers
  controlling incoming access by particular hosts or domains, 51
  sshd, built-in support for, 64
tcsh shell, terminating SSH agent on logout, 142
TCT (The Coroner's Toolkit), 280
tee command, 246
Telnet
  access control
    blocking all outgoing connections, 37
    restricting access by time of day, 63
    restricting for remote hosts (xinetd with libwrap), 60
  disabling/enabling invocation by xinetd, 54
  Kerberos authentication, using with, 96
  Kerberos authentication with PAM, 101
  passwords captured from sessions with dsniff, 245
  security risks of, 38
  testing TCP port by trying to connect, 223
telnetd, configuring to require strong authentication, 98
terminals
  Linux recording of for each user, 208
  preventing superuser (root) from logging in via, 71
testing systems for security holes (see monitoring systems for suspicious activity)
tethereal, 239
text editors, using encryption features for email, 183
text-based certificate format (see PEM format)
Thawte (Certifying Authority), 82
threading, listing for new service in inetd.conf, 56
tickets, Kerberos, 73
  for IMAP on the mail server, 99
  SSH client, obtaining for, 95
ticks, 277
time of day, restricting service access by, 62

timestamps
    recorded by system logger for each
        message, 259
    in Snort filenames, 255
    sorting log files by, 270
    verifying for RPM-installed files, 18
TLS (Transport Layer Security) (see SSL)
/tmp/ls (malicious program), 211
tracing network system calls, 226
Transport Layer Security (TLS) (see SSL)
Tripwire, 1–22
    checking Windows VFAT filesystems, 17
    configuration, 2
    database, 2
        adding files to, 16
        excluding files from, 17
        updating to ignore discrepancies, 15
    displaying policy and configuration, 5
    download site for latest version, 1
    download sites, 5
    highly secure integrity checks, 11
    integrity check, 2
    integrity checking, basic, 7
    manual integrity checks, using instead
        of, 20–22
    policy, 1
    policy and configuration, modifying, 6
    printing latest report, 14
    protecting files against attacks, 3
    read-only integrity checks, 8
    remote integrity checking, 9
    RPM-installed files, verifying, 18
    setting up, 4
        twinstall.sh script, 4
    using rsync instead of, 19
    weaknesses, 3
Trojan horses
    checking for with chkrootkit, 220
    planted in commonly-used software
        packages, 167
trust, web of, 148
trusted certificates, 72
trusted public keys (GnuPG), 157
trusted-host authentication, 135
    canonical hostname, finding for
        client, 137
    implications of
        strong trust of client host, 136
        weak authorization controls, 137
tty item (PAM), 78

tunneling
    TCP session through SSH, 144
    transferring your email from another ISP
        with SSH, 197
twcfg.txt file, 5
twinstall.sh script (Tripwire), 4
twpol.txt file, 5
twprint program, 15

U

UDP
    blocking packets on privileged ports, 29
    probing ports, difficulties of, 224
    stateful firewall, necessity for, 30
    testing for open port, 221
umask
    Linux chmod and umask commands, 149
    preventing files from being
        world-writable, 219
    setting as group writable, 112
unicast packets, 233
unique identifier for GnuPG keys, 154
unsecured IMAP connections, 187
unshadow command, 204
urlsnarf command, 247
Usenet news, tunneling NNTP connections
        through SSH, 144
user accounts
    allowing one account to access another
        with ksu, 121
    multiple root accounts, 103
    without a password, finding, 206
    restricting access to SSH server by, 64
    restricting hostbased authentication
        to, 138
    for SMTP authentication, 199
    superuser, finding, 207
    suspicious use, checking for, 207
        on multiple systems, 209–211
    usernames in remote file copying, 128
    usernames in trusted-host
        authentication, 136
user facility, system messages, 264
user ID of zero (0) (superuser), 207
user (inetd.conf file), 56
users
    administration of their own
        machines, 109
    authorizing to restart sshd, 116
    changes since last Tripwire check, 16
    Kerberos credentials for, 88
    login information about, printing, 207

/usr/share/ssl/cert.pem file, 80
utmp file, 210

V

/var/account/pacct, 274
variables (Mailcrypt), listing all, 177
/var/log/lastlog, 208
/var/log/messages, 260
/var/log/secure, unauthorized sudo attempts, listing, 117
/var/log/utmp, 210
/var/log/wtmp, 208
verifying RPM-installed files, 18
verifying signatures on downloaded software, 167
Verisign (Certifying Authority), 82
VFAT filesystems, checking integrity of, 17
vim editor
    composing encrypted mail, 177
    maintaining encrypted files, 170
violations (unexpected changes) in system files, 1
visudo program, editing sudoers file, 107
vulnerability to attacks
    factors in, 221
    measuring for operating systems, 225

W

web of trust, 148
    keys imported from keyserver, verifying, 167
    web site information on, 168
web page for this book, xvi
web servers, blocking outgoing access to all on a network, 33
web site, blocking outgoing traffic to, 32
Web-based mail packages, 187
well-known ports, scanning with nmap, 224
whois command, 282
wildcard expansion (shell-style), 114
Windows filesystems (VFAT), 17
worms, testing for with chkrootkit, 220
writable files, finding, 218
wtmp file, 208
    processing with Perl module Sys::Utmp, 210
www services, protecting dedicated server for, 38

X

X Window System
    disabling X forwarding for authorized keys, 141
    display name, Linux system record of, 208
    enabling X forwarding with ssh -X, 127
    running programs as root, 105
    ssh-agent, automatically run for logins, 139
X.509 certificates, 72
    generating self-signed, 192
xargs program
    0 (zero) option, for null-terminated filenames, 214
    collecting filename arguments to avoid long command lines, 214
    -n 1 option (one file at a time), 215
    searching filesystems effectively, 212
XAUTHORITY environment variable (X windows), 105
Ximian, Evolution mailer, 180
xinetd, 50
    access_times attribute, 62
    adding new network service controlled by, 55
    configuration files for services, 55
    configuring telnetd to require strong authentication, 98
    deleting service configuration file, 54
    enabling IMAP daemon within, 185
    home page, 54
    Kerberized Telnet, enabling, 97
    logging access to services, 70
    POP daemon, enabling, 185
    preventing DOS attacks with cps, instances, max_load, and per_source keywords, 67
    preventing invocation of TCP service by, 53
    redirecting connections with redirect keyword, 69
    server keyword, 69
    TCP services, access control, 58
        using with libwrap, 59
        using with tcpd, 60
xinetd.conf file
    confirming location of its includedir, 56
    modifying to invoke tcpd, 61
    only_from and no_access keywords, 58
XML::Simple module (Perl), 225

About the Authors

Daniel J. Barrett, Ph.D., has been immersed in Internet technology since 1985. Currently working as a software engineer, Dan has also been a heavy metal singer, Unix system administrator, university lecturer, web designer, and humorist. He has written several O'Reilly books, as well as monthly columns for *Computer and Keyboard* magazine. Dan and his family reside in Boston. Contact him at *dbarrett@oreilly.com*.

Richard E. Silverman has a B.A. in computer science and an M.A. in pure mathematics. Richard has worked in the fields of networking, formal methods in software development, public-key infrastructure, routing security, and Unix systems administration. He is the coauthor of *SSH, The Secure Shell: The Definitive Guide*. Contact him at *res@oreilly.com*.

Robert G. Byrnes, Ph.D., has been hacking on Unix systems for twenty years, and has been involved with security issues since the original Internet worm was launched from Cornell University while he was a graduate student and system administrator. He is currently a software engineer at Curl Corporation and has worked in the fields of networking, telecommunications, distributed computing, financial technology, and condensed matter physics. Contact him at *byrnes@oreilly.com*.

Colophon

Our look is the result of reader comments, our own experimentation, and feedback from distribution channels. Distinctive covers complement our distinctive approach to technical topics, breathing personality and life into potentially dry subjects.

Jane Ellin was the production editor and copyeditor for *Linux Security Cookbook*. Phil Dangler and Mary Brady provided quality control. Jaime Peppard provided production support. Ellen Troutman-Zaig wrote the index.

Hanna Dyer designed the cover of this book, based on a series design by herself and Edie Freedman. The cover image of a campfire scene is a 19th-century engraving from *American West*. Emma Colby produced the cover layout with QuarkXPress 4.1 using Adobe's ITC Garamond font.

David Futato designed the interior layout. Robert Romano chose the chapter opening images, which are from the Dover Pictorial Archive, *Marvels of the New West: A Vivid Portrayal of the Stupendous Marvels in the Vast Wonderland West of the Missouri River*, by William Thayer (The Henry Bill Publishing Co., 1888), and *The Pioneer History of America: A Popular Account of the Heroes and Adventures*, by Augustus Lynch Mason, A.M. (The Jones Brothers Publishing Company, 1884). This book was prepared in FrameMaker 5.5.6 by Andrew Savikas. The text font is Linotype Birka; the heading font is Adobe Myriad Condensed; and the code font is LucasFont's TheSans Mono Condensed. The illustrations that appear in the book were produced by Robert Romano and Jessamyn Read using Macromedia FreeHand 9 and Adobe Photoshop 6. The tip and warning icons were drawn by Christopher Bing.

Related Titles Available from O'Reilly

Linux

Building Embedded Linux Systems

Building Secure Servers with Linux

The Complete FreeBSD, *4th Edition*

CVS Pocket Reference, *2nd Edition*

Essential CVS

Even Grues Get Full

Extreme Programming Pocket Guide

Learning Red Hat Linux, *3rd Edition*

Linux Device Drivers, *2nd Edition*

Linux in a Nutshell, *4th Edition*

Linux iptables Pocket Reference

Linux Network Administrator's Guide, *2nd Edition*

Linux Server Hacks

Linux Web Server CD Bookshelf, *Version 2.0*

LPI Linux Certification in a Nutshell

Managing & Using MySQL, *2nd Edition*

Managing RAID on Linux

MySQL Cookbook

MySQL Pocket Reference

Practical PostgreSQL

Programming with Qt, *2nd Edition*

Root of all Evil

Running Linux, *4th Edition*

Samba Pocket Reference, *2nd Edition*

Understanding the Linux Kernel, *2nd Edition*

User Friendly

Using Samba, *2nd Edition*

O'REILLY®

Our books are available at most retail and online bookstores.
To order direct: 1-800-998-9938 • *order@oreilly.com* • *www.oreilly.com*
Online editions of most O'Reilly titles are available by subscription at *safari.oreilly.com*

Keep in touch with O'Reilly

1. Download examples from our books

To find example files for a book, go to:

www.oreilly.com/catalog

select the book, and follow the "Examples" link.

2. Register your O'Reilly books

Register your book at *register.oreilly.com*

Why register your books?
Once you've registered your O'Reilly books you can:

- Win O'Reilly books, T-shirts or discount coupons in our monthly drawing.
- Get special offers available only to registered O'Reilly customers.
- Get catalogs announcing new books (US and UK only).
- Get email notification of new editions of the O'Reilly books you own.

3. Join our email lists

Sign up to get topic-specific email announcements of new books and conferences, special offers, and O'Reilly Network technology newsletters at:

elists.oreilly.com

It's easy to customize your free elists subscription so you'll get exactly the O'Reilly news you want.

4. Get the latest news, tips, and tools

www.oreilly.com

- "Top 100 Sites on the Web"—PC Magazine
- CIO Magazine's Web Business 50 Awards

Our web site contains a library of comprehensive product information (including book excerpts and tables of contents), downloadable software, background articles, interviews with technology leaders, links to relevant sites, book cover art, and more.

5. Work for O'Reilly

Check out our web site for current employment opportunities:

jobs.oreilly.com

6. Contact us

O'Reilly & Associates, Inc.
1005 Gravenstein Hwy North
Sebastopol, CA 95472 USA

TEL: 707-827-7000 or 800-998-9938
      (6am to 5pm PST)

FAX: 707-829-0104

order@oreilly.com
For answers to problems regarding your order or our products. To place a book order online, visit:

www.oreilly.com/order_new

catalog@oreilly.com
To request a copy of our latest catalog.

booktech@oreilly.com
For book content technical questions or corrections.

corporate@oreilly.com
For educational, library, government, and corporate sales.

proposals@oreilly.com
To submit new book proposals to our editors and product managers.

international@oreilly.com
For information about our international distributors or translation queries. For a list of our distributors outside of North America check out:

international.oreilly.com/distributors.html

adoption@oreilly.com
For information about academic use of O'Reilly books, visit:

academic.oreilly.com

O'REILLY®

Our books are available at most retail and online bookstores.
To order direct: 1-800-998-9938 • *order@oreilly.com* • *www.oreilly.com*
Online editions of most O'Reilly titles are available by subscription at *safari.oreilly.com*